ALTERNATIVE BAKER

ALTERNATIVE BAKER

reinventing dessert with gluten-free grains and flours

WRITTEN AND PHOTOGRAPHED BY
ALANNA TAYLOR-TOBIN
CREATOR OF THE BOJON GOURMET

PAGE STREET
PUBLISHING CO.

PAGE STREET
PUBLISHING CO.

TO MY GRANDMOTHERS,
ANNE AND BUBBA, FOR ALWAYS
SHARING THE BEST COOKIES

CONTENTS

INTRODUCTION

At a birthday party the other day, my sweetie Jay and I were offered a chocolate cupcake from a local bakery. I had been testing recipes for this book for seven months and we were up to our ears in unconscionable amounts of baked goods that all boasted alternative grains and seasonal fruits and vegetables. Not wishing to be rude, Jay took a bite, and frowned. "It's bland," he whispered. I tasted the cupcake, expecting something super sweet and flat, and was pleasantly surprised. The cake was well seasoned, not too sweet and quite chocolaty, with enough salt to counter the sugar. The frosting was creamy and smooth, the cake rich and moist. What was missing? Before we left for the party, I'd baked a batch of the Buckwheat Pear Galettes with Walnuts and Salty Caramel (page 108) and Jay and I had shared one, still warm from the oven. The charcoal-hued crust shattered against tender pears coated in a nap of salty caramel, warm buckwheat exuding notes of chocolate and spice, earth and toasted nuts. It was then that I realized: our palates had become accustomed to alternative grains.

Baking with alternative grains opened up a whole new feast of flavors, textures and colors that I never knew existed. Culinary pioneers Kim Boyce and Alice Medrich have shown us that these flours aren't just desirable for their nutritional value, but also for the aesthetic pleasures—touch, taste and smell—that they bring to the kitchen. It's been a delight to see the look on friends' faces when they bite into a Chestnut Roulade Cake with Rum, Mascarpone and Roasted Pears (page 71) or Buckwheat Bergamot Double Chocolate Cookie (page 197) for the first time; their eyes widen, corners of the lips turn upward and a look of pure surprise crosses their faces. "What is this new flavor I'm tasting?" they ask.

Buckwheat flour sings of toasted hazelnuts mingling with cocoa and cinnamon. Teff flour tastes of malted milk and chocolate, mesquite flour of baked earth and chestnut flour is wildly sweet and rich. Sorghum and millet are nutty and grassy; amaranth is potently vegetal and almost herbaceous. Coconut flour is sweet with notes of the tropics, and almond flour has a delicate nuttiness. Replace the all-purpose flour in gingersnaps with sweet rice and mesquite flours, add teff flour to cobbler biscuits or whip up some scones made with oat and amaranth flours—all of a sudden what was once rather ordinary when made with everyday white flour becomes extraordinary.

In my kitchen, flavor comes first, but there are other benefits to playing with alternative grains and flours, too. Each has its own fragrance, color, history and nutritional profile. I always look forward to opening a jar of teff flour, whose malty smell takes me back to kindergarten and glasses of malted chocolate milk at recess. The lactic, whole-grain scent of oat flour reminds me of baking cookies on a rainy day. When I pull out my bag of mesquite flour with its reddish tan hue and scent of baked earth, I'm instantly transported to the red, rocky deserts of Arizona and New Mexico, where I traveled as a teen. The sunny yellow of corn flour never fails to cheer me, and I could gaze at buckwheat flour, with its heathered gray hue and charcoal flecks, for hours. It's a sensory experience.

Once I'd grown to love these flours and developed my own associations with them, researching their histories was even more fascinating. For example, protein-rich amaranth is strongly linked to the Aztec empire, where it accounted for 80 percent of diets, was used in religious rites and when popped and mixed with honey, embodied statues of the Aztec gods. Mesquite flour, on the other hand, nourished desert-dwellers native to North America, and has the unique ability to slow the metabolization of food and stabilize blood sugar levels. Teff, the world's tiniest grain, hails from the isolated Ethiopian highlands and is the only grain to contain significant levels of vitamin C. And chestnut flour, now considered the upper echelon of alternative flours with a price tag to match, was pooh-poohed as peasant food for centuries.

My journey to alternative grains and flours began nearly fifteen years ago. My sister had been diagnosed with a gluten allergy before most people even knew what the stuff was. Wondering whether the gluey wheat protein might account for my own lifelong digestive troubles, I began experimenting with alternatives. There's an inherent learning curve to baking with gluten-free (GF) flours (see my first disastrous GF cookie experience on page 191), but balancing them with sticky ingredients—sweet white rice flour, tapioca, ground chia seeds and eggs, to name a few—allows their good qualities to shine. Most of my recipes now come together with a minimum of fuss, and with tastes and textures that surpass their refined wheat counterparts, piquing the palate of the most sensitive celiac to the most ardent wheat-eater.

So it is with this new palette of flavors, textures and histories that we make new of what was once old. I'm delighted to share this collection of recipes based on alternative grains and flours and punctuated by all manner of delicious ingredients, from peak-of-season fruit to sweeteners to chocolate and spirits.

So let's get baking. Let's reinvent dessert.

Alanna T. T.

HOW TO USE THIS BOOK

Some of these recipes can seem intimidating at first, particularly if you are new to baking, to alternative flours or to working with seasonal ingredients. Here are some suggestions on how to approach these recipes without hating life. (Read more about alternative grains and flours on pages 236–249.)

FLOUR CHILD

If you're just beginning to dabble in GF baking (or baking at all) and are looking to stock your pantry with a few alternative grains, start with recipes that use just two or three flours.

These flours are easy to find and even easier to love with their mild flavors and multipurpose uses:

- Almond flour
- Millet flour
- GF oat flour and old-fashioned rolled oats
- Polenta/corn grits, cornmeal and corn flour
- Sweet white rice flour (a.k.a. glutinous rice flour; NOT regular white rice flour)

Try these easy-peasy recipes:

- Tart Cherry, Chocolate and Hempseed No-Bake Oat Bars (page 41)
- Blueberry Corn Flour Muffins (page 26)
- Creamy Baked Grits with Sweet Corn and Berries (page 171)
- Millet Skillet Cornbread with Cherries and Honey (page 29)
- Vanilla Butter Cake with Whipped Mascarpone and Summer Berries (page 59)
- Fig and Olive Oil Cake (page 67)
- Peach Brown Butter Crème Fraîche Tart (page 123)
- Chocolate Cranberry Pecan Tart (page 128)
- Blueberry Plum Cobbler with Corn Flour Biscuits (page 155)
- Blackberry Crisp Frozen Yogurt (page 175)
- Apricot Clafoutis with Honey and Cardamom (page 167)
- Pear and Pomegranate Clafoutis with Vanilla, Saffron and Pistachios (page 179)
- Meyer Lemon Bars with Vanilla-Almond Crust (page 210)
- Summer Stone Fruit and Marzipan Crumble (page 152)

FLOUR POWER

If you have some experience with gluten-free, alternative flour baking and wish to expand your repertoire, try these slightly less common flours:

- Teff flour
- Buckwheat flour
- Coconut flour
- Sorghum flour

And the sometimes fussier recipes that use them:

- Boozy Chocolate Cherry Teff Pots (page 172)
- Apple, Buckwheat and Gruyère Puff Pancake (page 37)
- Huckleberry Buckwheat Cheese Blintzes (page 34)
- Buckwheat Bergamot Double Chocolate Cookies (page 197)
- Poppy Seed, Pluot and Buckwheat Streusel Muffins (page 33)
- Rustic Plum, Teff and Hazelnut Tart (page 103)
- Roasted Banana Teff with Muscovado Sugar Glaze (page 42)
- Maple Bourbon Peach Cobbler with Cinnamon Teff Biscuits (page 151)
- Blackberry Buckwheat Crisps (page 156)
- Buckwheat Hazelnut Pear Financiers (page 64)
- Chocolate Zucchini Cake with Matcha Cream Cheese Frosting (page 60)
- Sorghum Peach Oven Pancake (page 26)
- Cashew Lime Blondies (page 206)

GRAINIAC

If you're an adventurous baker who wants ALL the flours, look for:

- Mesquite flour
- Chestnut flour
- Amaranth flour

And try these recipes:

- Apple Chestnut Tart with Salty Caramel (page 127)
- Cherry Chestnut Chocolate Chip Cookies (page 193)
- Salty Caramel Banana Cream Tart with Mesquite Crust (page 131)
- Strawberry Rhubarb Cobbler with Ginger-Amaranth Biscuits (page 140)
- Mesquite Gingersnaps and Chewy Double-Ginger Molasses Cookies (page 198) (and the recipes that use them)
- Chestnut Fig Scones (page 25)
- Chestnut Plum Financiers (page 64)
- Cinnamon Amaranth Peach Scones (page 25)
- Any of the pie or pandowdy recipes; the dough takes some getting used to but produces stunning results

HOW TO
WIN AT BAKING

I've heard it said that there are two types of people in the world: cooks and bakers. Cooks are hot-tempered creative types who break all the rules and don't follow directions. A little of this, a bit of that, they can throw together a genius meal using the dregs of your crisper drawer and a skillet. Recipes are tiresome words meant to be skimmed rather than analyzed. Then there are meticulous, exacting bakers. With their obsessive attention to detail and love of structure, they will follow a recipe to the letter.

My advice to you when making these recipes is to be a bit of a cook *and* a baker. Yes, these recipes have been carefully formulated to work with these exact measurements, ingredients, temperatures, baking pans, etc. So be like a baker and measure accurately, and make the recipe as written, at least the first time around. That said, each kitchen has its own set of variables—weather, oven temperature, baking pan size and material, brands of ingredients used and measuring techniques all have their own bizarre effects on baking. So be like a cook, too: use your senses and intuition to determine if that cake needs a longer baking time than called for, or if your scone dough needs more liquid. If something seems done to you before the timer goes off, pull it out; if it seems underdone, leave it in longer.

Along these lines, here are some general baking tips that should help you be a better baker (and cook).

1. **Read, read, read.** Before you get started, read through a recipe from start to finish; this will give you a sense of timing and flow before you begin, and there will be no nasty surprises, like chilling times, ingredients or equipment. I always give the recipe a final read-through once my batter is mixed, checking off ingredients in my head to make sure I haven't left any out. Once you place the goodies in the oven, refresh your memory about what to look for in terms of doneness and bake time. And make sure you pay attention to ingredients. **For example, sweet white rice flour is quite different from regular rice flour and the two are not interchangeable.** (Read more in "Alternative Grains and Flours," page 236.)

2. *Mise en place.* I never do this because I have a tiny kitchen and all my baking supplies are already in one place, but many bakers I know like to gather and measure all their ingredients before getting started. This way, you won't accidentally leave anything out.

3. **Know how to measure.** Ingredients in this book are given in volume (cups, tablespoons, teaspoons) as well as metric measurements (grams, which are weight, and milliliters, which are volume). To measure by volume, use dry measuring cups for flours, sugars and the like (those little metal cups with handles that come in ¼-cup increments) and use wet measuring cups for liquids (usually glass or plastic pitchers that come in 1- and 2-cup sizes). Weight measurements will give you the most accurate results, particularly for alternative flours that can have wide variations in weight due to the coarseness of the grind, moisture content and clumpiness. If measuring by volume, see step 4.

4. **Dip and sweep.** When measuring dry ingredients such as flours, grab your bag or jar of flour, a dry measuring cup and a straight knife or (my favorite) a small, offset spatula. If the flour has been sitting for a while, such as a new bag from the grocery store, stick your cup in the bag and fluff it up a bit. Conversely, if your flour is fluffy (say you just bought it in bulk, or you just poured your bag into a storage jar), rap the container on the counter a few times to settle it back down. Now, dip your measuring cup into the container and lift it up so that it's mounded with flour. Give it the gentlest of taps on the rim of the jar or with your hand to settle any large air pockets. Use your knife or offset spatula to sweep away the excess flour to make a level cup, letting the excess fall back into the jar or bag. Do the same thing when measuring with teaspoons or tablespoons.

5. **Use the utensils and mixing techniques called for.** When called for, whip, beat, stir, fold or rub in. Beating whipped egg whites into a batter with a spoon will give different results than gently folding them in with a spatula.

6. **Use the pan size called for.** An inch (2.5 cm) may not seem like a big difference, but a 9-inch (23-cm) round pan has 25 percent more volume than an 8-inch (20-cm) round pan, and this will have a big effect on the shape of your cake and its baking time. Similarly, the material of your baking vessel may transfer heat differently. Glass, ceramic, steel, aluminum and cast iron will give slightly different outcomes, making it essential to channel your inner cook and use visual cues and your instincts to determine doneness.

7. **Oven placement matters.** Take care to arrange your oven racks as specified in the recipe. For instance, scones burn easily on their bottoms, so baking them toward the top of the oven is essential. Pie, on the other hand, tends to get soggy on the bottom; baking it on the lower rack helps keep the bottom crisp.

8. **Oven temperature—it's anyone's guess!** Most ovens don't run true to temperature, no matter how fancy and new. My oven is about as ancient as some of the grains in this book, so I am at the mercy of my external oven thermometers, of which I always have two. But these can be inaccurate, too. The best way to see that your oven runs at the proper temperature is to hire a professional to come calibrate it. The second way is to make like a cook and adjust your oven according to your instincts. Are things not browning when they should? Maybe your oven runs cold and you need to turn it up. Are your cookies incinerated? Your oven probably runs a little warm and you should dial down the temperature a bit. Opening the oven door frequently will lower the temperature, too, so try to keep the peeking to a minimum.

9. **Use a timer.** And also, don't use a timer. Bake times are approximate and will differ depending on myriad factors, including oven temperature, pan material, the temperature of your kitchen and ingredients, how you measured your ingredients and how frequently you open the oven to check for doneness. So use your eyes, nose and fingers or a toothpick (when applicable) to determine if something is fully baked, regardless of the times given. That said, do set a timer for a little before the earliest done time so you know when to start checking on things.

10. **Keep your cool.** Freshly baked goods are still cooking from residual heat even after you've removed them from the oven, so it's best to obey the recipe and let things cool or chill for the specified time. Before storing baked goods, let them cool completely so they don't steam themselves.

DESSERT FOR BREAKFAST

"When you wake up in the morning, Pooh," said Piglet at last, "what's the first thing you say to yourself?"
"What's for breakfast?" said Pooh. "What do you say, Piglet?"
"I say, I wonder what's going to happen exciting today?" said Piglet.
Pooh nodded thoughtfully. "It's the same thing," he said.
—A. A. Milne

Breakfast is my favorite meal of the day because it's the one where you're allowed to eat dessert. Muffins are essentially cake in individual form. Oven pancakes resembling clafoutis puff around gently sweetened fruit. Scones are doused with honey, and glazed biscuits wrap around berries. In the case of chocolate-topped oat bars, you can even eat cookies for breakfast and none will be the wiser. There's a reason why bitter beverages like coffee and black tea star at breakfast—they're the perfect thing to wash down these sweet breakfast treats.

Alternative grains have the power to create breakfast snacks and pastries that taste good in addition to being good for you. I've kept most of the recipes in this section on the less-sweet side, using alternative grains and flours to add nutritional value and a bit of staying power to some favorite breakfast treats that are worth getting out of bed for any day of the week.

Sorghum adds sweet nuttiness to a custardy oven pancake encasing honey-roasted peaches. Melt-in-your-mouth cream scones get their tender texture from millet and oat flours, as well as amaranth and chestnut flours in the variations. Teff flour makes wildly flavorful roasted banana scones slathered in a butterscotchy glaze. Buckwheat stars in buttery poppy seed muffins as well as blintzes filled with sweet cheese and huckleberries. Don't miss the pumpkin cranberry loaf, which is barely sweet and made from a host of nuts, seeds and oats. With unique tastes and textures, these breakfast treats are sure to add a bit of excitement to your day, too.

LEMON RICOTTA BISCUITS

{OAT, MILLET}

These craggy biscuits are rich with butter, whole-milk ricotta and a touch of cream, and they get sweetness from sugar and a scraping of lemon zest. When warm from the oven, their delicate crumb positively melts in your mouth; cooled, they have a slightly chewy texture from the ricotta. Oat and millet flours combined with cornstarch for crispness and tapioca for extensibility give them a wheaten texture and delicate taste. They tend to spread a bit more than conventional biscuits, but it's the extra moisture that causes them to bake up light and crisp. These hold their shape best when chilled prior to baking, but you can bake them right away when you need biscuits in a hurry; they'll just sit a bit flatter.

Spread them with some softened butter and Rhubarb Preserves (page 232) for breakfast, or top them with ricotta cream, strawberries and tarragon for a sensational shortcake (page 143). Leftovers can be baked into a berry-filled bread pudding drizzled with honey (page 168).

MAKES 6 BISCUITS

½ cup (55 g) GF oat flour, plus extra for dusting the surface

¼ cup plus 2 tbsp (50 g) millet flour

2 tbsp (13 g) tapioca flour

2 tbsp (15 g) cornstarch

2 tbsp (25 g) organic granulated cane sugar

1½ tsp (8 g) baking powder

¼ tsp fine sea salt

Finely grated zest from ½ large lemon

3 tbsp (42 g) cold, unsalted butter, diced

½ cup (120 g) whole-milk ricotta cheese

3 tbsp (45 ml) cold heavy cream, plus 2 tsp (10 ml) for brushing the biscuits

Coarse sugar such as turbinado or demerara, for sprinkling

In a large bowl, whisk together the oat, millet and tapioca flours with the cornstarch, sugar, baking powder, salt and lemon zest. Add the butter pieces, and work with a pastry blender or your fingertips until the butter is broken down into the size of small peas. Chill the mixture until cold, 20–30 minutes.

Position a rack in the upper third of the oven and preheat to 425ºF (220ºC). Stack a rimmed baking sheet atop a second rimmed baking sheet and line with parchment paper (this will keep the bottoms from over-browning).

Remove the flour mixture from the refrigerator, add the ricotta and 3 tablespoons (45 ml) cream, and stir and/or knead with your hands until the dough comes together in a rough ball. The dough should feel fairly firm, but evenly moistened.

Working quickly to keep the dough cold, turn the dough out onto a surface dusted lightly with oat flour and form it into a disk. Cut the disk into 6 equal pieces. Shape each piece into a ball, place on the sheet pan spaced well apart, and flatten slightly. Brush the tops of each biscuit with the remaining 2 teaspoons (10 ml) cream and sprinkle with a bit of coarse sugar. (Optionally for taller biscuits: chill the biscuits until firm, 30–60 minutes.)

Bake the biscuits on the upper rack of the oven until golden on top, 15–20 minutes. Let cool for at least 15 minutes; they are still cooking from residual heat. The biscuits are best the day of baking, but they will keep at room temperature for a day or two. Toast before serving.

RASPBERRY SWIRL BISCUITS

{SWEET RICE, MILLET, OAT}

These swirled biscuits stuffed with fresh raspberries and drizzled with vanilla bean glaze fall somewhere between a muffin and a biscuit. The edges get crisp in the oven while the middles stay tender. Bright raspberries play off the sweet richness of the buttery biscuits, enhanced with nutty millet and oat flours, and the pretty presentation makes these perfect for a brunch or potluck. As you work, the dough will feel more fragile than wheat biscuits, but don't worry—the sweet rice flour provides enough stickiness to hold these together as they bake. Just be sure to use sweet rice flour (such as Mochiko) rather than regular rice flour. Feel free to skip the glaze for a less sweet breakfast treat. And don't miss the variations on page 22. Do give yourself 2 hours to complete these biscuits as the dough requires some chill time.

MAKES 8 OR 9 BISCUITS

BISCUITS

1 cup (155 g) sweet white rice flour

½ cup (65 g) millet flour

½ cup (50 g) oat flour, plus extra for dusting the surface

¼ cup (50 g) organic granulated cane sugar, plus 1 tbsp (10 g) for sprinkling

1 tbsp (12 g) baking powder

½ tsp fine sea salt

6 tbsp (85 g) cold, unsalted butter, sliced, plus 1 tsp, softened, for greasing the pan

6 tbsp (90 ml) whole milk, plus up to 4 tbsp (60 ml) more as needed

1 large egg

1 tsp vanilla extract

1½ cups fresh raspberries (about a 6-oz [170-g] package)

FOR BRUSHING BISCUITS

1 tbsp (15 ml) whole milk

1 tsp organic granulated cane sugar

VANILLA BUTTERMILK GLAZE

Seeds from ½ vanilla bean

½ cup (40 g) powdered sugar

1 tbsp (15 ml) well-shaken buttermilk or milk, or enough to make a pourable glaze

To make the biscuits, in a large bowl, combine the sweet rice, millet and oat flours with the ¼ cup (50 g) sugar, baking powder and salt. Add the 6 tablespoons (85 g) butter and blend with a pastry cutter or your fingertips until the butter is broken down into the size of small peas. Chill this mixture until cold, 10–20 minutes.

Meanwhile, whisk together the 6 tablespoons (90 ml) milk, the egg and the vanilla extract in a measuring pitcher. Chill until needed.

Remove the flour mixture from the refrigerator. Gradually add the milk mixture, working with a flexible silicone spatula until the dough holds together when you give it a squeeze. Stop adding liquid if the dough seems overly wet; we want it to be firm enough to roll out. Conversely, if the dough is dry or floury, work in 1–4 more tablespoons (15–60 ml) milk until it comes together. The amount of liquid needed will vary depending on the temperature and humidity of your kitchen, so add as little or as much as you need to make a firm but hydrated dough. Knead the dough about 20 times in the bowl to bring it together in a ball (unlike wheat biscuits, these gluten-free biscuits require more kneading to bring the dough together, so don't be shy). Cover and chill the dough for 15 minutes or up to several hours.

While the dough chills, rinse, dry and slice the berries in half.

When ready to bake, position a rack in the upper third of the oven and preheat to 350ºF (175ºC). Grease the bottom and sides of an 8-inch (20-cm) round or square cake pan with the remaining 1 teaspoon softened butter and line with parchment paper.

Remove the dough from the refrigerator and place on a large piece of parchment paper dusted lightly with oat flour. Use your hands and a rolling pin to pat and roll the dough out into roughly a 10 by 14-inch (25 by 35-cm) rectangle, dusting the dough as needed to prevent sticking. If the dough cracks or breaks at any point, don't worry, just pinch and squish it back together. When the dough begins to stick to the parchment, top with a second sheet of parchment and, grasping both pieces of parchment and the dough, bravely flip the whole thing over. Gently peel away the top piece of parchment and continue rolling out the dough.

(continued)

RASPBERRY SWIRL BISCUITS (CONT.)

Sprinkle the halved berries evenly over the dough, use your palms to press them gently into the dough and sprinkle with the remaining 1 tablespoon (10 g) sugar. Starting with a long end, use the parchment to help roll the dough into a log, rolling it as tightly as possible and ending with the seam side down. Use a sharp chef's knife to cut the log into 8 equal pieces (if using a round pan) or 9 pieces (if using a square pan), cutting straight down in an assertive manner. Place each round with a cut side up in the prepared pan, using a thin spatula to help transfer the biscuits if needed. Gently press the tops of the biscuits to flatten them slightly. Brush the tops of the biscuits with the 1 tablespoon (15 ml) milk and sprinkle with 1 teaspoon sugar to encourage browning.

Bake the biscuits until golden and cooked through, 40–55 minutes. Remove from the oven and let cool completely, 1 hour; their texture improves upon cooling.

To make the glaze, whisk together the vanilla seeds, powdered sugar and enough buttermilk or milk to make a pourable glaze until smooth. When the biscuits have cooled, drizzle with the glaze. Use a knife or small offset spatula to coax the biscuits out of the pan.

The biscuits are best within a few hours of baking, but extras will keep, airtight at room temperature, for an additional day.

VARIATIONS

BLUEBERRY CARDAMOM SWIRL BISCUITS
Use 1½ cups (170 g) whole fresh blueberries (or huckleberries or wild blueberries) in place of the raspberries. Add ½ teaspoon ground cardamom to the sugar sprinkled over the berries, and ⅛ teaspoon ground cardamom to the glaze. Pictured on page 16.

CINNAMON SWIRL BISCUITS WITH CREAM CHEESE ICING
Omit the raspberries and additional tablespoon (10 g) of granulated sugar. In a small bowl, stir together ⅓ cup (70 g) packed organic dark brown sugar or muscovado sugar, 1 teaspoon ground cinnamon, a good grating of fresh nutmeg and ⅛ teaspoon fine sea salt. Brush the rolled-out dough all over with 2 tablespoons (30 ml) melted and cooled butter, sprinkle with ⅓ cup (45 g) dried currants, raisins or golden raisins and sprinkle all over with the brown sugar mixture. Pat down the filling mixture into the dough and proceed with the recipe. For a simple cream cheese glaze, use the back of a spoon to mash 2 tablespoons (30 g) softened cream cheese with ½ cup (40 g) powdered sugar. Beat in 1 tablespoon (15 ml) milk or buttermilk, a few drops of vanilla extract and a pinch of fine sea salt, adding more liquid if needed to make a thick but pourable glaze. Drizzle the glaze over the biscuits.

NOTE: Making biscuit and scone doughs by hand gives you the best control over the finished product, since it's easier to overprocess the butter if using a machine. However, once you've gotten the hang of how to handle these doughs, feel free to give them a whirl using a stand mixer fitted with the paddle attachment to work in the butter, add the liquid and knead the dough. Alternatively, use a food processor to pulse the butter into the flour mixture, dump the mixture into a bowl and add the liquid ingredients by hand. If your kitchen is cool and you work quickly, you can also skip the additional step of chilling the flour/butter mixture; I list it as an extra precaution for newer bakers and/or warm kitchens.

BLACKBERRY CREAM SCONES

{SWEET RICE, MILLET, OAT}

Gluten-free scones are one of the hardest pastries to get right, texture-wise, and it took me a dozen or so tries to settle on this combination of ingredients and techniques. Sandwiching the tender berries between two layers of dough keeps things neat and tidy, and the berries bake into a chunky jam of sorts. (I love blackberries, but any summer berry, or a combination, will work here.) Cream makes for the most lusciously tender scones, and an egg helps the dough hold together. Sweet rice, millet and oat flours give the dough a mild flavor with a bit of nuttiness and textural interest. On the day of baking, the scones are crisp on the outside with tender middles; after a day they soften from the moisture in the fruit and gain a slightly cakey texture.

Do give yourself 2 hours to make these scones; most of the time is inactive, and the extra chilling steps ensure tender scones that hold their shape as they bake.

MAKES 8 MEDIUM-SIZED SCONES

1 cup (155 g) sweet white rice flour

½ cup (65 g) millet flour

½ cup (50 g) oat flour

¼ cup (50 g) organic granulated cane sugar, plus 1 tsp for the berries

1 tbsp (12 g) baking powder

½ tsp fine sea salt

5 tbsp (70 g) cold, unsalted butter, sliced

6 tbsp (90 ml) heavy cream, more as needed, plus 1 tbsp (15 ml) for brushing the scones

1 large egg

1 tsp vanilla extract

1 cup (130 g) fresh blackberries, halved

1 tbsp (10 g) coarse sugar such as demerara or turbinado, for sprinkling

FOR SERVING (OPTIONAL)
Crème Fraîche (page 223)

Honey

In a large bowl, combine the sweet rice, millet and oat flours with the ¼ cup (50 g) sugar, baking powder and salt. Add the butter and blend with a pastry cutter or your fingertips until the butter is broken down into the size of small peas. Chill this mixture until cold, 15–30 minutes.

Meanwhile, whisk together the 6 tablespoons (90 ml) cream, egg and vanilla in a measuring pitcher. Chill until needed.

Remove the flour mixture from the refrigerator. Gradually add the cream mixture, working with a flexible silicone spatula until the dough holds together when you give it a squeeze; you may need to add 1–6 tablespoons (15–90 ml) of cream to properly hydrate the dough and the amount will vary depending on the temperature and humidity of your kitchen and how much you've worked in your butter. Knead the dough 20 or so times in the bowl to bring it together in a ball; unlike wheat scones, these gluten-free scones require more kneading to bring the dough together, so don't be shy. Cover and chill the dough for 15 minutes or up to several hours.

While the dough chills, rinse, dry and slice the berries in half, and set aside until needed.

Remove the dough from the refrigerator and place on a surface dusted lightly with oat flour. Divide the dough into 2 equal portions (they will weigh about 10 ounces [285 g] each) and flatten each into a 6-inch (15-cm) diameter round a scant ½-inch (1.3-cm) thick. Place the berries atop one of the rounds in an even layer, leaving a ½-inch (1.3-cm) border. Sprinkle with the remaining 1 teaspoon cane sugar and top with the second dough round. Squish the edges together to seal and smooth into an even round.

Wrap the scone in plastic wrap and chill until firm, 30 minutes or up to overnight.

When ready to bake, position a rack in the upper third of the oven and preheat to 400ºF (200ºC). Stack a rimmed baking sheet atop a second rimmed baking sheet and line with parchment paper (this will keep the bottoms from over-browning).

Remove the scone from the refrigerator, unwrap and place on a cutting board. Brush the scone with the remaining 1 tablespoon (15 ml) cream and sprinkle with the 1 tablespoon (10 g) coarse sugar. Use a large, sharp chef's knife to cut the scone into 8 wedges and place the wedges on the prepared baking sheet, spaced well apart.

(continued)

Bake the scones until golden on top and cooked through, 20–30 minutes. Remove from the oven and let cool until warm, 20 minutes; they are still baking from residual heat. The scones are best the day of baking but will keep, airtight at room temperature, for a day or two.

VARIATIONS

CHESTNUT FIG SCONES
The earthy flavor and jammy fig filling of this variation reminds me a bit of really delicious Fig Newtons. Chestnut flour creates a softer, cakier texture than the originals.

Omit the millet and oat flours and replace with 1 cup (105 g) chestnut flour. In place of the berries, use ¾ cup (130 g) sliced fresh figs (about 3 medium figs). To slice the figs, trim away the stems, halve, place cut side down and slice ¼-inch (6-mm) thick. Pictured on page 10.

CINNAMON AMARANTH PEACH SCONES
This version has a strong amaranth flavor when hot, but when cool, the scones taste complex and nutty.

Omit the millet flour and substitute ½ cup (65 g) amaranth flour, adding 1 teaspoon ground cinnamon along with the flours. In place of the berries, use 1 cup (150 g) sliced ripe but firm peaches or nectarines. Sprinkle the tops of the cream-brushed scones with 1 tablespoon (10 g) organic granulated cane sugar mixed with ¼ teaspoon ground cinnamon.

ORANGE CURRANT CREAM SCONES
Classic, with a bit of brightness. Serve these with a bit of clotted cream, honey and a pot of Earl Grey.

Add the finely grated zest from 1 small orange to the dough along with the butter. When the butter is worked in, add in ⅓ cup (55 g) lightly packed, plump dried currants. Omit the vanilla, berries and additional sugar, form the dough into one 6-inch (15-cm) diameter round rather than two and proceed with the recipe.

A FEW TIPS FOR SCONE SUCCESS

- When making scones, keep your ingredients and dough cool. Scone dough is similar to pie dough in that small pebbles of butter not fully incorporated into the dough add flake to the finished product. Make sure your butter is cold to start with, work quickly and chill the dough as directed and more often if your kitchen is on the warm side.

- How much cream you add is dependent on several factors: how much you've worked in the butter, how warm it is in your kitchen (i.e., how soft the butter has become), the humidity in the air and the way you've measured your flours. I always need the full ¾ cup (180 ml), but other testers needed only a scant ½ cup (120 ml). Add the cream mixture slowly, tossing with a spatula as you go, and stop when the dough holds together when you grab a handful and squeeze, and there are no dry, floury bits in the bottom of the bowl.

- Wheat scones need barely a squeeze to bring the dough together, but this gluten-free dough likes a bit of assertive kneading in the bowl to help it adhere due to the absence of sticky glutens or gums. Once the dough is properly saturated, give it a good firm kneading in the bowl until it forms a sturdy ball.

- Scones' bottoms tend to darken rapidly when baking, so always stack two baking sheets on top of each other, line with parchment and bake in the upper third of the oven.

- Do ahead: The dough can be made, shaped and refrigerated airtight overnight. Cut, unbaked scones can be frozen for longer storage and baked to order from frozen at 375°F (190°C) for about 20 minutes.

BLUEBERRY CORN FLOUR MUFFINS

{SWEET RICE, CORN, OAT}

These pillow-soft muffins are threaded with the warm flavor of corn flour, which soaks up moisture from juicy blueberries while keeping the batter delicate and tender. They're easy to throw together and even easier to love: sweet and cakelike, with some whole-grain oomph from nutty oat and corn flours. Be sure to use powder-fine corn flour and not cornmeal or polenta. If you come across fresh huckleberries (or wild blueberries), their tart flavor and small size make these even more addictive. In this case, decrease the amount of this intense fruit to 1 cup (170 g).

MAKES 12 MUFFINS

8 tbsp (113 g) unsalted butter, at room temperature

½ cup (100 g) organic granulated cane sugar

2 large eggs, at room temperature

½ cup plus 2 tbsp (95 g) sweet white rice flour

½ cup plus 2 tbsp (75 g) corn flour

½ cup (55 g) GF oat flour

1½ tsp (6 g) baking powder

½ tsp baking soda

½ tsp fine sea salt

½ cup (120 ml) well-shaken buttermilk

1 tsp vanilla extract

1½ cups (215 g) fresh blueberries, plus a handful for the tops

Coarse sugar such as turbinado or demerara, for sprinkling

Position a rack in the upper third of the oven and preheat to 350ºF (175ºC). Line a standard muffin pan with 12 paper liners. (Alternatively, skip the liners and grease the pans well with softened butter.)

In the bowl of a stand mixer fitted with the paddle attachment (or in a large bowl with a wooden spoon), beat together the butter and sugar until light and fluffy, scraping down the sides of the bowl occasionally, 2–3 minutes. Beat in the eggs one at a time; it's okay if the mixture looks broken at this point.

Meanwhile, in a medium bowl, sift together the sweet rice, corn and oat flours with the baking powder, baking soda and salt. Stir together the buttermilk and vanilla in another small measuring pitcher or bowl.

With the mixer on low, stir in one-third of the flour mixture, stirring until just combined, then stir in half of the buttermilk mixture, stirring just until combined and scraping the bowl as needed. Continue until you've used up all the ingredients.

Remove the bowl from the mixer and use a flexible silicone spatula to gently fold in the berries. Divide the batter among the muffin cups, filling them nearly to the top (a #25 spring-loaded ice cream scoop makes this a snap). Sprinkle the tops with the coarse sugar and dot with a few extra berries.

Bake the muffins until their tops are golden and a toothpick inserted into the center of one comes out mostly clean with a few moist crumbs, 22–28 minutes, rotating the pan after 15 minutes for even baking. Let the muffins cool in their pan for 5–10 minutes, then remove to a cooling rack. Serve warm or at room temperature.

The muffins are best the day of baking but will keep, airtight at room temperature, for up to 2 days.

MILLET SKILLET CORNBREAD WITH CHERRIES AND HONEY

{CORN, SWEET RICE, OAT, MILLET}

This cornbread was inspired by a millet muffin from the best breakfast place I know of, Plow on Potrero Hill in San Francisco. If you're lucky enough to grab a millet muffin, you'll find it packed with whole millet seed kissed with butter and honey. For days when a simpler, homemade breakfast is in order, I stir together this easy batter studded with toasted millet seed and juicy sweet cherries. When cherries aren't about, make this with 1 cup (115 g) blackberries in their place.

This recipe fits perfectly into an 8-inch (20-cm) cast-iron skillet, and the hot, buttered skillet makes the edges extra crisp and golden. However, it's essential that you turn the bread out of the pan shortly after baking lest it pick up the metallic-tasting seasoning from the pan. You can also bake this in an 8-inch (20-cm) round cake pan; in this case, skip the pan-heating step, grease the pan with 1 teaspoon room-temperature butter and line the bottom with a round of parchment paper cut to fit. See the variation below for baking a double batch of this cornbread.

MAKES ONE 8-INCH (20-CM) BREAD, 6 SERVINGS

2 tbsp (20 g) uncooked whole millet seed

3 tbsp (42 g) unsalted butter

½ cup (80 g) yellow cornmeal (NOT polenta; preferably Arrowhead Mills GF Yellow Cornmeal)

¼ cup (40 g) sweet white rice flour

¼ cup (25 g) GF oat flour

2 tbsp (25 g) organic granulated cane sugar

½ tsp baking powder

½ tsp baking soda

⅜ tsp fine sea salt

1 large egg

2 tbsp (30 ml) honey, plus more for serving

½ cup (120 ml) well-shaken buttermilk

4 oz (115 g) pitted sweet cherries (1 cup) (frozen and not defrosted works, too)

Position a rack in the center of the oven and preheat to 375°F (190°C).

Place the millet seed in a small, dry skillet set over medium heat, and toast, shuffling the pan frequently, until the millet smells fragrant, pops a bit and takes on a bit of color, 2–4 minutes. Tip the millet into a large heatproof bowl to stop the cooking.

Place the butter in an 8-inch (20-cm) ovenproof skillet and place in the oven to melt while you prepare the batter, taking care not to let the butter burn.

In the large bowl containing the millet, whisk together the cornmeal, sweet rice and oat flours, sugar, baking powder, baking soda and salt to combine and eradicate clumps. Make a well in the flour mixture, crack in the egg and add the honey and buttermilk. Remove the hot pan from the oven, swirl the butter around the sides of the pan and pour the rest into the batter, whisking the batter vigorously just until well combined. Scrape the batter into the hot pan, spread into an even layer and dot the cherries evenly over the top; they will sink into the batter as it bakes. Bake the cornbread until golden on top and a tester inserted near the center comes out clean or with a few moist crumbs, 20–30 minutes.

Let the cornbread cool for a minute or two, then turn out of the pan and onto a plate or cutting board, invert again onto another serving board or plate, and let cool for at least 20 minutes and up to several hours; it is still baking from residual heat. Serve the cornbread warm or at room temperature. The cornbread is best the day of baking but will keep, airtight at room temperature, for up to 2 days.

VARIATION: MILLET SKILLET CORNBREAD {DOUBLE BATCH}

To feed a crowd, double all of the ingredients and bake the batter in a 9-inch (23-cm) square baking pan greased with 1 teaspoon room-temperature butter or a 10-inch (25-cm) cast-iron skillet, increasing the bake time to 30–40 minutes.

SORGHUM PEACH OVEN PANCAKE

{SORGHUM, SWEET RICE}

I call this an oven pancake, but the batter is really closer to a crepe, with a higher ratio of milk and eggs to flour that gives this baked breakfast a custardy texture not unlike the clafoutis on pages 167 and 179. Sorghum flour has a mild, nutty flavor that pairs beautifully with floral honey and peaches, and it retains a bit of texture in the finished product that reminds me of the cream of wheat cereal my dad would make on cool mornings when I was growing up. You can either top slices with an extra drizzle of honey or go all out and sprinkle the whole thing with powdered sugar for a dramatic presentation. Mine always sticks to the bottom a bit, so don't be alarmed if the first slice is difficult to get out of the pan; a thin metal spatula will unstick subsequent slices. If the batter separates a bit during baking, this is normal and doesn't detract from the deliciosity of this pancake. For a quicker breakfast, make the batter the night before and refrigerate overnight; whisk to combine in the morning and proceed with the recipe. And feel free to trade in apricots, pitted cherries or nectarines for the peaches.

MAKES 4 SERVINGS

PEACHES

2 tbsp (28 g) unsalted butter

2 large peaches (about 14 oz [400 g] total), cut into ½-inch (1.3-cm) thick wedges (enough for a single layer in the skillet)

2 tbsp (30 ml) honey

PANCAKE

½ cup (60 g) sorghum flour

½ cup (80 g) sweet white rice flour

¼ tsp fine sea salt

3 large eggs

1 tbsp (15 ml) honey

1 tsp vanilla extract

1¼ cups (295 ml) whole milk

FOR SERVING (OPTIONAL)

Powdered sugar or honey

Whipped Cream (page 224), Crème Fraîche (page 223) or plain Greek yogurt

Position a rack in the center of the oven and preheat to 400ºF (200ºC).

For the peaches, place the butter in a 10-inch (25-cm) ovenproof skillet with 2-inch (5-cm) high sides and place in the oven to melt, 2–3 minutes. Remove from the oven and swirl or brush the butter over the sides of the pan. Carefully add the peaches in a single layer to the buttery skillet and drizzle with the honey. Return to the oven and roast until the juices bubble thickly, about 15 minutes, turning the peaches once or twice.

Meanwhile, to make the pancake, in a large bowl, whisk together the sorghum and sweet rice flours with the salt. Add the eggs, honey, vanilla and a splash of the milk and whisk vigorously until very smooth. Gradually whisk in the rest of the milk until smooth. Alternatively, combine all ingredients in a blender and puree smooth. The batter will be very loose.

If the batter has separated, whisk to recombine, then pour the batter over the peaches in the hot skillet. Return to the oven and bake until the pancake is puffed, pale golden on top, deeply bronzed around the edges and cooked through, 25–35 minutes. Remove from the oven.

To serve, sprinkle all over with the powdered sugar, if desired. Cut the pancake into wedges with a sharp knife, then use a thin metal spatula to remove slices from the pan and onto plates. Optionally, top with whipped cream and honey if desired. Serve warm.

Leftover pancake keeps well, refrigerated airtight, for up to 3 days. Reheat before serving for best results.

POPPY SEED, PLUOT AND BUCKWHEAT STREUSEL MUFFINS

{SWEET RICE, OAT, BUCKWHEAT}

These muffins are essentially coffee cake in individual form. Earthy buckwheat, oats, brown sugar and cinnamon set off sweet-tart bursts of pluot lodged within a moist and tender crumb crowned with sandy streusel. Pluots are a plum-apricot hybrid that are three-fourths plum and come with all of the plum's sweet/tart/floral trappings but with a slightly firmer, sweeter flesh. That said, these muffins take well to variations, so try them with any summer berry or stone fruit, fresh figs or ripe chunks of pear in place of the pluots. The poppy seeds add a nice bit of crunch and depth of flavor, but the muffins will still explode with deliciousness should you decide to leave them out. Do be sure to press the streusel gently into the batter prior to baking to help it adhere.

MAKES 14 MUFFINS

STREUSEL

3 tbsp (42 g) cold, unsalted butter, cut into small pieces, plus 1 tsp for greasing the tops of the muffin tins

¼ cup (35 g) sweet white rice flour

2 tbsp (10 g) oat flour

1 tbsp (5 g) tapioca flour

½ cup (50 g) GF old-fashioned rolled oats

¼ cup (50 g) packed organic light or dark brown sugar

1½ tsp (4 g) poppy seeds

½ tsp ground cinnamon

¼ plus ⅛ tsp fine sea salt

MUFFINS

⅓ cup (80 ml) whole milk (or plant milk such as almond milk)

2 tbsp (15 g) poppy seeds

2 tsp (10 ml) vanilla extract

8 tbsp (113 g) unsalted butter, at room temperature

½ cup plus 2 tbsp (130 g) packed organic light brown sugar

2 large eggs, at room temperature

¾ cup (115 g) sweet white rice flour

½ cup (50 g) oat flour

¼ cup plus 2 tbsp (50 g) buckwheat flour

2 tsp (8 g) baking powder

½ tsp fine sea salt

9 oz (252 g) pluots (about 3), ripe but firm (1½ cups [252 g] pluot chunks)

Position a rack in the upper third of the oven and preheat to 350ºF (175ºC). Rub the tops of 2 standard muffin pans with the 1 teaspoon softened butter (this will prevent any overflow from sticking) and line with 14 paper liners. (Alternatively, skip the liners and grease the pans well with softened butter.)

To make the streusel, in the bowl of a stand mixer fitted with the paddle attachment, combine the sweet rice, oat and tapioca flours with the rolled oats, brown sugar, poppy seeds, cinnamon, salt and remaining 3 tablespoons (42 g) butter. Mix on medium-low speed until the butter is worked in and the streusel comes together in clumps, about 2 minutes. (Alternatively, rub the butter in with your fingertips.) Scrape the streusel into a small bowl and set aside; no need to wash the mixer bowl.

To make the muffins, in a measuring pitcher, stir together the milk, poppy seeds and vanilla and set aside. This will plump up the seeds a bit and draw out their unique flavor.

Meanwhile, in the now-empty bowl of the stand mixer (or in a large bowl with a wooden spoon), combine the butter and brown sugar. Beat on medium speed until light and fluffy, 3 minutes, scraping down the sides of the bowl once or twice. Add the eggs one at a time, beating to combine after each addition; the mixture may look broken at this point and that's okay.

While the butter does its thing, sift the sweet rice, oat and buckwheat flours with the baking powder and salt into a medium bowl. When the eggs are incorporated into the butter, turn the mixer to low. Add one-third of the flour mixture, mixing to combine, then add half of the milk mixture, mixing to combine. Continue until you've used up all the milk and flour mixtures, scraping down the sides and bottom of the bowl as well as the paddle to make sure the batter is homogenous.

To prepare the pluots, use a sharp paring or serrated knife to cut the flesh off of the pits, then into ½- to 1-inch (1.3- to 2.5-cm) chunks; you should have 1½ cups of prepared fruit. Remove the bowl from the mixer and use a flexible spatula to gently fold in the pluot chunks until evenly distributed.

Use a tablespoon or spring-loaded ice cream scoop to divide the batter among the muffin cups, filling them nearly to the top and mounding them in the center, and making sure to include some pluot pieces in the last couple of muffins. Sprinkle the streusel over the muffins and press it in slightly. Bake the muffins until the tops are golden and a tester inserted into the center of one comes out clean or with a few moist crumbs, 22–32 minutes. Remove the muffins from the oven and let cool for 10 minutes, then carefully remove from the pans and let cool to warm or room temperature, at least 10 more minutes. Store airtight at room temperature for up to 2 days.

HUCKLEBERRY BUCKWHEAT CHEESE BLINTZES

{BUCKWHEAT, SWEET RICE}

My paternal grandmother, whom we called Bubba, made the best cheese blintzes—little parcels of lightly sweetened farmer cheese wrapped in soft crepes and fried in butter, which we would eat with sour cream and applesauce. Not exactly health food. But adding fresh berries and loads of buckwheat flour, and frying them in the thinnest layer of ghee, helps lighten these up. A drizzle of maple syrup is just the thing to add earthy sweetness, and I confess to liking a dollop of sour cream or Greek yogurt to up the creamy factor. Ghee is your friend for frying, as it has a high smoke point and warm flavor. Huckleberries, with their intense flavor and low water content, make an ideal filling, though wild blueberries work beautifully (and are often available frozen) as do cultivated blueberries. Assembled blintzes freeze brilliantly; to serve, just fry them on both sides over low heat until golden and heated through. Look for farmer cheese that's like a firmer version of ricotta.

MAKES ABOUT 12 BLINTZES, 4–6 SERVINGS

BUCKWHEAT CREPES
1 cup (235 ml) whole milk

4 large eggs

1 tbsp (10 g) organic granulated cane sugar

¼ tsp fine sea salt

¾ cup (105 g) buckwheat flour

¼ cup (35 g) sweet white rice flour

1 tbsp (14 g) melted butter

FILLING
1 lb (450 g) farmer cheese

1½ tbsp (20 g) organic granulated cane sugar

1 egg yolk

Big pinch of salt (1/16 tsp)

1 tbsp (14 g) melted butter

¾ cup (100 g) fresh or frozen huckleberries (or wild blueberries)

FOR FRYING AND SERVING
2 tbsp (28 g) ghee or unsalted butter

Extra huckleberries

Maple syrup

Greek yogurt, sour cream or Crème Fraîche (page 223)

To make the crepes, in a blender, combine the milk, eggs, sugar, salt, buckwheat flour and sweet rice flour. Blend on low to combine, scraping down the sides of the blender once or twice. With the motor running, blend in the melted butter. Pour the batter into a measuring pitcher or bowl and stick a spatula in there; you'll need to stir the batter occasionally while cooking the crepes in order to incorporate the flecks of buckwheat that tend to sink to the bottom. Have a large plate by the stove on which to stack the cooked crepes.

To make the filling, in a medium bowl, stir together the cheese, sugar, egg yolk and salt. Quickly stir in the melted butter, then gently fold in the huckleberries.

To fry the crepes, heat an 8-inch (20-cm) crepe pan or skillet over medium heat, and use a scrunched-up paper towel to swipe it with a bit of ghee or butter. (Too much butter will cause the batter to slip as you swirl it to coat the pan.)

Pour a scant ¼ cup (59 ml) of batter onto the crepe pan, tilting, swirling and shuffling to coat it evenly with a thin layer of batter. Cook the crepe until just barely set on top, 30–60 seconds. Use a thin, metal spatula to ease the edges of the crepe up off the pan, then slide (or drag) the crepe onto the plate, cooked side down. It should be barely colored on the bottom.

Continue cooking the crepes, swiping the pan with a bit of butter between crepes, and adjusting the heat so that the pan doesn't burn but the crepes cook in 30–60 seconds each.

To fill the blintzes, place 2½ tablespoons (38 g) of cheese filling on the lower third of a crepe and fold the bottom up over the cheese. Fold the sides in so that they just touch, then roll the blintz up from the filled end up to form a parcel—it should look something like an egg roll. Stack the filled blintzes on a plate.

When the blintzes have all been filled, melt some butter or ghee in your crepe pan over medium heat (or use another large skillet if you like). (Preheat your oven to 200ºF [100ºC] if you're making these for a crowd and need to keep them warm while you fry the next batch.) Fry the blintzes until they are golden on the bottom, about 2 minutes, then flip and brown on the second side, another 2 minutes. Have the heat low enough so that the filling heats through without the bottoms burning.

Serve the warm blintzes with the berries, maple syrup and a dollop of yogurt.

Extra blintzes keep brilliantly, fried or unfried, in the refrigerator for up to 3 days or in the freezer for up to 2 months.

APPLE, BUCKWHEAT AND GRUYÈRE PUFF PANCAKE

{SWEET RICE, BUCKWHEAT, OAT}

My sole New Year's resolution for the past five years has been "eat more dessert," specifically, dessert made by someone else. I tend to eschew sweets when out and about, knowing there are usually goodies waiting for us back at home. But tasting what other cooks get up to in the kitchen is endlessly inspiring, thus the resolution. One January 1st, my request was answered. A few musician friends came over to welcome the New Year with tunes and comestibles. My friend's mother, Barbara, who was visiting from the Provençal village in which she lives, brought over a tub of buttery, caramelized apples and a container of batter, which she put together and popped into the oven. We feasted on apple puff pancake laced with cinnamon and lemon, and Barbara kindly shared her recipe with me. Barbara often adds slices of Brie cheese to her pancake, which is pure genius.

Here, I've adapted Barbara's recipe to work with alternative grains—oat flour for starchy sweetness, buckwheat for nutty flavor, and sweet rice for binding power—and added some cave-aged Gruyère (though sharp Cheddar or Brie work beautifully, too). The salty cheese sets off the sweet, caramelized apples brightened with lemon, the batter puffs up, forming a crackly crust that flakes as it cools, and if you're like us, you'll be stealing into the kitchen to sneak slices from the pan at all hours of the day—and year.

MAKES 4 SERVINGS

APPLES AND CHEESE

1 lb (450 g) tart, firm baking apples (such as Granny Smith; about 2 large or 4 medium)

4 tbsp (56 g) unsalted butter

¼ cup (25 g) organic granulated cane sugar

2 tbsp (30 ml) lemon juice

1 tsp ground cinnamon

⅛ tsp fine sea salt

3–4 oz (56–84 g) thinly sliced cave-aged Gruyère cheese (or sharp Cheddar or Brie)

BATTER

¼ cup (35 g) sweet white rice flour

¼ cup (30 g) buckwheat flour

¼ cup (25 g) GF oat flour

1 tbsp (12 g) organic granulated cane sugar

½ tsp fine sea salt

4 large eggs

1 cup (235 ml) whole milk

FOR SERVING (OPTIONAL)

Maple syrup or powdered sugar

Position a rack in the upper third of the oven and preheat to 425ºF (220ºC).

To prepare the apples, peel them, cut their flesh off the core, and slice them about ⅜-inch (1-cm) thick; you should have about 2¾ cups (412 g).

Melt the butter in a 10-inch (25-cm) ovenproof skillet (such as a well-seasoned cast-iron skillet) over medium-high heat. Add the apples and sprinkle with the sugar, lemon juice, cinnamon and salt. Cook, turning the apples occasionally with a metal spatula, until the apples are tender and their juices thicken, 8–10 minutes, decreasing the heat as needed.

Meanwhile, to make the batter, sift the sweet rice, buckwheat and oat flours with the sugar and salt into a large bowl. Whisk in the eggs 2 at a time, whisking until smooth, then gradually whisk in the milk to form a loose batter. If the batter is lumpy, strain it through a medium-mesh sieve. (Alternatively, throw everything in a blender and blend until smooth, about 1 minute.)

When the apples are cooked, give them a final stir, top them with the sliced cheese, and pour the batter over the top. Immediately transfer to the oven and bake until the pancake is puffed, golden and cooked through, 18–28 minutes, decreasing the oven temperature if the sides are browning too quickly and rotating the pancake halfway through for even baking.

Remove from the oven, cut into wedges, and serve hot or warm with maple syrup, if desired. Leftovers keep well, refrigerated airtight, for up to 2 days. Reheat in a 350ºF (175ºC) oven for best results.

NOTE: For a strictly sweet version, leave off the cheese and serve the pancake sprinkled with powdered sugar or drizzled with maple syrup and topped with a plume of Whipped Cream (page 224).

PUMPKIN CRANBERRY NUT AND SEED LOAF

{OATS}

This loaf was inspired by the Adventure Bread made at Josey Baker's The Mill in San Francisco, home of the infamous four-dollar toast. His adventure bread is packed with nuts, seeds and oats, held together by psyllium husk, chia seeds and flaxseeds, moistened with water, vegetable oil and maple syrup. Once you've sourced the ingredients (available in bulk at most health food stores), the bread is incredibly simple to mix up and bake. A loaf keeps, refrigerated, for up to 2 weeks. At first glance, the recipe seems impossible, as though it shouldn't work; but mix it all up, let it rest for a few hours, and bake it and you'll soon find yourself as hooked as I am.

I've updated Baker's loaf with the fall flavors of pumpkin, cranberries, walnuts and pepitas, and a hint of warming spices. Slices are heavenly when toasted and spread with whipped cream cheese, but the bread isn't so sweet that you couldn't use it to make toasted cheese sandwiches or to wrap around slices of leftover Thanksgiving turkey.

MAKES ONE 9 BY 5-INCH (23 BY 13-CM) LOAF

1½ cups (175 g) raw walnut halves

1 cup (140 g) raw pumpkin seeds (pepitas)

2¾ cups (250 g) GF old-fashioned rolled oats

1 cup (145 g) dried cranberries

½ cup (90 g) flaxseeds

⅓ cup (30 g) psyllium husks

¼ cup (40 g) chia seeds

2 tsp (9 g) fine sea salt

¾ tsp ground cinnamon

½ tsp freshly grated nutmeg

1 (15-oz [425-g]) can unsweetened pumpkin puree

1 cup (235 ml) water

¼ cup (60 ml) maple syrup

¼ cup (60 ml) sunflower oil (or light olive oil)

Position a rack in the center of the oven and preheat to 325ºF (165ºC). Spread the walnuts and pumpkin seeds on a small, rimmed baking sheet and toast until golden and fragrant, shuffling the pan occasionally, 10–15 minutes. Remove from the oven.

Meanwhile, in a large bowl, stir together the oats, cranberries, flaxseeds, psyllium husks, chia seeds, salt, cinnamon and nutmeg to combine. Stir in the hot walnuts and pumpkin seeds. Add the pumpkin puree, water, maple syrup and sunflower oil and stir well with a sturdy wooden spoon or your hands to make sure the "dough" is moistened through and evenly distributed.

Line a 9 by 5-inch (23 by 13-cm) loaf pan on all sides with parchment paper and scrape the dough into the prepared pan, packing it in and rounding it slightly on top; it won't rise in the oven. Cover tightly with a piece of plastic wrap and let sit at room temperature for 2–8 hours.

When ready to bake, preheat the oven to 400ºF (200ºC). Bake the loaf for 1 hour and 15 minutes; it will be deeply bronzed on top and feel firm to the touch. Let cool completely, at least 2 hours. The bread is best sliced fairly thinly and toasted well. It will keep, refrigerated airtight, for up to 2 weeks.

TART CHERRY, CHOCOLATE AND HEMPSEED NO-BAKE OAT BARS {VEGAN}

My mom, who's a bit of a health nut (understatement), used to disparage an ex by saying, "He ate COOKIES for BREAKFAST!" as if there were no worse crime. Call me rebellious, but I'm a fan of cookies for breakfast, particularly if there's chocolate involved, and that's essentially what these no-bake granola bars are.

I always assumed no-bake bars were inferior to the baked variety, but Laura of the blog Tutti Dolci changed my mind when she mixed hers up with plenty of almond butter and topped them with a smear of salted chocolate. I like mine with a dose of dried tart cherries, buttery hempseeds and crunchy cacao nibs, though feel free to switch up the nuts, seeds and fruit as you see fit; the recipe is quite forgiving. If you're anything like me, you'll find yourself dipping into your stash … any time of day.

MAKES 16 SMALL BUT RICH BARS

BARS
1 cup (235 ml) smooth, unsalted almond butter (preferably at room temperature, stirred if separated)

½ cup (120 ml) maple syrup

2 tsp (10 ml) vanilla extract

¼ tsp fine sea salt

2½ cups (225 g) GF old-fashioned rolled oats

½ cup (55 g) unblanched sliced almonds

½ cup (70 g) dried tart cherries (or cranberries)

¼ cup (30 g) hulled hempseeds

¼ cup (30 g) cacao nibs

TOPPING
1 tbsp (15 ml) extra-virgin coconut oil

¾ cup (130 g) chopped bittersweet chocolate

Flaky salt such as Maldon, cacao nibs and hempseeds, for sprinkling

To make the bars, in a large bowl, whisk together the almond butter, maple syrup, vanilla and salt until smooth. Set aside.

Place the oats in a wide, heavy-bottomed skillet set over low heat and toast until golden and fragrant, 8–12 minutes, stirring frequently. Pour the warm oats into the bowl with the almond butter mixture. Wipe out the skillet and add the almonds, toasting over low heat and stirring frequently until golden and fragrant, 4–6 minutes. Add the almonds to the bowl with the oats, then add the dried cherries, hempseeds and cacao nibs. Use a flexible spatula to fold the mixture until well combined. Let sit until cool enough to handle, 5–10 minutes.

Line an 8-inch (20-cm) square pan with a sling of parchment paper, leaving an overhang on each side to use as handles. Scrape in the oat mixture and use damp hands to pack the mixture firmly into an even layer.

To make the topping, place the coconut oil and chocolate in a small saucepan and set it over the lowest possible heat, stirring constantly with a heatproof silicone spatula until the chocolate is melted and smooth. Pour the melted chocolate over the bars, and tilt the pan gently to coat it in an even layer; there will be just enough. Sprinkle the top with a few small pinches of flaky salt and several large pinches of cacao nibs and hempseeds. Chill the bars until firm, at least 2 hours and up to 1 day.

Loosen the edges of the bar with a small, offset spatula or the tip of a knife, and use the parchment handles to lift it up and out of the pan and onto a cutting board. Use a large, sharp chef's knife to cut 16 squares.

Store the bars airtight in the refrigerator; they will soften if left at room temperature. They are crispest on the day of making but will keep well for up to 5 days.

NOTE: Natural nut butters often come with a slick of oil at the top of the jar, so be sure to give yours a good stir before you get started measuring.

ROASTED BANANA TEFF SCONES WITH MUSCOVADO SUGAR GLAZE

{SWEET RICE, TEFF, OAT}

These decadent scones are filled with the malty flavors of teff flour, molasses and roasted banana, with toothsome heft from whole grains and pecans. The scones themselves are minimally sweet to contrast a butterscotch-y muscovado sugar glaze that was inspired by a recipe from the West Oakland brunch spot Brown Sugar Kitchen.

MAKES 8 SCONES

ROASTED BANANAS AND PECANS

3 large bananas (1¼ lb [570 g] in peel)

2 tbsp (25 g) packed light or dark muscovado sugar (or organic brown sugar)

1 tbsp (14 g) unsalted butter

¾ cup (90 g) raw pecan halves

SCONES

1 cup (155 g) sweet white rice flour

¾ cup (100 g) teff flour, plus more for shaping the scones

¼ cup (25 g) GF oat flour

2 tbsp (25 g) packed light or dark muscovado sugar (or organic brown sugar)

1 tbsp (15 g) baking powder

½ tsp fine sea salt

5 tbsp (70 g) cold, unsalted butter, sliced

½ cup (120 ml) cold, heavy cream, plus another 1–7 tbsp (15–105 ml), as needed

1 large egg

1 tsp vanilla extract

GLAZE

¼ cup (25 g) organic powdered sugar

3 tbsp (45 ml) heavy cream

1 tbsp (14 g) unsalted butter

¼ cup (50 g) packed light or dark muscovado sugar (or organic brown sugar)

½ tsp vanilla extract

⅛ tsp fine sea salt

Position a rack in the upper third of the oven and preheat to 400ºF (200ºC). To prepare the bananas and pecans, peel the bananas, slice them into ½-inch (1.3-cm) rounds, and place them on a small baking sheet lined with parchment paper for easy cleanup. Sprinkle with the muscovado sugar and dot with the butter. Roast in the oven until the bananas are golden and tender, 20–30 minutes, flipping them once halfway through roasting and being gentle with them so they stay intact. Remove from the oven, immediately scrape into a shallow, heatproof bowl, and refrigerate until completely chilled, at least 20 minutes. Lower the oven temperature to 350ºF (175ºC). Spread the pecans on a small, rimmed baking sheet and toast in the oven until fragrant and crisp, 8–10 minutes. Let cool completely, then break up into rough quarters.

Meanwhile, to make the scones, in a large bowl, combine the sweet rice, teff and oat flours with 2 tablespoons (25 g) muscovado sugar, baking powder and salt. Add the butter and blend with a pastry cutter or your fingertips until the butter is broken down into the size of small peas. Chill this mixture until cold, 15–30 minutes. In a measuring pitcher, whisk together the ½ cup (120 ml) cream, egg and vanilla and refrigerate until needed. Increase the oven temperature to 425ºF (220ºC). Stack a rimmed baking sheet atop a second rimmed baking sheet and line with parchment paper (this will keep the bottoms from over-browning).

Add the cooled pecans and bananas to the butter/flour mixture and toss gently to combine. Gradually add the cream mixture, working with a flexible silicone spatula until the dough holds together when you give it a squeeze; you may need to add 1–6 tablespoons (15–90 ml) more cream to properly hydrate the dough. Knead the dough 20 or so times in the bowl to form a ball; unlike wheat scones, these gluten-free scones require more kneading to bring the dough together, so don't be shy. Cover and refrigerate the dough for 15 minutes or up to several hours.

Place the dough on a board dusted lightly with teff flour. Dust the top of the dough round lightly with more teff flour, and use clean, dry hands to pat it into a 7-inch (18-cm) round, 1¼ inches (3 cm) high. Use a sharp chef's knife to cut the round into 8 wedges, and use a thin metal spatula or bench scraper to transfer the scones to the lined baking sheet, spacing them 3 inches (7 cm) apart. Brush the tops of the scones with 1 tablespoon (15 ml) cream. Bake the scones until deeply golden and firm to the touch, 18–25 minutes. Remove from the oven and let cool until barely warm; they are still cooking from residual heat.

While the scones bake, make the glaze. Sift the powdered sugar into a small bowl and set aside. In a small saucepan placed over medium-low heat, melt together the cream, butter, muscovado sugar, vanilla and salt to dissolve the sugar, stirring occasionally, 3 minutes. Pour the hot cream mixture into the powdered sugar and whisk smooth. Let cool to a spreadable consistency, 30–60 minutes. Spoon and spread the glaze over the cooled scones and let it set for 20 minutes or so to firm. These are the best the day of baking, but extras keep for 1–2 days.

MAPLE ORANGE AMARANTH GRANOLA

{OATS, AMARANTH}

Homemade granola is worlds away from the store-bought stuff; even expensive brands tend to taste stale and rancid compared to fresh-baked. This granola tastes like a big, crunchy oatmeal cookie studded with bits of crispy popped amaranth that gives the granola a toasty flavor reminiscent of popcorn. A hot skillet and amaranth seeds are all you'll need to make a bowl of tiny, popped grains; these tend to burn easily, so have extra on hand just in case. The maple, orange and vanilla create a bright, floral flavor not unlike the honey that was traditionally mixed with amaranth by the ancient Aztecs for use in religious rituals. But maple keeps the granola crisper than does honey, which is hygroscopic (which means that it grabs moisture from out of the air), thus maple is a better choice for granola. Either way, a bowl of this crunchy cereal topped with fresh fruit and good yogurt or almond milk is a religious experience.

You'll need two rimmed baking sheets that stack and a couple of pieces of parchment paper to bake this granola. Spreading the uncooked granola into the pan in a thin layer, then covering it with parchment and a second sheet pan, eliminates the need to stir the granola as it bakes, and it ensures fat clusters that clump, almost like a thin granola bar. The salt level here seems high, but it ensures full-flavored granola. Do be sure to use fine sea salt or kosher salt, not table salt or an unrefined salt with lots of ocean flavor. And do be sure to give the raw granola a good stir to evenly distribute the salt.

MAKES ABOUT 4 CUPS (600 G)

6 tbsp (70 g) whole, raw amaranth seeds

2½ cups (270 g) GF old-fashioned rolled oats

1 cup (110 g) unblanched, sliced almonds

¼ cup (40 g) maple sugar (or packed organic light brown sugar)

¼ cup plus 2 tbsp (90 ml) maple syrup

¼ cup plus 2 tbsp (85 g) melted, unsalted butter

¾ tsp fine sea salt (not table salt)

1 tsp vanilla extract

Finely grated zest from 1 large orange

Position a rack in the center of the oven and preheat to 325ºF (165ºC).

Heat a medium, heavy-bottomed skillet over medium heat until very hot (I use an 8-inch [20-cm] cast-iron skillet). Add 2 teaspoons (23 g) of the amaranth seeds and shuffle the pan so they're in a single layer; they should begin popping immediately. Shake the pan frequently, every few seconds, and keep the amaranth in a single layer, until about half of the seeds have popped and the rest are golden in color. Tip these into a large bowl. Repeat until you've popped all the amaranth.

To the bowl of popped amaranth, add the oats, almonds, maple sugar, maple syrup, melted butter, salt, vanilla and orange zest. Stir very well to combine, making sure to evenly distribute the salt and amaranth seeds.

Scrape the mixture onto the lined baking sheet, and spread it into a thin sheet. Ideally, the edges will be slightly thicker than the center, as they will bake faster. Lay the second piece of parchment over the granola, and place the second sheet pan on top, right side up, making a little granola sandwich.

Slide the whole thing into the oven and bake for 20 minutes. Rotate and continue baking for 10–20 minutes for a total of 30–40 minutes, peeking under the parchment to make sure the edges aren't burning, until the granola is a rich golden brown. It will still be soft, but should crisp up as it cools. If the granola is still soft after cooling, break it up and return it, uncovered, to a low oven (around 150ºF [65ºC]) and let it dry out for 20 minutes or so.

Let the granola cool completely in the sheet pan sandwich, 1–2 hours, then break up into large sheets or clumps and store in an airtight container for up to 1 month.

NOTE: To make this vegan, trade the melted butter for 5 tablespoons (75 ml) sunflower oil, melted coconut oil or light olive oil.

CAKE

Alternative flours have the power to create cakes full of moisture and tenderness that wheat-based cakes can only dream of. Here, there are none of the pitfalls of all-purpose flour, which can toughen when overworked and obliterate flavors with bland starches. From rustic skillet cakes to refined roulades, the cakes in this chapter explode with the tastes of whole grains, natural sweeteners and peak-of-season produce. Liqueurs, creams, herbs, spices and compotes build layers, making each cake well worth its calories in gustatory pleasure.

Here you'll find a cake for every occasion. There are Bundt cakes, rolled cakes, upside-down cakes and layer cakes. There are spring berries (Blueberry Lemon Verbena Bundt Cake with Vanilla Bean Glaze, page 55), summer stone fruit (Chai-Spiced Nectarine Skillet Cake, page 63), fall pomes (Chestnut Roulade Cake with Rum, Mascarpone and Roasted Pears, page 71) and winter citrus (Petite Blood Orange Cornmeal Upside-Down Cake, page 79).

Vanilla cupcakes get an update from millet and oat flours. Sorghum flour adds textural interest to a chocolate zucchini cake slathered in cream cheese frosting laced with grass-green matcha. Cozy up with a cup of tea and an olive oil pear cake studded with chocolate, rosemary and flaky salt for an eye-opening pick-me-up. And for special occasions, turn to a twist on a berry layer cake topped with mascarpone, or a spiced persimmon number slathered with whiskey cream cheese frosting.

VANILLA CHIFFON CAKE

{SWEET RICE, MILLET, OAT}

During my stint at pastry school, we spent what felt like an inordinate amount of time on cakes. Genoise, chiffon, angel food, white cakes, yellow cakes … they all tasted bland and boring to me. And they're supposed to. These light, spongy cakes are designed to soak up flavors from other ingredients, making the possibilities endless. I find chiffon to be the easiest and most foolproof, with a moist, springy crumb that gets a double lift from baking powder and whipped egg whites. Here, millet and oat flours add their nutty, buttery flavors with subtle flecks of grain, while sweet rice flour helps maintain an airy crumb that no one would EVER guess was gluten-free. Sunflower oil gives it a slightly warm, clean flavor along with a good dose of vanilla. You might think that being made with vegetable oil would put chiffon at a disadvantage, but au contraire: unlike butter-based cakes, chiffon stays soft even when chilled, making it ideal for cream-filled cakes and custards that need refrigeration.

Unlike the refined wheat cakes from pastry school, slices of this version are tasty enough to serve on their own alongside mugs of tea or coffee, dusted with powdered sugar, or dolloped with whipped cream and fresh berries. For special occasions, it can be sliced into thirds horizontally, brushed with liqueurs or syrups, and layered with favorite fillings or frostings. Cut it into strips, soak it with coffee-nocino syrup and layer it with whipped mascarpone and shaved chocolate for an easy tiramisù (page 180). In slightly different configurations, it becomes a base for rolled cakes filled with jam, berries or rhubarb preserves (page 51), a boozy chestnut-pear roulade (page 71), a bright citrus trifle (page 187), and a killer tres leches cake doused with rum and smothered in fresh mango (page 188).

MAKES ONE 8-INCH (20-CM) ROUND CAKE

¼ cup (60 ml) sunflower oil (or other neutral oil)

¼ cup plus 2 tbsp (90 ml) water

3 large egg yolks

1 tsp vanilla extract

½ cup plus 2 tbsp (120 g) organic granulated cane sugar

¼ cup plus 2 tbsp (55 g) sweet white rice flour

¼ cup plus 2 tbsp (50 g) millet flour

¼ cup plus 2 tbsp (40 g) oat flour

1¼ tsp (6 g) baking powder

½ tsp fine sea salt

5 large egg whites (½ cup plus 2 tbsp [150 ml]), at room temperature

¼ tsp cream of tartar

Position a rack in the center of the oven and preheat to 325ºF (165ºC). Line an ungreased 8-inch (20-cm) round cake pan with a piece of parchment paper cut to fit.

In a large bowl, whisk together the oil, water, egg yolks and vanilla, then whisk in the ½ cup (100 g) sugar. Place a strainer over the bowl and sift the sweet rice, millet and oat flours with the baking powder and salt directly into the yolk mixture, adding back any bits left behind in the strainer. Whisk until very smooth.

In the clean, dry bowl of a stand mixer fitted with the whip attachment, whip the egg whites with the cream of tartar on medium-high speed until soft peaks form. Slowly add the remaining 2 tablespoons (20 g) sugar and whip until the whites are glossy and just hold a firm peak when lifted from the bowl, 1–3 more minutes.

Use a flexible silicone spatula to fold one-third of the whites into the batter, then gently fold in the remaining whites until just combined and no streaks remain. Immediately pour the batter into the prepared pan and quickly but gently use an offset spatula to spread the batter into a thin, even layer. Transfer to the oven and bake until the cake is golden, springs back to the touch and a toothpick inserted near the center comes out clean, 40–50 minutes. Remove to a rack and let cool completely in the pan. Loosen the edges with a thin knife or offset spatula, and invert the cake onto a rack or board. Peel away the parchment paper.

The cake can be made a day or two in advance and stored airtight at room temperature until needed.

(continued)

VANILLA CHIFFON CAKE (CONT.)

VARIATIONS

CITRUS CHIFFON CAKE

Use this as the base for the Citrus Trifle with Lillet Sabayon (page 187), or serve slices dressed up with fresh berries and whipped cream and dusted with powdered sugar for an elegant teatime treat.

Place the ½ cup (100 g) sugar in a large bowl. Add the finely grated zest from 1 Meyer lemon, 1 blood orange (or small regular orange) and 1 tangerine and rub with your fingertips until the sugar feels moist. Proceed with the recipe, omitting the vanilla extract.

COCONUT FLOUR CHIFFON CAKE

Coconut flour makes a sweet, springy cake with a touch of texture. It's super absorbent, hence the higher water content of this cake. To make this into a Triple Coconut Rum "Tres Leches" Cake with Mango and Lime (page 188), bake the cake in an 8- or 9-inch (20- or 23-cm) square baking dish with 2-inch (5-cm) sides lined with parchment paper on the bottom only until it springs back to the touch and a tester inserted into the center comes out clean, 40–50 minutes, and proceed with the recipe on page 49.

Increase the water to ¾ cup (175 ml). Omit the flours and make the cake with ⅓ cup (50 g) sweet white rice flour, ⅓ cup (40 g) coconut flour and ¼ cup (30 g) millet flour.

NOTE: This cake can also be baked in a 9-inch (23-cm) round pan or an 8-inch (20-cm) square pan for thinner cakes. Reduce the baking time as needed.

ROSY RHUBARB ROULADE CAKE

{SWEET RICE, OAT, MILLET}

Rolled cakes (sometimes called Swiss rolls or jelly rolls) used to intimidate me until I learned the secret to preventing cracking: roll the warm cake up in a clean tea towel to help set its shape, then spread it with all manner of goodies and roll it up. When sliced, the pinwheels of color are so pleasing to look at, and it's much easier than making a layer cake. Feel free to go wild with the fillings: brush the cake with liqueur and spread with preserves, whipped cream and chopped fresh fruit. I've included a few favorite variations below.

This version gets a rosy filling of pink rhubarb puree. Along with airy sponge cake and rose water–infused crème fraîche, it is the prettiest dessert for a Mother's Day brunch, springtime birthday or high tea.

MAKES ONE 12-INCH (30-CM) LONG ROLLED CAKE, 10-12 SERVINGS

ROLLED CHIFFON CAKE

¼ cup (60 ml) sunflower oil (or other neutral oil)

¼ cup plus 2 tbsp (90 ml) water

3 large egg yolks

1 tsp vanilla extract

½ cup plus 2 tbsp (120 g) organic granulated cane sugar

¼ cup plus 2 tbsp (55 g) sweet white rice flour

¼ cup plus 2 tbsp (40 g) oat flour

¼ cup (40 g) millet flour

2 tbsp (11 g) tapioca flour

1¼ tsp (6 g) baking powder

½ tsp fine sea salt

5 large egg whites (½ cup plus 2 tbsp [150 ml]), at room temperature

¼ tsp cream of tartar

¼ cup (25 g) powdered sugar

FILLING

⅓ cup (80 ml) Crème Fraîche (page 223)

¼ cup (60 ml) heavy whipping cream

Seeds from ½ vanilla bean (or ½ tsp vanilla extract)

1 tbsp (12 g) organic granulated cane sugar

½ tsp rose water (or more to taste)

1¼ cups (297 ml) Rhubarb Puree (page 232), chilled

Powdered sugar, for dusting

To make the cake, position a rack in the center of the oven and preheat to 325ºF (165ºC). Line a 12 by 17–inch (30 by 43–cm) ungreased rimmed baking sheet with a piece of parchment paper cut to fit.

In a large bowl, whisk together the oil, water, egg yolks and vanilla, then whisk in the ½ cup (100 g) sugar. Place a strainer over the bowl and sift the sweet rice, oat, millet and tapioca flours with the baking powder and salt directly into the yolk mixture, adding back any bits left behind in the strainer. Whisk until very smooth.

In the clean, dry bowl of a stand mixer fitted with the whip attachment, whip the egg whites with the cream of tartar on medium-high speed until soft peaks form. Slowly add the remaining 2 tablespoons (20 g) sugar and whip until the whites are glossy and just hold a firm peak when lifted from the bowl, 1–3 more minutes. Use a flexible silicone spatula to fold one-third of the whites into the batter to lighten it, then gently fold in the remaining whites until just combined and no streaks remain.

Immediately pour the batter onto the prepared baking sheet, and quickly but gently use an offset spatula to spread the batter into a thin, even layer. Rap the pan on the counter once or twice to pop any large air bubbles. Transfer to the oven and bake until the cake is golden on top, pulls away from the sides of the pan and feels fairly firm when you press the top gently with the pads of your fingers, 18–22 minutes.

Working quickly, dust the top of the cake with the powdered sugar and loosen it from the sides of the pan using a small offset spatula or knife. Place a large, clean kitchen towel over the cake and top with a second baking sheet or large cutting board. Wearing oven mitts, grab the whole thing and flip it over. Remove the hot pan and carefully peel away the parchment paper. Trim away ¼ inch (6 mm) from each edge of the cake, and roll up the cake with the towel; this will help set the shape and the steam will keep it moist and pliant. You can either roll the cake from a short end for a fatter roll (as shown here) or from a long end for a skinnier roll. Either way, let the cake hang out in its towel roll until mostly cool, about 1 hour.

(continued)

To make the filling, in the bowl of a stand mixer fitted with the whip attachment, combine the crème fraîche, heavy cream, vanilla seeds, sugar and rose water. Whip on medium-high speed until the mixture holds firm peaks. (Err on the side of overwhipping so the cake will hold its shape when rolled.) Taste, adding more rose water if you like. Cover and chill until needed.

Leaving a 1-inch (2.5-cm) border, spread the rhubarb puree evenly over the cake. Dollop the whipped crème fraîche over the rhubarb and spread into an even layer. Re-roll the cake up into a log the same way it was rolled before (but without the towel this time), ending with the seam down. Use a wide spatula or two to transfer the cake to a board. For the cleanest slices, cover the cake and chill until firm, at least 30 minutes and up to 1 day.

When ready to serve, dust the cake with a little more powdered sugar and slice into rounds. The cake will keep, refrigerated airtight, for up to 3 days.

VARIATIONS

APRICOT CRÈME FRAÎCHE ROULADE

Omit the rhubarb puree and spread the cake with 1 cup (235 ml) good apricot jam. Omit the rose water from the whipped crème fraîche and proceed with the recipe.

STRAWBERRY ELDERFLOWER ROULADE

Elderflower liqueur, such as St-Germain, adds sweetness and nectar-like floral notes to this cake that offsets tangy berries. If you don't have any on hand, use an orange liqueur such as Cointreau in its place, or leave it out altogether. And feel free to use other berries or diced poached quince (page 73) in place of the strawberries.

Omit the rhubarb puree. Hull 2 cups (240 g) ripe strawberries and cut them into a small dice. Whip the cream, omitting the rose water. Brush the cake with ¼ cup (60 ml) elderflower liqueur, spread with the whipped crème fraîche, sprinkle the berries over the cream and roll up.

COCONUT CREAM ROULADE {DAIRY-FREE}

Omit the cream and crème fraîche. Place a 13.5-ounce (400 ml) can of full-fat coconut milk (such as Thai Kitchen brand) in the refrigerator for 12–24 hours, until solid. Without tipping or shaking the can, remove the lid and scoop the solidified cream at the top into the bowl of a stand mixer fitted with the whip attachment, leaving behind the watery liquid at the bottom of the can. Whip on medium-high speed until thickened, then add 2 tablespoons (12 g) powdered sugar and ½ teaspoon vanilla extract (or a few drops of rose water, to taste) and continue whipping until the mixture holds firm peaks, like whipped cream. You should have about 1 cup (115 g). Use this in place of the whipped cream/crème fraîche in any of the variations.

NOTE: This cake base is a variation of the chiffon cake on page 49 with a few tweaks to make it conducive to rolling.

BLUEBERRY LEMON VERBENA BUNDT CAKE WITH VANILLA BEAN GLAZE

{SWEET RICE, OAT, MILLET}

To me, fresh lemon verbena smells like happiness—bright, citrusy and floral. The leaves make a tasty tisane when brewed in hot water, or they can be added to custards or cocktails. Here, they perfume a buttery pound cake studded with blueberries and a few scrapes of lemon zest. Once you've tried it, you may start noticing it growing in backyards, and sneaking handfuls when no one's looking. But don't let the hard-to-find herb stop you from making this cake; you can leave it out and still have a happy Bundt.

Cream cheese is the magic ingredient that makes for a moist pound cake dense enough to keep the berries aloft. Be sure to thoroughly grease the crevices of the Bundt pan with a pastry brush dipped in butter softened to the texture of mayonnaise, and dust it thoroughly with flour, tapping out the excess. This will ensure a Bundt that releases easily from the pan every time. This recipe can also be baked in two standard-size loaf pans lined with parchment.

MAKES ONE 10-INCH (25-CM) BUNDT CAKE, 12–16 SERVINGS

CAKE

1 cup (226 g) unsalted butter, at room temperature, plus 2 tbsp (30 g) for the pan

¾ cup (85 g) GF oat flour, plus 2 tbsp (25 g) for the pan

6 oz (¾ cup [175 g]) cream cheese, softened

1 cup (210 g) organic granulated cane sugar

Finely grated zest from 2 large lemons

4 large eggs, at room temperature

1½ cups (235 g) sweet white rice flour

½ cup (70 g) millet flour

¼ cup (30 g) tapioca flour/starch

1 tbsp (12 g) baking powder

1 tsp fine sea salt

2½ cups (340 g) fresh blueberries

⅓ cup (17 g) chopped fresh lemon verbena leaves

GLAZE

1 cup (120 g) powdered sugar

Seeds from 1 vanilla bean

2–4 tbsp (30–60 ml) lemon juice (or enough to make a drizzle-able glaze)

Tiny lemon verbena leaves and extra blueberries, for garnish (optional)

To make the cake, position a rack in the center of the oven and preheat to 350°F (175°C). Use a pastry brush dipped in the 2 tablespoons (30 g) soft butter to grease a 10-cup (10-inch [25-cm]) Bundt pan thoroughly. Sprinkle the pan with 2 tablespoons (25 g) oat flour and tap and shake the pan to coat it evenly, rapping it on the counter to release excess flour.

In the bowl of a stand mixer fitted with the paddle attachment (or in a large bowl with your arm and a wooden spoon), cream together the remaining 1 cup (226 g) butter, cream cheese, sugar and lemon zest on medium speed until light and fluffy, 3–4 minutes. Add the eggs one at a time, mixing to combine after each addition, scraping down the sides of the bowl as needed. The mixture may look broken or curdled; this is okay, as it will come together in the next step.

Meanwhile, sift together the remaining ¾ cup (85 g) oat, sweet rice, millet and tapioca flours with the baking powder and salt into a medium bowl. With the mixer on low, stir the flour mixture into the butter mixture until just thoroughly combined, scraping down the sides of the bowl as needed. Remove the bowl from the mixer, add the blueberries and lemon verbena, and use a flexible silicone spatula to fold gently to combine, scraping the bottom and sides of the bowl to make sure the batter is homogenous. Scrape the batter into the prepared pan and smooth the top, tapping the pan a few times on the counter to settle it into the pan's crevices and release any large air pockets.

Bake the cake until the top is lightly golden and a toothpick inserted near the center comes out clean, or with a few moist crumbs, 55–65 minutes. Let the cake cool slightly, then invert a large plate or platter over the pan, grasp the whole thing and flip it over, tapping it on the counter a few times. The cake should release easily from the pan. Let the cake cool completely.

To make the glaze, in a small bowl, whisk together the powdered sugar, vanilla bean seeds and enough lemon juice to make a drizzle-able glaze. Whisk well to eradicate lumps. Use a pastry brush to drizzle and brush the glaze all over the cake.

Serve the cake at room temperature, scattered with tiny lemon verbena leaves and extra berries if you like. The cake keeps well, airtight at room temperature, for up to 2 days, or refrigerated for up to a few days (let come to room temperature before eating for best results).

MESQUITE CHOCOLATE CAKES WITH WHIPPED CRÈME FRAÎCHE AND RASPBERRIES

{MESQUITE}

These little chocolate cupcakes fall somewhere between a flourless chocolate cake and a more traditional cupcake. Mesquite flour makes the batter sturdier while adding a touch of warm, earthy flavor that underscores the bittersweet chocolate. Topped with whipped crème fraîche and raspberries, they'll win fans at any party or potluck.

The cakes are best at room temperature, so assemble them shortly before serving for best results. They are a bit messier to eat than traditional cupcakes, so do hand out napkins. If you don't have mesquite flour on hand, these work well with an equal measure of almond flour.

MAKES 10 INDIVIDUAL CAKES

CAKES

6 tbsp (85 g) unsalted butter

6 oz (170 g) bittersweet chocolate (60–70% cacao mass), chopped (about 1 cup)

¼ cup plus 2 tbsp (80 g) organic granulated cane sugar

¼ cup plus 2 tbsp (40 g) mesquite flour, sifted

¼ tsp fine sea salt

1 tsp vanilla extract

3 large eggs, at room temperature, separated

TOPPING

½ cup (120 ml) Crème Fraîche (page 223)

⅓ cup (80 ml) heavy cream

1 tbsp (12 g) organic granulated cane sugar

½ tsp vanilla extract

1 pint (~200 g) raspberries, rinsed and dried

A handful of cacao nibs (optional, for serving)

To make the cakes, position a rack in the center of the oven and preheat to 350°F (175°C). Fill a standard muffin pan with 10 paper liners.

In a large heatproof bowl set over a pot of barely simmering water, combine the butter and chocolate. Stir occasionally until the mixture is melted and smooth, 5 minutes. Remove from the heat and whisk in 3 tablespoons (40 g) of the sugar and all of the mesquite flour, salt, vanilla and finally the egg yolks.

In the bowl of a stand mixer fitted with the whip attachment, whip the egg whites on medium-high speed until foamy. Slowly sprinkle in the remaining 3 tablespoons (40 g) sugar and continue whipping until the whites hold soft peaks (when you pull the whip out and turn it upside down, the egg whites form a peak that flops over). Be careful not to overwhip the whites or they will be difficult to incorporate into the batter and will make for denser cakes.

Stir one-third of the egg whites into the chocolate mixture until just combined, then gently fold in the remaining two-thirds until no streaks remain. Divide the batter among the lined muffin cups, filling them three-fourths of the way to the top. Bake the cakes until puffed and cracked, and a toothpick inserted into the centers comes out with moist crumbs, 20–25 minutes. Let cool completely. The cakes can be made up to 1 or 2 days ahead and stored airtight at room temperature for up to 2 days.

To make the topping, combine the crème fraîche, heavy cream, sugar and vanilla extract in the chilled bowl of a stand mixer fitted with the whip attachment. Whip on medium-high speed until the mixture holds firm peaks. Chill until needed.

When ready to serve, dollop the cooled cakes with the whipped crème fraîche and top with a handful of raspberries and a few cacao nibs. Serve soon after assembling.

NOTE: When baking these, be sure to have your eggs at room temperature; cold eggs can cause the batter to seize and firm up, making it difficult to work with. To quickly warm your eggs, place them, still in their shells, in a bowl of hot tap water for 5 minutes or so.

VANILLA BUTTER CAKE WITH WHIPPED MASCARPONE AND SUMMER BERRIES

{SWEET RICE, OAT, MILLET}

This buttery yellow layer cake filled with billows of cream and loads of summer berries is not unlike a giant berry shortcake. Slices always remind me of my dad, who each summer would top store-bought pound cake with whipped cream and ripe strawberries, which he'd toss in a little Triple Sec. Though impressive to look at, it's stupid easy to put together and it tastes even better after a day in the fridge. Mascarpone adds body to the whipped cream and helps it hold its shape, and a double dose of vanilla (bean and extract) adds sweetness to a neutral cake base made soft and springy from sweet rice, oat and millet flours. Serve this cake at cool room temperature so the butter in the cake softens up but the cream stays firm. And if you want to try this Dad-style, brush the cake layers with a bit of Triple Sec or another GF orange liqueur before layering with the berries.

MAKES ONE 8-INCH (20-CM) 2-LAYER CAKE, ABOUT 10 SERVINGS

CAKE

8 tbsp (113 g) unsalted butter, at room temperature, plus 1 tsp for the pan

¾ cup (150 g) organic granulated cane sugar

Seeds from 1 vanilla bean

2 large eggs, at room temperature

¾ cup (105 g) sweet white rice flour

½ cup (50 g) GF oat flour

¼ cup plus 2 tbsp (45 g) millet flour

1½ tsp (6 g) baking powder

½ tsp baking soda

½ tsp fine sea salt

½ cup (120 ml) well-shaken buttermilk

1 tsp vanilla extract

WHIPPED MASCARPONE AND BERRIES

¾ cup (170 g) mascarpone

1 cup (235 ml) heavy whipping cream

Seeds from ½ vanilla bean, split lengthwise and scraped

2 tbsp (25 g) organic granulated cane sugar

5 cups (500 g) mixed summer berries (strawberries, raspberries, blackberries and blueberries)

Honey or sugar for the berries (optional, if berries are tart)

To make the cake, position a rack in the center of the oven and preheat to 325°F (165°C). Grease an 8-inch (20-cm) round cake pan with 2-inch (5-cm) sides with the 1 teaspoon softened butter and line the bottom with a round of parchment paper cut to fit.

In the bowl of a stand mixer fitted with the paddle attachment, beat the remaining 8 tablespoons (113 g) butter, sugar and vanilla seeds together on medium speed until light and fluffy, 2–3 minutes. Add the eggs one at a time, beating well after each addition, and scraping down the sides of the bowl as needed. In a medium-sized bowl, sift together the sweet rice, oat and millet flours with the baking powder, baking soda and salt.

Add half of the flour mixture to the butter mixture and beat on low speed until just combined. Beat in the buttermilk and vanilla, mixing until just combined, then beat in the remaining flour mixture, beating until well combined, scraping down the sides of the bowl once or twice. Remove the bowl from the mixer and stir with a flexible silicone spatula to make sure the batter is homogenous. Scrape the batter into the prepared pan and spread into an even layer. Bake the cake until the top springs back to the touch and a toothpick inserted into the center comes out clean or with a few moist crumbs, 35–45 minutes. Remove from the oven and let cool completely, 1–2 hours.

To make the whipped mascarpone, place the mascarpone, heavy cream, vanilla bean seeds and sugar in the bowl of a stand mixer fitted with the whip attachment (or use a large bowl and a handheld whisk or hand blender). Beat the mixture on low speed until combined, then increase to medium and whip until the mixture holds firm peaks, a minute or so. If you overwhip and the mixture becomes grainy, you can rescue it by folding in several more tablespoons of heavy cream until the mixture loosens up. Cover and chill until needed, up to 1 day.

To assemble the cake, rinse the berries and let them dry on paper towels. Hull and quarter the strawberries, and halve the blackberries if large. Turn the cooled cake out of its pan and peel away the parchment paper. Place the cake on a cutting board and use a large serrated knife to slice the cake in half horizontally, making the halves as even as possible. Place the bottom half cut side up on a serving plate or stand. Spread the cake with half of the whipped mascarpone and top with 2 cups (200 g) of the berries, pressing the berries into the cream slightly. If the berries are tart, drizzle with a bit of honey or sugar. Top with the remaining cake half, cut side down, and spread with the remaining mascarpone and berries, mounding the berries on top. Sprinkle with honey or sugar if you like. Serve the cake immediately, or chill for up to 1 day.

CHOCOLATE ZUCCHINI CAKE WITH MATCHA CREAM CHEESE FROSTING

{SORGHUM, SWEET RICE}

Perhaps it's all the sugar I eat as a professional baker, but I love going to the dentist. And while it may seem wrong, I often show up with a box of baked goods in tow. Some dentists might give you a talking-to for tempting them with evil sugar, but mine has a wicked sweet tooth. When I proffered a box of this cake on my last visit, she called all the hygienists into her office for a slice, and one after another they trooped into the waiting room with brown crumbs about the lips to profess their love for this cake. I can't blame them. This tastes a bit like a classic chocolate cake, but with a fudgy texture from zucchini and sweet rice and sorghum flours and an eye-opening finish of matcha cream cheese frosting. It's sure to win you fans in the unlikeliest of places.

Be sure to measure the zucchini by weight or volume; they can vary greatly in size and too much zucchini will lead to a soggy cake. For cupcakes, divide the batter among 12 paper-lined muffin cups and bake for 18–22 minutes. Do feel free to leave the matcha out of the frosting if making this for kiddos, or decrease the amount if you're not accustomed to its assertive flavor.

MAKES ONE 8-INCH (20-CM) SQUARE CAKE, 9 LARGE SERVINGS OR 16 SMALL SERVINGS

CAKE

8 oz (225 g) zucchini (about 2 small)

1 cup (215 g) packed organic light brown sugar

2 large eggs

¼ cup (60 ml) light olive oil or sunflower oil

¼ cup (60 ml) whole milk

1 tsp vanilla extract

¾ cup (60 g) Dutch-process cocoa powder

¾ cup plus 2 tbsp (115 g) sorghum flour

¼ cup (35 g) sweet white rice flour

2 tsp (8 g) baking powder

½ tsp fine sea salt

FROSTING

6 oz (¾ cup [170 g]) cream cheese, softened

3 tbsp (42 g) unsalted butter, softened

¾ cup (85 g) powdered sugar

1 tbsp (5 g) good-quality culinary-grade matcha

⅛ tsp fine sea salt

To make the cake, position a rack in the center of the oven and preheat to 350ºF (175ºC). Line an 8-inch (20-cm) square baking pan with 2 crisscrossing pieces of parchment paper, leaving an overhang on each side. (Alternatively, grease the pan with 1 teaspoon softened unsalted butter.)

Trim the zucchini and grate them on the medium holes of a box grater (the ones that measure ⅛ inch [2–3 mm]); you should have 1 cup (about 200 g) packed grated zucchini. Place the grated zucchini in a large bowl and add the brown sugar, eggs, oil, milk and vanilla extract, stirring to combine well. Place a strainer over the bowl and sift the cocoa powder, sorghum flour, sweet rice flour, baking powder and salt into the zucchini mixture, pushing through any clumps, then stir well to combine.

Scrape the batter into the prepared pan and smooth into an even layer. Bake the cake until a toothpick inserted near the center comes out with moist crumbs, 45–55 minutes. Let cool completely, at least 30 minutes and up to 1 day. The cake can be wrapped and stored for up to 2 days.

To make the frosting, combine the cream cheese, butter, powdered sugar, matcha powder and salt in the bowl of a stand mixer fitted with the paddle attachment. Beat the frosting on low speed, increasing to medium speed until smooth, light and fluffy, 2–3 minutes, scraping down the sides of the bowl occasionally.

Place the cake on a serving board or platter and use a small, offset spatula or butter knife to spread the frosting over the top and sides, making swirls as you go. The cake can sit at cool room temperature for up to 2 hours. If not serving right away, chill for up to 1 day but bring back to room temperature before serving to soften the frosting.

CHAI-SPICED NECTARINE SKILLET CAKE

{SWEET RICE, MILLET, OAT}

A yellow cake laced with the sweet spices commonly used in masala chai—cinnamon, ginger and cardamom—this is a simply stunning way to showcase nectarines with flavors that straddle the line between summer and fall. A blend of sweet rice, millet and oat flours creates a flavorful base with a delicate crumb that drinks up the juices of the fruit. Use flavorful nectarines that are fragrant but still firm enough to slice. Feel free to trade the nectarines for peeled peaches. The cake can also be baked in a 9-inch (23-cm) cake pan lined with a round of parchment paper.

MAKES ONE 9- TO 10-INCH (23- TO 25-CM) CAKE, 8-10 SERVINGS

SPICED SUGAR

¾ cup (165 g) organic granulated cane sugar

1½ tsp (4 g) ground cardamom

1 tsp ground ginger

¾ tsp ground cinnamon

CAKE

8 tbsp (113 g) unsalted butter, plus 2 tsp (9 g) for greasing the pan and 2 tsp (9 g) for dotting the fruit topping, all at room temperature

Spiced sugar from above (2 tbsp [20 g] reserved for topping; see instructions)

2 large eggs, at room temperature

¾ cup (115 g) sweet white rice flour

½ cup (55 g) oat flour

¼ cup plus 2 tbsp (50 g) millet flour

2 tsp (8 g) baking powder

¾ tsp fine sea salt

⅓ cup (80 ml) Crème Fraîche (page 223) or sour cream

2 tsp (10 ml) vanilla extract

1 lb (450 g) ripe but firm nectarines (about 4 medium; white, yellow or a blend)

Position a rack in the upper third of the oven and preheat to 350°F (175°C). Butter a 9- or 10-inch (23- or 25-cm) ovenproof skillet with 2-inch (5-cm) sides (such as a well-seasoned cast-iron skillet) with the 2 teaspoons (9 g) softened butter. To make the spiced sugar, in a small bowl, stir together the sugar, cardamom, ginger and cinnamon. Set aside 2 tablespoons (20 g) to top the cake.

To make the cake, combine the remaining spiced sugar with the 8 tablespoons (113 g) butter in the bowl of a stand mixer fitted with the paddle attachment (or in a large bowl with a wooden spoon). Beat on medium speed until light and fluffy, scraping down the sides of the bowl occasionally, 3 minutes. Add the eggs one at a time, beating well after each addition.

In a medium bowl, sift together the sweet rice, oat and millet flours with the baking powder and salt. Add half of the flour mixture to the butter mixture and mix on low speed until just combined. Add the crème fraîche and vanilla, mix on low speed until just combined, then add the remaining flour mixture, beating on low until well combined. Remove the bowl from the mixer and give it a good stir with a rubber spatula, scraping the bottom and sides to make sure the batter is homogenous.

If the nectarines are freestones, halve them and remove their pits. Otherwise, cut the fruit off of the pit following the curve of the pit with the knife. Cut some of the nectarine pieces into enough ½-inch (1.3-cm) cubes to equal 1 cup (145 g), and slice the rest into ¼-inch (6-mm) thick wedges. Gently fold the chunks into the batter, then spread the batter evenly into the greased skillet. Fan the nectarine slices over the top of the cake, pressing them into the batter a bit. Sprinkle the reserved 2 tablespoons (20 g) spiced sugar evenly over the top, and dot the fruit with the remaining 2 teaspoons (9 g) butter.

Bake the cake until the top is golden and set, the sides are pulling away from the pan, and a toothpick inserted into the center comes out clean, 45–55 minutes. Let cool completely, 1–2 hours, then use a sharp paring knife to cut the cake into wedges and remove them from the pan using a small offset spatula or cake server. The cake is best the day of baking but leftovers keep well, covered at room temperature, for up to 1 day or refrigerated airtight for up to 3 days.

VARIATION: CHAI-SPICED PEAR SKILLET CAKE

Omit the nectarines and substitute 1 pound (450 g) ripe but firm pears, peeled, cored and prepared in the same manner as the nectarines, tossing the pear slices with 2 teaspoons (10 ml) lemon juice before you fan them over the top of the cake. Proceed with the recipe.

CHESTNUT PLUM FINANCIERS

{ALMOND, CHESTNUT}

These dense little cakes bursting with browned butter were the invention of a bakery near the Paris stock exchange, where they were baked to resemble small gold bricks and named for the money men of the area. Financiers are by far my favorite way to make use of extra egg whites, which I often have after making a batch of ice cream (page 227). The egg whites magically do the work of fluffing the cakes, no leavening necessary, and all that protein makes for a satisfying texture sans gluten. Financiers avail themselves to myriad flavorings, and I often change up the fruit and flours based on what's in season. Here they soak up moisture from tart plums, and they gain dimension from earthy, sweet chestnut flour. Flour from Ladd Hill will make for mild, blond cakes (as pictured here); the darker conventional flour works equally well, but will make for more deeply colored cakes with a more pronounced flavor. If you don't have access to chestnut flour, try these with ⅓ cup (35 g) GF oat flour in its place, or the buckwheat variation below. See "How to Brown Butter," page 219, for tips.

MAKES 10–12 INDIVIDUAL CAKES

8 tbsp (113 g) unsalted butter, plus 1–2 tsp (5–10 g) softened butter for greasing the pans

½ vanilla bean, split lengthwise and scraped

¾ cup (80 g) blanched almond flour

⅓ cup (35 g) chestnut flour

1½ tbsp (11 g) cornstarch

½ cup (100 g) organic granulated cane sugar, plus 1–2 tbsp (10–20 g) for sprinkling

¼ tsp fine sea salt

4 large egg whites (½ cup [120 ml])

3 medium ripe but firm plums (225 g)

VARIATION: BUCKWHEAT HAZELNUT PEAR FINANCIERS

Omit the almond and chestnut flours, using ¾ cup (75 g) hazelnut flour/meal and ⅓ cup (40 g) buckwheat flour. Omit the plums, using 2 medium ripe but firm pears (225 g). Peel the pears, halve them lengthwise, cut out the cores and stems, and halve again crosswise. Slice into ¼-inch (6-mm) thick pieces and proceed with the recipe.

Position a rack in the center of the oven and preheat to 350°F (175°C). Use a pastry brush or scrunched-up paper towel to rub 10–12 standard muffin tins with the 1–2 teaspoons (5–10 g) softened butter. (Alternatively, line the cups with paper liners.)

Place the remaining 8 tablespoons (113 g) butter in a medium, heavy-bottomed saucepan with the vanilla pod and scrapings. Cook over medium heat, swirling occasionally. After 3–5 minutes, the butter will foam up, turn golden and smell nutty, with brown flecks mingling with black vanilla bean seeds on the bottom of the pan. At this point, remove the pan from the heat. Pour the butter into a small heatproof bowl to stop the cooking, and let cool for 10–15 minutes. Remove the vanilla bean and discard.

In a large bowl, sift together the almond and chestnut flours with the cornstarch, ½ cup (100 g) sugar and salt, adding back any bits that get stuck in the strainer. Whisk in the egg whites vigorously until the batter is smooth, then whisk in the melted, cooled butter little by little until well combined. Let sit while you prepare the plums; the batter will thicken slightly. It can also be covered and chilled for up to 2 days prior to baking.

Using a sharp knife, cut the plums off their pits and slice thinly, discarding the end pieces that are mostly skin. Divide the batter among the greased or lined cups, filling them halfway. (A spring-loaded ice cream scoop makes quick work of this.) Top with a fan of plum slices and sprinkle the tops with the remaining 1–2 tablespoons (10–20 g) sugar, using more for tart plums and less for sweeter ones.

Bake the cakes until golden on top and a tester inserted into the center comes out clean, 30–35 minutes. Remove from the oven and let cool for 10 minutes, then use a thin knife or small offset spatula to loosen the edges and release the cakes from the pans. Financiers are best the day of baking, but they keep well, airtight at room temperature, for an additional day or two.

NOTE: Be sure to grease your molds with softened butter the consistency of mayonnaise, as the sticky batter will gladly adhere to less well-greased pans. Alternatively, line the muffin pan with paper liners.

FIG AND OLIVE OIL CAKE

{ALMOND, SWEET RICE, OAT, MILLET}

This cake was inspired by a flat of gorgeous Black Mission figs that arrived at my door, hand-picked by my dear friend Amelia from her grandmother's tree. The figs were enormous—it took only four, each cut into eighths, to cover the top of this cake. The base is the same as the Chocolate Pear Tea Cakes with Rosemary, Olive Oil and Sea Salt on page 68, but with a good grating of lemon zest mixed in to contrast the sweet figs. Almond flour and Greek yogurt form a nubby base that supports the juicy figs, and the lemon plays off the olive oil to add a bit of mysterious complexity. A good sprinkle of sugar over the top makes a crunchy crust. If figs aren't about, try this cake crowned with sliced plums instead.

MAKES ONE 9-INCH (23-CM) ROUND CAKE, 10 SERVINGS

1 tsp (5 g) unsalted butter, for the pan

1 cup (120 g) blanched almond flour

½ cup (80 g) sweet white rice flour

½ cup (55 g) GF oat flour

¼ cup (35 g) millet flour

2 tsp (8 g) baking powder

½ tsp baking soda

¼ tsp fine sea salt

½ cup (100 g) organic granulated cane sugar, plus 2 tbsp (20 g) for sprinkling on top

2 large eggs

½ cup (120 g) whole-milk plain Greek yogurt (I use Straus Family Creamery)

6 tbsp (90 ml) flavorful extra-virgin olive oil

Finely grated zest from 1 medium lemon

4–6 large (200 g) fresh figs

Position a rack in the center of the oven and preheat to 350ºF (175ºC). Grease a 9-inch (23-cm) springform pan with the unsalted butter and place on a rimmed baking sheet to catch any drips.

Sift the almond, sweet rice, oat and millet flours together into a medium bowl along with the baking powder, baking soda and salt, adding back any bits that get caught in the sifter. Set aside.

In a large bowl, whisk together the ½ cup (100 g) sugar, eggs, yogurt, olive oil and lemon zest. Stir the flour mixture into the egg mixture until smooth and homogenous. Scrape the batter into the prepared pan, and smooth into an even layer.

Trim the stems from the figs, halve each lengthwise, and cut each half into 4 wedges (for large figs) or 2 wedges (for smaller figs). Place the fig wedges over the top of the cake batter in concentric rings (or just drop them over the top willy-nilly—that looks nice, too). Sprinkle all over with the remaining 2 tablespoons (20 g) sugar.

Bake the cake until golden on top and a tester inserted near the center comes out clean, 40–50 minutes.

Remove the cake from the oven and let cool completely, 45 minutes, then remove the sides from the pan. Slide the cake onto a serving platter and cut into wedges to serve.

The cake is best within the first 2 days of baking but will keep at room temperature for up to 3 days.

CHOCOLATE PEAR TEA CAKES WITH ROSEMARY, OLIVE OIL AND SEA SALT

{ALMOND, SWEET RICE, OAT, MILLET}

These little cakes were inspired by a cast-iron muffin pan I scored at the Alemany Flea Market in San Francisco. They straddle the line between sweet and savory with the additions of peppery olive oil, bittersweet chocolate, flakes of sea salt and a whisper of rosemary. The combination of sweet rice, millet, oat and almond flours keeps them delicate but never crumbly, despite the lack of gums or starches, and the neutral flavor of the grains allows the subtle nuances of ripe pear to star. These little cakes are incredibly moist from olive oil and whole-milk yogurt, and the almond flour adds a bit of nubby texture. I like to top the muffins with extras of the flavorings to pretty them up and let everyone know what's hiding inside: juicy pear chunks, shavings of chocolate and woodsy rosemary. These make a first-rate afternoon treat alongside a cup of tea, though I won't tell if you have one for breakfast …

MAKES 12 INDIVIDUAL CAKES

CAKES

1 tbsp (14 g) unsalted butter, at room temperature, for greasing the pan

1 cup (120 g) blanched almond flour

½ cup (80 g) sweet white rice flour

½ cup (55 g) GF oat flour

¼ cup (35 g) millet flour

2 tsp (8 g) baking powder

½ tsp baking soda

¼ tsp fine sea salt

½ cup (100 g) organic granulated cane sugar

2 large eggs

½ cup (120 ml) whole-milk plain yogurt (I use Straus European-style whole-milk yogurt)

6 tbsp (90 ml) extra-virgin olive oil

2 tsp (1 g) finely chopped fresh rosemary

⅔ cup (3.5 oz [100 g]) chopped bittersweet chocolate

1½ cups (140 g) chopped ripe but firm pear

TOPPING

Pear pieces

Chocolate chunks

Chopped rosemary

Coarse sugar, such as demerara or turbinado

Flaky salt, such as Maldon

To make the cakes, position a rack in the upper third of the oven and preheat to 350ºF (175ºC). Brush the cups and top of a standard 12-cup muffin tin with the softened butter (or fill with paper liners).

Sift the almond, sweet rice, oat and millet flours together into a medium bowl along with the baking powder, baking soda and salt, adding back any bits that get caught in the sifter. Set aside.

In a large bowl, whisk together the sugar, eggs, yogurt, olive oil and rosemary. Gently stir the flour mixture into the egg mixture until smooth, then fold in the chocolate and pears until evenly distributed.

Divide the batter among the muffin cups, filling them almost to the top. Top each cake with a pear piece, chocolate bits, a few bits of rosemary, a flutter of coarse sugar and a few flakes of salt.

Bake the cakes until golden on top and a toothpick inserted into the center comes out clean or with a few moist crumbs, 23–30 minutes. They are still baking from residual heat, so let cool until warm, at least 20 minutes, then release them from the pan and let cool completely. Extra cakes will keep, airtight at room temperature, for up to 3 days.

CHESTNUT ROULADE CAKE WITH RUM, MASCARPONE AND ROASTED PEARS

{CHESTNUT, SWEET RICE}

My favorite-ever job was baking at a short-lived, all-organic patisserie run by two sisters. The owner and head baker Rachel would go to any length to obtain organic products, which included candying our own citrus peels, blanching our own almonds and roasting and peeling chestnuts to puree into chocolate cakes. Luckily, the chestnut thing happened only once. We spent several days heating and peeling the little buggers around the clock, only to end up with burnt fingertips and a handful of dense cakes that didn't sell. I swore off chestnuts for a while after that, until my dear friend and yoga teacher Gizella, who hails from Hungary and has a sadistic streak when it comes to core work (though, thankfully, not chestnut peeling), made a tiramisù of sorts filled with chestnut cream whipped with mascarpone. I thought I'd died and gone to heaven.

Here, that same deliciousness fills a springy cake flavored with earthy chestnut flour, plenty of dark rum and brown sugar all rolled up with roasted pears. A taste tester described it as "light and fluffy, but still wintery and warm-tasting." In the United States, chestnut products only appear in stores around the holidays, but you can scour Italian grocers to find them year-round. Look for chestnut spread or cream made with sugar (as opposed to puree made from just chestnuts and water). Perrotta makes a less-sweet version that tastes as though made by angels, but others will work just fine. You'll have a little extra filling left over to "taste" or serve along slices. If you like your desserts extra-boozy, up the rum or whiskey to ⅓ cup (80 ml). This makes an ideal do-ahead dessert as it stores well for a day or two and needs only to be sliced and plated when it comes time for dessert. Watch them swoon.

MAKES ONE 12-INCH (30-CM) LONG ROLLED CAKE, 12 SERVINGS

CAKE

¼ cup (60 ml) sunflower oil (or other neutral-tasting vegetable oil)

½ cup (120 ml) water

2 large egg yolks

1 tsp vanilla extract

½ cup plus 2 tbsp (135 g) fresh, packed organic light or dark brown sugar

½ cup (80 g) sweet white rice flour

½ cup (55 g) chestnut flour

2 tbsp (15 g) tapioca flour

1¼ tsp (6 g) baking powder

½ tsp fine sea salt

5 egg whites (½ cup plus 2 tbsp [150 ml]), at room temperature

¼ tsp cream of tartar

2 tbsp (25 g) organic granulated cane sugar

¼ cup (25 g) powdered sugar, plus more for finishing

¼ cup (60 ml) GF black or spiced rum (such as The Kraken)

To make the cake, position a rack in the center of the oven and preheat to 325°F (165°C). Line a 12 by 17–inch (30 by 43–cm) ungreased rimmed baking sheet with a piece of parchment paper cut to fit.

In a large bowl, whisk together the oil, water, egg yolks and vanilla, then whisk in the brown sugar. Place a mesh strainer over the bowl and sift in the sweet rice, chestnut and tapioca flours with the baking powder and salt directly into the bowl, adding back any bits left behind in the strainer. Whisk until very smooth.

In the clean, dry bowl of a stand mixer fitted with the whip attachment (or in a large bowl with a hand blender or balloon whisk), whip the egg whites with the cream of tartar on medium-high speed until soft peaks form. Slowly add the sugar and whip until the whites are glossy and hold a firm peak when lifted from the bowl.

Use a flexible silicone spatula to fold one-third of the whites into the batter to loosen, then gently fold in the rest until just combined and no streaks remain. Immediately pour the batter onto the prepared baking sheet, and quickly but gently use an offset spatula to spread the batter into a thin, even layer. Transfer to the oven and bake until the cake springs back to the touch, 20–30 minutes. While the cake bakes, gather the following to have at the ready: powdered sugar in a strainer, small offset spatula or knife, large clean kitchen towel, a second baking sheet and kitchen shears or a sharp knife.

(continued)

CHESTNUT ROULADE CAKE WITH
RUM, MASCARPONE AND ROASTED PEARS (CONT.)

ROASTED PEARS

1 tbsp (14 g) unsalted butter

8 medium-sized pears such as Bartlett or Anjou, ripe but firm (2 lb [900 g])

2 tbsp (20 g) packed organic light or dark brown sugar

CHESTNUT CREAM

1 cup (225 g) mascarpone

1 cup (225 g) sweetened chestnut spread (sometimes called "chestnut cream")

1 cup (235 ml) heavy whipping cream

1 vanilla bean, split lengthwise, seeds scraped (pod reserved for Vanilla Extract, page 220), or 1 tsp vanilla extract

Big pinch of fine sea salt

2 tbsp (20 g) packed organic light or dark brown sugar, as needed (depending on sweetness of chestnut spread)

NOTES

- If you can't find chestnut spread, no worries; leave it out and add 2–4 tablespoons (25–50 g) packed organic brown sugar to taste.

- Roulade cakes can be tricky even for seasoned bakers. If your cake cracks in too many places when you roll it up, never fear: cut it up, stick it in individual serving glasses or bowls, dust with a little extra powdered sugar and call it trifle.

Working quickly, dust the top of the baked cake with the powdered sugar and use the knife or spatula to loosen it from the sides of the pan. Place a large, clean kitchen towel over the cake and top with a second, inverted baking sheet. Wearing oven mitts, grab the whole thing and flip it over. Remove the hot pan and carefully peel away the parchment paper. Trim away ¼ inch (6 mm) from each edge of the cake, and roll up the cake with the towel; this will help set the shape and the steam will keep it moist and pliant. You can either roll the cake from a short end for a fatter roll (as shown here) or from a long end for a skinnier roll. Either way, let the cake hang out in its towel roll until mostly cool, about 1 hour.

While the cake cools, roast the pears. Increase the oven temperature to 400°F (200°C). Rub a rimmed baking sheet with a little of the butter and cut the rest into small pieces. Peel the pears, cut them off the core and slice into ¼- to ½-inch (6- to 13-mm) thick slices. Spread in a single layer on the buttered pan, sprinkle with the brown sugar and dot with the butter pieces. Roast the pears until golden on the underside, about 20 minutes, then turn each slice and roast on the second side until golden, 10–20 more minutes; it's okay if they get broken up a little. Remove from the oven and use a thin metal spatula to scrape the pears onto a large plate. Chill until cool, 15 minutes.

To make the chestnut cream, place the mascarpone in the bowl of a stand mixer fitted with the whip attachment. Mash with a flexible spatula to smooth out any lumps, then add the chestnut spread, heavy cream, vanilla seeds and salt. Whip on medium speed until the mixture holds firm peaks (we want it fairly firm so that the cake will hold its shape). Taste, adding a tablespoon or two (15 or 30 g) of brown sugar if you feel the filling needs it. Cover and chill until needed.

Gently unroll the cake. Use a pastry brush to drizzle and dab the rum evenly over the cake. Leaving a 1-inch (2.5-cm) border on the inner and outer edges, cover the cake with about three-fourths of the chestnut cream, reserving the rest, and top with the roasted pears. Re-roll the cake into a log, ending with the seam side down and using the towel to help. Use a wide spatula to transfer it to a baking sheet or board, and cover it with plastic wrap. Chill the cake until sliceable, at least an hour and up to 1 day. (If the cake isn't perfectly round, or if it cracks, you can usually smoosh it together once chilled.)

When ready to serve, dust the cake with a little more powdered sugar. Use a sharp chef's knife to slice the cake into rounds and serve with the extra chestnut cream if you like. The cake will keep for up to 3 days.

VARIATION: CHESTNUT ROULADE WITH MASCARPONE, CINNAMON ROASTED APPLES AND WHISKEY (OR CALVADOS)

Omit the pears, using 2 pounds (900 g) tart baking apples (6 medium) and sprinkling the raw apples with ¾ teaspoon ground cinnamon in addition to the brown sugar. Replace the rum with an equal amount of GF whiskey (such as Queen Jennie Sorghum Whiskey), or try this with Calvados, an apple brandy from the Normandy region of France.

GINGER, VANILLA AND QUINCE UPSIDE-DOWN CAKE

{SWEET RICE, MILLET, OAT}

I have a hard time letting go of summer produce come fall, but fun fruits such as quinces and persimmons help ease the transition. Quinces are a member of the pome family along with apples and pears, and they look like a knobby combination of the two. Their flesh is pithy and must undergo a long, slow cook to be rendered edible. When they do, they turn a delightful shade of pink, and their mysterious flavors get teased out. Pomes are part of the rose family, which makes sense given the floral notes inherent in a quince. I like to accentuate quince's flowery qualities, so here I've paired it with vanilla, Meyer lemon and fresh ginger all wrapped up in a buttery cake. Sweet rice, oat and millet flours make a neutral base with a meltingly tender texture that allows the subtle tastes in this cake to star. Serve slices with a dollop of Whipped Crème Fraîche (page 223) for a pretty fall dessert or teatime treat. And if you haven't any quinces about, try the equally delicious pear version, below.

MAKES ONE 8-INCH (20-CM) CAKE, 8-10 SERVINGS

POACHED QUINCES

1 vanilla bean

½ large lemon (preferably Meyer)

4 cups (950 ml) water, plus more as needed

1 cup (235 ml) dry white wine

¾ cup (125 g) organic granulated cane sugar

1¾ lb (800 g) quince (about 3 large or 6 small)

CAKE

8 tbsp (113 g) unsalted butter, softened, plus 2 tsp (10 g) for the pan

Vanilla bean seeds (from above)

½ cup (100 g) organic granulated cane sugar

2 large eggs, at room temperature

2 tbsp (30 g) finely grated, packed fresh ginger

½ cup (80 g) sweet white rice flour

½ cup (65 g) millet flour

½ cup (55 g) GF oat flour

1½ tsp (6 g) baking powder

½ tsp baking soda

½ tsp fine sea salt

½ cup plus 2 tbsp (150 g) Crème Fraîche (page 223)

To poach the quinces, split the vanilla bean down the center and use the back of a knife to scrape away the seeds. Set the seeds aside to use in the cake, and place the pod in a large saucepan. Use a vegetable peeler (T-shaped works best) to pare away the lemon peel and add to the pot. Juice the lemon and add the juice to the pot along with the water, wine and sugar. Bring the liquid to a boil while you prepare the quinces.

Use a T-shaped vegetable peeler to pare away the skin of each quince. Cut it in half, leaving the seeds in for now, and add it to the pot. Continue with the remaining quinces. Place a small, heatproof plate (or round of parchment paper cut to fit) over the quinces to keep them submerged, cover partially with the lid of the pot and adjust the heat to keep the liquid at a simmer. Cook until the quinces are rosy and tender, about 1½ hours, adding more water as needed to keep the quinces submerged. When done, carefully remove the quinces and let them drain, reserving the liquid (or let the quinces cool in their juices if using later). Cut the cores, stems and blossoms from the quinces and cut them into ¼-inch (6-mm) thick slices, then chop some of the slices into ½ cup (75 g) chunks (these will get stirred into the batter).

Return the poaching liquid to the saucepan and simmer until reduced by about half and bubbling thickly, 10–20 minutes. Reserve.

To make the cake, position a rack in the center of the oven and preheat to 350ºF (175ºC).

Grease an 8- or 9-inch (20- or 23-cm) round cake pan with some of the 2 teaspoons (10 g) softened butter and line with a round of parchment cut to fit. Butter the parchment. Lay the quince slices, slightly overlapping, in concentric circles over the buttered parchment and set aside.

In the bowl of a stand mixer fitted with the paddle attachment (or in a large bowl fitted with your arm and a wooden spoon), combine the remaining 8 tablespoons (113 g) butter, vanilla bean seeds and sugar. Beat on medium speed until light and fluffy, 3 minutes. Add the eggs one at a time, beating until combined after each and scraping down the sides and bottom of the bowl as needed, then beat in the grated ginger.

Meanwhile, sift the sweet rice, millet and oat flours with the baking powder, baking soda and salt into a medium bowl.

(continued)

GINGER, VANILLA AND QUINCE UPSIDE-DOWN CAKE (CONT.)

With the mixer on low, stir half of the flour mixture into the butter mixture until just combined. Stir in the crème fraîche until just combined, then the rest of the flour, scraping down the sides and bottom of the bowl as needed. Stir in the chopped quince and give the batter a final stir by hand to make sure it is well combined. Gently spread the batter over the quinces.

Bake the cake until the top is golden and a toothpick inserted near the center comes out clean or with a few moist crumbs, 40–50 minutes. Let the cake cool completely, then invert onto a serving platter and gently peel away the parchment. If the reduced poaching liquid has solidified, warm it in a small saucepan until liquid. Brush some of this glaze over the top of the cake. Serve the cake at room temperature with a dollop of cream, if you like. Extras will keep at room temperature for up to 2 days or refrigerated airtight for up to 3 days.

VARIATION: GINGER PEAR UPSIDE-DOWN CAKE

Omit the quinces and poaching liquid. Place 3 tablespoons (42 g) unsalted butter in the prepared pan and place in the oven to melt, 3 minutes. Remove from the oven and sprinkle ¼ cup (50 g) packed organic light or dark brown sugar and a big pinch of salt evenly over the melted butter. Peel and core 3 large ripe but firm pears (1¼ pounds [565 g]) and slice lengthwise into ¼-inch (6-mm) slices. Chop enough of the slices to make ½ cup (75 g) pear chunks. Fan the slices over the brown sugar, overlapping slightly in concentric circles, and fold the pear chunks into the batter. Proceed with the recipe, turning out the cake while still warm. Optionally, drizzle the top of the cake with any variation of Salty Vanilla Bean Caramel Sauce (page 231).

TWO-PERSIMMON LAYER CAKE WITH VANILLA BOURBON CREAM CHEESE FROSTING

{ALMOND, SWEET RICE, MILLET, OAT}

Persimmons rarely get the love they deserve, particularly the oblong variety (Hachiya), which must be squishy-ripe to lose astringency and burst with soft, sweet flesh. This cake makes use of both Hachiyas, which get pureed into a gently spiced batter full of nubby almond flour, and Fuyus, which crown the layers in electric orange cubes. A bourbon-infused vanilla cream cheese frosting makes this a unique cake for the winter holidays. Baking the cake in a 6-inch (15-cm) pan gives you a petite cake with three layers, pictured here. Alternatively, make an 8-inch (20-cm) cake with two shorter layers, or try the cupcake variation on page 78.

MAKES ONE 6-INCH (15-CM) CAKE WITH 3 LAYERS OR ONE 8-INCH (20-CM) CAKE WITH 2 LAYERS, 8-10 SERVINGS

CAKE

½ cup (60 g) blanched almond flour

½ cup (80 g) sweet white rice flour

½ cup (75 g) millet flour

½ cup (55 g) GF oat flour

1 tsp baking soda

1 tsp ground cinnamon

½ tsp ground cardamom

½ tsp fine sea salt

8 tbsp (113 g) unsalted butter, at room temperature

½ cup (100 g) packed organic light or dark brown sugar

2 large eggs, separated

1 tsp vanilla extract

1 cup (235 ml) Hachiya persimmon puree (see Note)

To make the cake, position a rack in the lower third of the oven and preheat to 350ºF (175ºC). Line a 6-inch (15-cm) round cake pan with 2-inch (5-cm) sides with a round of parchment paper cut to fit. Cut a 4-inch (10-cm) wide strip of parchment paper that's longer than the circumference of the pan and use it to make a collar around the inside of the pan (this will keep the batter from overflowing as it bakes and make the cake easier to unmold). You can skip the collar if baking this in an 8-inch (20-cm) pan.

Place a strainer over a medium bowl and add the almond, sweet rice, oat and millet flours along with the baking soda, cinnamon, cardamom and salt. Sift the dry ingredients into the bowl, adding back in any bits that get caught in the strainer.

Combine the butter and brown sugar in the bowl of a stand mixer fitted with the paddle attachment and beat on medium speed until light and fluffy, 3 minutes, scraping down the sides of the bowl a few times. Beat in the egg yolks and vanilla. With the mixer on low, beat in a third of the flour mixture until combined. Beat in half of the persimmon puree until combined. Repeat until you've added everything.

In a separate, clean bowl, use a whisk to whip the egg whites until they hold firm peaks when the whisk is lifted out of the bowl. (Hint: This is easier if they're at room temperature. You can also do this in a clean bowl for your stand mixer with the whip attachment.) As soon as the whites are whipped, stir a third of them into the cake batter. Gently fold in the remaining egg whites until no streaks remain.

Scrape the cake batter into the prepared cake pan (don't forget the parchment collar if using a 6-inch [15-cm] pan!). Bake the cake until a toothpick inserted near the center comes out clean, 60–75 minutes for a 6-inch (15-cm) pan and 50 minutes for an 8-inch (20-cm) pan. Let the cake cool completely in the pan, about 2 hours.

When the cake is cool, us a small offset spatula or butter knife to loosen the edges and bottom from the pan. Invert it into your hand, and pry off the pan. Remove the parchment collar and bottom and discard. Place the cake upright on a board, plate or cake stand (if you have one that rotates, bonus points!). Use a large, serrated knife to trim the top of the cake flat. Mark the cake horizontally into even thirds. With your palm on the top of the cake and the knife held parallel to the work surface, use a sawing motion to cut the cake into thirds as you rotate it, taking care to make the layers as even as possible.

(continued)

FROSTING AND FILLING

8 oz (225 g) cream cheese, at room temperature

4 tbsp (56 g) unsalted butter, at room temperature

¾ cup (85 g) powdered sugar

Seeds from 1 vanilla bean or 1 tsp vanilla extract

Pinch of fine sea salt

2 tbsp (30 ml) bourbon or GF whiskey (such as Queen Jennie) (or a squeeze of lemon juice)

2 large Fuyu persimmons, ripe but firm

A squeeze of lemon juice

To make the frosting, in the bowl of a stand mixer fitted with the paddle attachment, whip together the cream cheese, butter, powdered sugar, vanilla seeds and salt on medium speed until light and fluffy. Be careful not to overbeat, or the mixture could break and become grainy or liquidy. Add the bourbon and beat to incorporate. (Mine always becomes slightly grainy at this point due to the low amount of powdered sugar, but I find that preferable to being too sweet.) The frosting can be covered and kept at cool room temperature for up to a few hours.

For the filling, slice the tops off the Fuyu persimmons and cut them into an even dice about ¼-inch (6-mm) square or a little larger. Place in a small bowl and toss with a squeeze of lemon juice to keep them from oxidizing.

To assemble the cake, place the bottom cake layer on a fresh round of parchment paper or small plate. Lay the other layers on a clean surface. Divide the frosting among the three layers. Starting with the bottom layer, smooth the frosting over the surface, taking it almost to the edge. Top with about a quarter of the diced persimmon, and press the persimmons into the frosting. Top with a second cake layer. Repeat this process, using the remaining half of the diced persimmon to top the cake.

Serve immediately, or, for the cleanest slices, chill the cake for at least 1 hour. The cake is best at room temperature when the butter in the cake and frosting have softened, so let individual slices come to room temperature before enjoying for best results.

The cake is best on the day of baking, but it will keep refrigerated (ideally in a cake dome or large, inverted container) for up to 3 days.

VARIATION: TWO-PERSIMMON CUPCAKES

Divide the batter among 12 muffin cups fitted with paper liners. Bake for 28–32 minutes. Let cool. When ready to serve, spread or pipe with the frosting and sprinkle with the diced Fuyus.

NOTES

- To make the Hachiya persimmon puree, make sure your Hachiya persimmons are so squishy-ripe that they feel like water balloons about to burst. I let mine ripen on the counter for at least a week or two, stem side down to protect their delicate bottoms, transferring them to a container in the refrigerator as they ripen. They'll keep there for up to a week. When ready to bake, cut the blossom off the persimmon, squeeze out the jellylike flesh into a mesh strainer placed over a large bowl, and use a flexible silicone spatula to work the flesh through. It will be the consistency of a runny jelly. This puree can also be frozen to use later.

- If you or your cake eaters are sensitive to trace amounts of gluten, be sure to use a certified GF spirit such as Queen Jennie whiskey, or a GF rum or brandy. Otherwise, I like Bulleit bourbon here.

PETITE BLOOD ORANGE CORNMEAL UPSIDE-DOWN CAKE

{CORN, SWEET RICE, OAT}

My best friend and I spent our junior year of college studying in Bologna, Italy, at one of the oldest universities in the world. Having lived our whole lives in mild California, and having spent only a couple of summers in Italy, we were in for a rude awakening when the weather turned gray and icy from October all the way through April. Thank goodness for Prosecco, gelati and blood oranges, called *aranci tarocchi*. That winter, we would buy up the ruby-hued fruits in abundance at the open-air markets (on the rare occasion that it wasn't raining). After simple, homemade dinners of risotto or pasta, we would sit at the table peeling and eating the oranges, admiring their bright flesh that whispered of the colorful sunsets we hoped to see again someday.

Here, blood orange rounds are bathed in honey butter and baked beneath a sturdy cake flecked with cornmeal to soak up the fruit's copious red juices. When turned out, the sunny topping reminds me a little of pineapple upside-down cake, only more brightly hued. Serve wedges of cake at room temperature with a cup of tea on a wintry afternoon when you're longing for sunnier days. It will help. This makes a petite 6-inch (15-cm) cake, but the recipe can be doubled and baked in a 9-inch (23-cm) round cake pan, increasing the bake time as needed.

MAKES ONE 6-INCH (15-CM) ROUND CAKE, 6 SERVINGS

TOPPING

1½ tbsp (21 g) unsalted butter, in a few pieces, plus 1 tsp for greasing the pan

2 tbsp (30 ml) honey

1 lb (450 g) blood oranges (about 4 medium)

CAKE

4 tbsp (56 g) unsalted butter, at room temperature

¼ cup (50 g) organic granulated cane sugar

1 tbsp (15 ml) honey, plus more for drizzling

1 tsp finely grated zest from 1 blood orange (above)

Finely grated zest from ½ large lemon (preferably Meyer)

1 large egg, at room temperature

¼ cup plus 2 tbsp (55 g) yellow cornmeal (NOT polenta)

¼ cup (60 g) Crème Fraîche (page 223) or sour cream

¼ cup plus 2 tbsp (55 g) sweet white rice flour

¼ cup plus 2 tbsp (35 g) GF oat flour

1 tsp baking powder

⅜ tsp fine sea salt

¼ cup or a little more (60 g) chopped blood oranges, from above

Position a rack in the center of the oven and preheat to 350ºF (175ºC). Grease a 6-inch (15-cm) round baking pan with 2-inch (5-cm) sides with the 1 teaspoon butter and line the bottom with a 6-inch (15-cm) round of parchment paper. Place the pan on a rimmed baking sheet lined with parchment for easy cleanup and to catch drips.

To make the topping, place the butter and honey in the pan and put it in the oven to melt together, 5 minutes.

Meanwhile, zest 1 blood orange and set the zest aside to use in the batter. Use a sharp paring knife to slice ¼ inch (6 mm) off the top and bottom of each blood orange. Place cut side down, and, following the curve of the orange, cut away the peel and white pith. Cut the orange crosswise into thin rounds roughly ¼-inch (6-mm) thick. Repeat with the remaining oranges.

Using the larger rounds, lay the orange slices over the buttery honey in concentric circles, starting from the outside and overlapping the slices slightly. Fill in the center with a few more slices. Cut any remaining slices into small chunks and reserve for the cake batter (you should have roughly ¼ cup [60 g]).

To make the cake, in the bowl of a stand mixer fitted with the paddle attachment (or in a large bowl fitted with your arm and a wooden spoon), beat together the softened butter, sugar, honey and blood orange and lemon zests on medium speed until light and fluffy, 3 minutes, scraping down the sides of the bowl occasionally. Beat in the egg, then the cornmeal, then the crème fraîche, stirring until smooth after each addition. (The mixture may look curdled; this is okay.)

Place a mesh strainer over the bowl and sift in the sweet rice and oat flours along with the baking powder and salt. Stir to combine well, then gently fold in the chopped blood oranges.

(continued)

PETITE BLOOD ORANGE CORNMEAL UPSIDE-DOWN CAKE (CONT.)

Dollop the batter over the blood orange slices in the pan, and spread it gently and evenly. Bake the cake until a tester inserted in the center of the cake comes out completely clean, 35–45 minutes. Let the cake cool in the pan for 10 minutes, then use a small, offset spatula or thin knife to loosen the cake from the sides of the pan. Invert a plate or small cake stand over the pan, and, wearing oven mitts, flip the whole thing over. Remove the cake pan and gently peel away the parchment.

Let the cake cool to warm, 20 minutes, then drizzle the top with more honey. Cut into wedges and serve slightly warm or at room temperature. The cake is best shortly after baking, but leftovers will keep at room temperature for an additional day, or in the refrigerator for up to 3 days. Bring to room temperature before serving.

VARIATION: PETITE TANGERINE CORNMEAL UPSIDE-DOWN CAKE

Omit the blood oranges, using 1 pound (450 g) tangerines or mandarins such as satsumas or clementines (about 4 large) in their place.

NOTE: I prefer the finer grind of Arrowhead Mills' cornmeal here to Bob's Red Mill's coarser GF cornmeal. If that's what you've got, break it up in a coffee grinder before measuring.

VANILLA BEAN CUPCAKES WITH KUMQUAT CREAM CHEESE FROSTING

{SWEET RICE, OAT, MILLET}

These sunny cupcakes taste a bit like Creamsicles, with loads of vanilla in the batter and tangy candied kumquats in the topping. The kumquat syrup moistens the cakes, and a slice makes a pretty garnish. The recipe, which I adapted from my dear friend and seasoned gluten-free baker Sarah Menanix, who writes the blog SnixyKitchen.com, turns out the most tender and tasty vanilla cupcakes I've ever had. Sweet rice, oat and millet flours create a neutral base with a touch of nutty flavor dotted with vanilla beans and lightened with buttermilk. These are easy to whip up should you have candied kumquats on hand. Alternatively, leave them off and you'll still have the most killer vanilla cupcakes imaginable.

MAKES 14 CUPCAKES

CUPCAKES

8 tbsp (113 g) unsalted butter, at room temperature

¾ cup (150 g) organic granulated cane sugar

Seeds from 1 vanilla bean

2 large eggs, at room temperature

¾ cup (105 g) sweet white rice flour

½ cup (50 g) GF oat flour

¼ cup plus 2 tbsp (45 g) millet flour

1½ tsp (6 g) baking powder

½ tsp baking soda

½ tsp fine sea salt

½ cup (120 ml) well-shaken buttermilk

1 tsp vanilla extract

FROSTING

½ cup (130 g) Honey Candied Kumquats (page 235) in their syrup, plus more for garnish

8 oz (225 g) cream cheese, at room temperature

4 tbsp (56 g) unsalted butter, at room temperature

¾ cup (85 g) powdered sugar

Pinch of fine sea salt

A few drops of lemon juice, as needed

To make the cupcakes, position a rack in the center of the oven and preheat to 350°F (175°C). Line 14 standard muffin cups with paper liners.

In the bowl of a stand mixer fitted with the paddle attachment (or in a large bowl with a wooden spoon), beat the butter, sugar and vanilla seeds together on medium speed until light and fluffy, 2–3 minutes. Add the eggs one at a time, beating well after each addition and scraping down the sides of the bowl as needed.

In a medium-sized bowl, sift together the sweet rice, oat and millet flours with the baking powder, baking soda and salt.

Add half of the flour mixture to the butter mixture and beat on low speed until just combined. Beat in the buttermilk and vanilla, mixing until just combined, then beat in the remaining flour mixture, beating until well combined, scraping down the sides of the bowl once or twice. Remove the bowl from the mixer and stir with a flexible silicone spatula to make sure the batter is homogenous.

Divide the batter among the lined muffin cups, filling them two-thirds of the way. Bake until the tops spring back to the touch and a toothpick inserted into the center of one comes out clean or with a few moist crumbs, 20–25 minutes. Remove from the oven and let cool completely.

To make the frosting, place the kumquats in a strainer set over a bowl and press as much liquid out of them as you can. Reserve the syrup for brushing the cupcakes; you should have 3–4 tablespoons (45–60 ml). Chop the kumquats finely. Beat the cream cheese, butter, powdered sugar and salt together in the bowl of a stand mixer fitted with the paddle attachment on medium speed until smooth and fluffy, 2–3 minutes, scraping down the sides of the bowl occasionally. With the mixer on low, beat in the drained, chopped kumquats. Taste the frosting, adding a few drops of lemon juice if you like to sharpen the flavors.

To finish the cupcakes, poke the tops of the cupcakes several times with a toothpick. Brush with a few coats of the reserved kumquat syrup, letting the syrup soak into the cakes, until you've used it all up. Pipe or spread the frosting over the cakes, and top each with a candied kumquat or two. The cakes will keep at cool room temperature for up to a few hours, or refrigerated airtight for a day or two. Serve the cakes at room temperature.

PIE

Whoever coined the term "easy as pie" was clearly not a baker. Pies are one of the more fussy desserts to get right, not just at home but in professional kitchens, too. With pie, so many things can go wrong. Too much liquid in the crust and it turns tough. Too little and the dough cracks all over the place. Underbake and the crust is sodden and pasty; overbake and the edges burn. Custard fillings can leak, adhering the pie to the pan like superglue, and fruit fillings can turn into puddles of soup when sliced.

And yet when pie goes right, it goes so very right. Flaky pastry shatters against fillings of sliceable custard infused with citrus or spice. Chunks of fruit soften in the heat of the oven, their flavors condensing into something greater than the sum of their parts, all wrapped up in a buttery shell.

I've adapted my flaky pie dough to be full of alternative flours and free from gluten and gums. Chia seed is the magic ingredient that takes the place of the usual xanthan gum. Cornstarch adds crunch and tapioca makes the dough more pliable. And a trio of flours—sweet rice, oat and millet (as well as a couple of variations)—make a crust that tastes like a perfectly flaky whole wheat pastry and is nearly as easy to work with. The key to flaky pie dough is to leave the butter in large chunks. When worked into sheets through the classic French technique of *fraisage* and given a few folds in the manner of puff pastry, the pockets of butter give off steam in the heat of the oven, lifting up the layer of dough above it.

This flaky dough makes a buttery base for ginger peach and strawberry raspberry rhubarb pies, a floral lemon buttermilk custard flecked with vanilla bean, and savory-sweet fig and chèvre bites. Teff creates a malty, warm-tasting base for apple pie or hazelnut frangipane and fresh plums. Buckwheat lends an earthy, charcoal hue to a dough with lots of crunch and flake. Try this around walnuts and pears for individual tarts kissed with salty caramel, or in a dreamy pumpkin pie made with maple syrup and crème fraîche.

FLAKY PIE DOUGH

{SWEET RICE, OAT, MILLET}

Flaky pie dough is the holy grail of alternative flour baking, with most recipes turning out heavy, crumbly doughs or requiring loads of gums and starches to bake up well. I tested this dough dozens of times to get it just right, with various ingredients and techniques. A trio of flours—sweet rice, millet and oat—work together with cornstarch, tapioca flour and ground chia seed to create a dough that's sturdy enough to trap air from steaming butter and flake into layers not unlike puff pastry, all without the use of gluten or gums. When done right, the result tastes like whole wheat puff pastry. All who try this recipe or the resulting product agree—it's downright miraculous.

I find it all too easy to overmix pie dough in a stand mixer or food processor, so I highly recommend making this by hand the first few times, preferably using a sturdy metal pastry blender. You want the butter kept in large chunks—not the small peas generally asked for by other recipes, but ½-inch (1.3-cm) pieces the size of almonds. There will be lots of small pieces of butter, too, but be sure to leave lots of big chunks, as well.

The next key point is that of the liquid. Before you start, fill a ½-cup (120-ml) measure with ice cubes and top it off with water. Stir this together with buttermilk (or vinegar or lemon juice if you prefer) and add the liquid 1 tablespoon (15 ml) at a time, tossing with a flexible silicone spatula until it's barely moistened and there are no floury bits. A chunk of dough should hold together when you give it a squeeze, but it should not feel wet or sticky. How much liquid you add will vary greatly on a number of different factors, so it must be done by feel rather than a fixed amount. Like any pie dough recipe, it may take a few tries before you get a feel for how much liquid should be added. I do tend to moisten this dough a little bit more than wheat doughs, as this helps it hold together better when you work it.

METHOD

The fraisage method may be new to you; it was to me when I came across it in a baking cookbook several years ago. It's a quick process that takes only a minute or two, wherein you drag portions of dough across the counter with the heel of your hand. This flattens the butter chunks into sheets, creating many flaky layers and helping to bring the dough together. If this sounds intimidating, you can try a method that I learned in a pastry kitchen: after cutting in the butter, but before working in the liquid, go through the dough and squeeze every butter chunk between your fingers to flatten them out. Work quickly so the butter doesn't melt. Proceed with the recipe, skipping the fraisage, doing the turns if you like. And if none of this sounds like any fun, just give the dough 10–20 good kneadings in the bowl and go from there; you'll still have a lovely pie dough, just a bit less tender and flaky than the fully flaky versions. For even flakier dough that is smoother and easier to handle, do the optional turns, detailed below. This is the same technique used to give croissants, Danish and puff pastry their flaky layers.

TIPS FOR ROLLING

This dough is more fragile than wheat dough due to its lack of gluten and gums, so you'll want to baby it a bit. Having the dough at the proper temperature can help. Too cold, and it will crack. Too warm and it will melt and stick. I usually let my dough rest at room temperature for 5–10 minutes prior to rolling if it has chilled through completely. My preferred rolling situation is to use a countertop dusted lightly with oat flour. Other testers have preferred rolling the dough between two pieces of parchment paper, which keeps the dough from sticking and makes it easier to maneuver. With either rolling method, be sure to dust the counter with just enough oat flour to keep the dough from sticking, and use a pastry brush to sweep excess flour off of the dough so you don't end up with chunks of flour.

(continued)

FLAKY PIE DOUGH (CONT.)

As you begin to roll out the dough, start by pressing down on the pin gently, lifting it up, moving it outward and pressing down, until you've pressed the length of the dough. This helps to soften the dough slightly and minimize the cracking that will happen around the edges.

When the edges crack, use your hands and fingers to press them back together. As you work, use a bench scraper to lift the dough, flipping it over if you can do so without it breaking (or just dusting underneath with flour) and continuing. After a minute or two of this when the dough is flatter, begin to use a gentle yet firm rolling motion, rolling in all directions, continuing to move and dust the dough and countertop frequently, brushing away excess flour, until the dough is the correct shape for the recipe. If it cracks or breaks, just use your fingers to stick it back together. If it begins to soften and stick, drag it onto a rimless cookie sheet and chill it for 5–10 minutes.

DO AHEAD

You can make the dough up to 2 days ahead; it actually benefits from a day's rest, which allows the starches in the flours to absorb moisture and create a sturdier, smoother dough. I often make a double batch of pie dough, use half in a recipe, and freeze the other half airtight until I'm ready to make another pie. You can also wrap a shaped, frozen shell, baked or unbaked, for up to several months.

TIMING

Give yourself at least 3–4 hours to complete a parbaked crust if you plan to do the turns, or 2 hours if you're skipping this step. Most of this time is inactive. Ideally, make the dough a day ahead and let it rest overnight.

TOOLS AND EQUIPMENT

- Pastry blender
- Metal or plastic bench scraper
- Flexible silicone spatula
- Rolling pin
- Pastry brush (for sweeping excess flour off of the dough)

- Scissors (for trimming dough)
- Plastic wrap or a large, zip-top bag
- Pie weights and parchment paper (if parbaking)
- Parchment paper, for rolling out the dough (optional)

NOTES

- Once you get a feel for this dough, it can also be made in a food processor. Place all the dry ingredients in the bowl fitted with a steel blade. Scatter the butter pieces over the top, but don't pulse just yet. Place the lid on and open up the pouring chute. Gradually pour in the ice water mixture, pulsing all the while and adding liquid in a slow, steady stream. Remove the lid and give the dough a squeeze; it should feel moist but not sticky, and hold together, with lots of pea-sized butter pieces in there.

- If you don't have buttermilk on hand, or don't care to use it, stir 8 tablespoons (120 ml) of ice water together with 1 teaspoon of apple cider (or white) vinegar or lemon juice to use in place of the ice water/buttermilk mixture.

FLAKY PIE DOUGH (CONT.)

MAKES ONE STANDARD 9-INCH (23-CM) PIE SHELL FOR A SINGLE-CRUST PIE

¼ cup (60 ml) ice water

½ cup (80 g) sweet white rice flour (Mochiko)

¼ cup plus 2 tbsp (40 g) GF oat flour, plus more for dusting

¼ cup (35 g) millet flour

¼ cup (30 g) cornstarch

2 tbsp (13 g) tapioca flour

2½ tbsp (15 g) finely ground chia seed (preferably white)

1 tbsp (12 g) organic granulated cane sugar

½ tsp fine sea salt

8 tbsp (113 g) cold, unsalted butter (preferably European style), sliced ¼-inch (6-mm) thick

¼ cup (60 ml) cold buttermilk

Make the ice water by filling a ½-cup (120-ml) measure with ice and topping it off with cool water.

In a large bowl, combine the rice, oat and millet flours with the cornstarch, tapioca flour, ground chia seed, sugar and salt. Scatter the butter pieces over the top, and work in with a pastry blender or your fingertips until the mixture resembles gravel, with lots of butter chunks the size of large almonds and some smaller bits.

Stir together ¼ cup (60 ml) of the ice water with the buttermilk, and drizzle the mixture into the flour mixture 1 tablespoon (15 ml) at a time, tossing the dough with a flexible silicone spatula to moisten evenly. Add just enough water for the dough to hold together when you give it a squeeze, and add it directly to the dry floury bits that like to hang out on the bottom of the bowl; you may not need all the liquid, or you may need to add more ice water.

OPTION 1: KNEAD
Knead the dough in the bowl 10–20 times to bring it together.

OPTION 2 (RECOMMENDED): FRAISAGE
Skip the kneading option, above. Working quickly, dump the dough out onto the counter. Grab a handful of dough, place it on the counter, put the heel of your hand on the dough and push it away from you, scraping it across the surface several inches. Use a bench scraper to scrape the dough up off the counter and place it back in the bowl. This is called *fraisage*. Repeat with the remaining dough. It should only take a minute or two to complete this process.

With either method, gather the dough up into a ball, wrap it loosely in plastic wrap and flatten it into a disk. Chill the dough until firm, 30–60 minut*es*.

OPTION 3: TURN
This classic technique is used to give puff pastry and croissant dough their layers. Here, it also helps to make a smoother, more pliable dough that will be easier to manipulate. Dust your surface lightly with oat flour and use a rolling pin to roll the dough out into a rough rectangle that is about ¼-inch (6-mm) thick, lifting and turning the dough, dusting underneath the dough to keep it from sticking, flipping it over and sweeping away excess flour with a pastry brush. (Alternatively, roll the dough between two pieces of parchment paper dusted with oat flour to prevent sticking.) When the dough is rolled out, fold it into thirds, as though folding a letter, then fold it in thirds again the other way. Gently press to flatten it slightly, re-wrap and chill for 30–60 more minutes.

OPTION 4: ANOTHER TURN
For the absolute flakiest dough, repeat the turning step one more time, making a second turn. This will only be effective if you started out with those big chunks of butter.

You're done! Chill the dough until cold, at least 30–60 minutes and up to 2 days. Alternatively, slip the dough into a freezer bag and freeze for up to 2 months. Refer to individual recipes for how to use your beautiful masterpiece. If shaping the dough in a pie pan, continue with the instructions below.

SHAPE THE CRUST

Remove the dough from the refrigerator, unwrap and place on a lightly floured surface. If it is very cold, let it soften for 5–10 minutes until malleable; this will minimize cracking. Roll out the dough into a 12-inch (30-cm) round, dusting the dough lightly with oat flour as needed, rotating and flipping it to prevent it from sticking. (Alternatively, roll the dough between two pieces of parchment paper dusted with oat flour to prevent sticking.) Ease the dough into a 9-inch (23-cm) glass pie plate, fit it into the corners, and trim it to a 1-inch (2.5-cm) overhang. (Save the scraps to patch any tears in the dough post-parbaking.) Fold the overhang of the crust under itself, and flute the crust by pressing it between the thumb of one hand and the index finger and thumb of the other hand. Prick the bottom of the crust all over with the tines of a fork. Chill the crust for 30 minutes, or until firm.

BAKE OR PARBAKE

Position a rack in the lower third of the oven and preheat to 400ºF (200ºC). Remove all other racks from the oven. If you have a baking stone, put it on the rack.

Place the chilled crust on a rimmed baking sheet. Line it with a piece of parchment paper, and fill to the top with pie weights, dry beans or clean pennies, pressing the weights into the sides and corners of the crust.

Bake the crust for 15–30 minutes, until the dough holds its shape when you lift off the parchment. Carefully remove the weights and parchment and bake until the bottom is dry and lightly golden, about 8–12 minutes longer (for a parbaked crust) or until deeply golden, 15–20 minutes (for a fully baked crust). Use the saved scraps of dough to patch any holes, cracks, or tears in the dough, baking for a few more minutes post-patching.

VARIATIONS

BUCKWHEAT PIE DOUGH
Omit the millet flour, substituting ¼ cup plus 2 tablespoons (45 g) buckwheat flour and decreasing the oat flour to ¼ cup (25 g).

TEFF PIE DOUGH
Omit the millet flour, substituting ¼ cup (35 g) teff flour.

COCONUT OIL PIE DOUGH {VEGAN}
This dough is more fragile to work with, but doing the fraisage and turns helps make it more cohesive. Since coconut oil is harder than butter when chilled, the dough is easier to handle when slightly warmer than refrigerator temperature. Because the dough is more fragile, it's easier to use in hand pies and galettes that need less manipulation, as opposed to larger pies. The flavor of the coconut oil doesn't carry through; this pie dough tastes just like any other fabulously flaky whole-grain pie dough.

Omit the butter. Scoop 8 tablespoons (105 g) of firm, room-temperature (or slightly chilled) unrefined, extra-virgin coconut oil over the flour mixture in tablespoon-sized blobs. Chill the whole bowl until the coconut oil is firm, 20 minutes or longer. Work in the oil as you would the butter, but break it up into finer particles the size of peas. Omit the buttermilk, stirring together 8 tablespoons (120 ml) ice water with 1 teaspoon lemon juice, and work in the ice water mixture as per usual. Proceed with the recipe.

PIE DOUGH FOR CUTOUT PIES AND PANDOWDIES

{SWEET RICE, OAT, MILLET}

This recipe is one and a half times the Flaky Pie Dough recipe on page 87. I just did the math for you—you're welcome.

MAKES ENOUGH FOR 1 BOTTOM CRUST AND A CUTOUT UPPER CRUST FOR A 9-INCH (23-CM) PIE, OR 2 PANDOWDIES

¼ cup plus 2 tbsp (90 ml) ice water

¼ cup plus 2 tbsp (90 ml) well-shaken buttermilk

¾ cup (110 g) sweet white rice flour

½ cup (55 g) GF oat flour

¼ cup plus 2 tbsp (50 g) millet flour

¼ cup plus 2 tbsp (45 g) cornstarch

3 tbsp (25 g) tapioca flour

4 tbsp (25 g) finely ground white chia seed

1½ tbsp (20 g) organic granulated cane sugar

¾ tsp fine sea salt

12 tbsp (170 g) cold, unsalted butter (preferably European style such as Straus Family Creamery), sliced ¼-inch (6-mm) thick

Follow the directions for the Flaky Pie Dough (page 87), preferably with the fraisage and 1–2 turns.

If making a cutout double-crust pie, divide the finished dough into one-third and two-third portions, wrap each in plastic wrap, flatten into disks and chill until firm, at least 1 hour and up to 2 days. Using the larger portion of dough, follow the instructions for shaping a bottom crust on page 90. Use the smaller portion for the top cutout crust (see individual recipes for method).

For pandowdies, divide the dough in half, wrap each in plastic wrap and chill.

Place the dry ingredients in a large bowl.

Add the sliced butter.

Use a pastry blender to work the butter …

. . . into chunks the size of almonds and peas.

Gradually add the liquid by the tablespoon (15 ml),

tossing the dough to distribute evenly.

Fraisage by scraping portions of dough . . .

. . . across the counter to form thin sheets.

Alternatively, make the dough in a food processor.

hill the dough until cold.

Dust with flour to prevent sticking.

Slowly press and roll into an even round.

old the dough in thirds . . .

. . . and in thirds again for extra layers.

Shape the crust in the pan, tucking the edges under.

se your thumb and forefingers . . .

. . . to form a fluted edge.

Pierce, chill again and bake!

STRAWBERRY RASPBERRY RHUBARB CUTOUT PIE

{SWEET RICE, OAT, MILLET}

Raspberries make a bright addition to the classic combination of strawberries and rhubarb. Along with a bit of lemon, the three turn out a crimson filling that is downright refreshing, studded with fat chunks of red fruit. Topping the pie with rounds of dough creates a pretty top that is far easier to execute than a lattice or double crust, and it keeps the fruit-to-crust ratio in check while allowing plenty of steam to escape from the fruit. I learned this topping method from Laura Kasavan, who writes the beautiful dessert blog Tutti Dolci.

This well-balanced pie needs no accompaniment, though a scoop of Vanilla Bean, Cardamom or Fresh Ginger Ice Cream (pages 227–228) is always welcome.

MAKES ONE 9-INCH (23-CM) PIE, ABOUT 10 SERVINGS

CRUST
1 recipe Pie Dough for Cutout Pies (page 93)

GF oat flour, for dusting

FILLING
2½ cups (270 g) rhubarb trimmed and sliced ½-inch (1.3-cm) thick

2 cups (230 g) hulled and quartered strawberries

2 cups (230 g) raspberries

Finely grated zest from 1 medium-sized lemon (preferably Meyer)

1 tbsp (15 ml) lemon juice

¾ cup (150 g) organic granulated cane sugar

¼ cup (30 g) cornstarch

⅛ tsp fine sea salt

FOR FINISHING
1 tbsp (15 ml) milk or cream

1 tbsp (15 g) coarse sugar (demerara or turbinado)

For the crust, prepare and chill the pie dough as directed.

Position a rack in the lower third of the oven, top with a baking stone if you've got one and preheat to 425ºF (220ºC). Line a rimmed baking sheet with parchment paper for easy cleanup.

Make a bottom crust with the larger round of pie dough (see page 89). Chill the crust until firm, 30 minutes (or wrap and chill up to 1 day). On a surface dusted lightly with oat flour, roll out the smaller round of dough to a 9-inch (23-cm) round about ¼-inch (6-mm) thick. Use a fluted biscuit cutter (or small glass) to cut 1½- and/or 2-inch (3.8- and/or 5-cm) rounds close together. Stack the rounds on a plate and chill until firm, 20 minutes. Optionally, press the dough scraps together, wrap and chill until firm, and repeat the rolling/cutting process once more.

To make the filling, place the prepared rhubarb, strawberries and raspberries in a large bowl and add the lemon zest and juice, sugar, cornstarch and salt. Use a flexible silicone spatula to stir gently to combine, and let sit for a few minutes to draw out the juices a bit.

Spoon the fruit and juices into the chilled crust, smoothing it flat. Place the chilled dough rounds over the top of the fruit, overlapping them slightly and leaving lots of windows for the steam to escape. To finish, brush the rounds with the cream or milk and sprinkle with the coarse sugar.

Place the pie on the lined baking sheet and place in the oven on the baking stone. Bake at 425ºF (220ºC) for 15 minutes, then decrease the oven temperature to 375ºF (190ºC) and continue baking until the crust is golden and the fruit is bubbling furiously, 35–50 more minutes. Let the pie cool completely to set the fruit, at least 2 hours, then cut into wedges and serve at room temperature. The pie is best shortly after baking and will keep at room temperature for up to 1 day, or refrigerated for up to 3 days.

NOTE: When preparing rhubarb, be sure to trim away the leaves completely, as they are toxic.

BLUEBERRY HAND PIES {VEGAN}

{SWEET RICE, OAT, MILLET}

It's hard to go wrong with fresh blueberries. Here, they're given minimal sweetening, tossed with lemon and nutmeg, and tucked into flaky coconut-oil dough. The clean taste of coconut lets the deep purple berries star, baking into tender little nubs within crust that shatters and flakes. These not-too-sweet treats work equally well for breakfast with a cup of tea or to travel on a picnic. If you want them a bit sweeter, give them a drizzle of vanilla bean glaze (page 55) and they will remind you of really classy Pop-Tarts.

Placing the rounds of dough on individual pieces of parchment paper helps shape the hand pies, so be sure to have some handy when making this recipe. Fresh berries work better here, as frozen ones will cause the dough to harden, making it crack as you fold it around the filling.

MAKES 6 INDIVIDUAL HAND PIES

CRUST

1 recipe Coconut Oil Pie Dough (page 90), prepared with the fraisage and 1–2 turns, chilled

GF oat flour, for dusting

FILLING

1½ cups (190 g) blueberries (preferably fresh, otherwise frozen and not defrosted)

3 tbsp (40 g) organic granulated cane sugar

Finely grated zest from 1 small lemon

2 tsp (10 ml) lemon juice

1 tsp cornstarch

¼ tsp fine sea salt

⅛ tsp freshly grated nutmeg

FOR FINISHING

1–2 tbsp (30 ml) plant milk, for brushing the dough

Organic granulated cane sugar, for sprinkling

For the crust, prepare and chill the pie dough as directed.

To make the filling, in a medium bowl, toss together the blueberries, sugar, lemon zest and juice, cornstarch, salt and nutmeg to combine. Set aside.

Divide the dough into 6 equal portions, letting it stand at cool room temperature for 5–10 minutes to soften slightly. On a surface dusted lightly with oat flour (or between 2 squares of parchment paper dusted with oat flour), roll each portion of dough out into a 5- to 6-inch (13- to 15-cm) round about ¼-inch (6-mm) thick, turning the dough and dusting with more oat flour to prevent sticking. Trim each round to make an even circle (a pizza wheel works well here), and place on a 6-inch (15-cm) square of parchment. If the rounds have become soft or sticky, chill them for about 10 minutes (this will depend on the temperature of your kitchen).

Lay the dough rounds, still on their pieces of parchment, on your work surface. Divide the blueberries among the rounds, mounding them toward the center and a little off to one side. Use the parchment to help fold the dough over itself, making a half-moon shape. If the dough cracks, use your fingers to squish it back together. Repeat with the remaining pies. Use the tines of a fork to crimp the edges closed and seal the pies, and trim away excess dough from the edges. Lay the pies on a rimmed baking sheet lined with parchment paper and chill until firm, 20 minutes.

Position a rack in the upper third of the oven and preheat to 400ºF (200ºC).

To finish, remove the pies from the refrigerator, brush with the milk and sprinkle with the sugar. Use the tip of a paring knife to cut a few slits in the top of each pie to allow the steam to escape.

Bake the pies until the dough is golden and the fruit is bubbling, 22–30 minutes. Remove from the oven, and, while hot, use a thin metal spatula to remove the pies from their parchment and onto a cooling rack (otherwise, the caramelized juices will cause them to stick). Let cool to warm, then enjoy warm or at room temperature. They are best the day of baking when the crust is crisp, but will keep for up to 2 days airtight at room temperature.

GINGER PEACH CUTOUT PIE

{SWEET RICE, OAT, MILLET}

Peach pie always seems like a big production. There are hundreds of different recipes out there and everyone's got an opinion on flavorings, thickeners, lattice vs. double crusts, white vs. yellow peaches, to peel or not to peel … and that doesn't even touch on the hotly debated topic of shortening vs. butter in the crust. It really needn't be so difficult. I threw this one together with an extra batch of pie dough left over from another project, some white and yellow peaches that were cluttering my counter, and a smattering of crystallized ginger hiding in my cupboard. The whole project was simply satisfying. Bring this to a party and watch them treat you like the domestic god or goddess you are.

Half a cup of ginger will thrill true ginger fiends like myself; take it down to ¼ or ⅓ cup (40 or 60 g) if you prefer just a hint. Use whatever shade of peach (or nectarine) you have on hand. I find no need to peel most peaches; just give them a rinse and rub off some of the fuzz with a clean kitchen towel. Cornstarch is my thickener of choice, as it leaves behind not a trace of flavor or texture, and I'll give another shout-out to the cutout top crust, which is both stupid easy to make and oh so pretty to look at. Serve slices of this pie with any of the ice creams on pages 227–228, or with a plume of softly Whipped Cream (page 224) or Whipped Crème Fraîche (page 224).

MAKES ONE 9-INCH (23-CM) PIE, ABOUT 10 SERVINGS

CRUST
1 recipe Pie Dough for Cutout Pies (page 93)

GF oat flour, for dusting

FILLING
6–7 medium peaches (2¼ lb [1 kg]), ripe but firm (about 6½ cups [900 g], sliced)

Finely grated zest from 1 medium lemon

1 tbsp (15 ml) lemon juice

¾ cup (150 g) organic granulated cane sugar

3 tbsp (17 g) cornstarch

⅛ tsp fine sea salt

⅓–½ cup (60–90 g) finely chopped crystallized ginger

FOR FINISHING
1 tbsp (15 ml) milk or cream

1 tbsp (15 g) coarse sugar (demerara or turbinado)

For the crust, prepare and chill the pie dough as directed.

Position a rack in the lower third of the oven, top with a baking stone if you've got one and preheat to 425ºF (220ºC). Line a rimmed baking sheet with parchment paper for easy cleanup.

Make a bottom crust with the larger round of pie dough (see page 93). Chill the crust until firm, 30 minutes (or wrap and chill for up to 1 day). On a surface dusted lightly with oat flour, roll out the smaller round of dough to a 9-inch (23-cm) round about ¼-inch (6-mm) thick. Use a fluted biscuit cutter (or small glass) to cut 1½- and/or 2-inch (3.8- and/or 5-cm) rounds close together. Stack the rounds on a plate and chill until firm, 20 minutes. Optionally, press the dough scraps together, wrap and chill until firm, and repeat the rolling/cutting process once more.

To make the filling, halve the peaches and remove the pits, then cut each half into 8 wedges; you should have about 6½ cups (900 g). Place the peaches in a large bowl and add the lemon zest and juice, sugar, cornstarch, salt and ginger. Toss gently to combine and let sit for a few minutes to draw out the juices a bit.

Spoon the fruit and juices into the chilled crust, smoothing it flat. Place the chilled dough rounds over the top of the fruit, leaving lots of windows for steam to escape. To finish, brush the rounds with the milk and sprinkle with the coarse sugar.

Place the pie on the lined baking sheet and place in the oven on the baking stone. Bake at 425ºF (220ºC) for 15 minutes, then decrease the oven temperature to 375ºF (190ºC) and continue baking until the crust is golden and the fruit is bubbling furiously, 35–50 more minutes. Let the pie cool completely to set the fruit, at least 2 hours, then cut into wedges and serve at room temperature. The pie is best the day of baking and will keep at room temperature for up to 1 day or refrigerated for up to 3 days.

RUSTIC PLUM, TEFF AND HAZELNUT TART

{SWEET RICE, OAT, TEFF}

Plums' high water content makes them a challenge in the kitchen. Here, a hazelnut frangipane absorbs some of their liquid, puffing up around the slices and melding with a flaky teff flour pastry. The malty flavor of the teff pairs well with the toasted hazelnuts and tart, juicy plums, all drizzled with a touch of floral honey. The sugared edges become wildly crisp in the oven and make an addictive contrast to the tender middles. Do be sure to use parchment paper for rolling out the dough; it's difficult to transfer the large piece of dough onto the baking sheet without it. And give the tart a thorough bake on the lowest oven rack, letting the frangipane turn a deep golden all over; otherwise, the bottom crust will be soggy from those pesky plums.

MAKES 1 LARGE FREE-FORM TART, 12-15 SERVINGS

CRUST

1 recipe Teff Pie Dough (page 90), chilled

Teff flour, for dusting

FRANGIPANE AND PLUMS

1 cup (120 g) raw hazelnuts

¼ cup plus 2 tbsp (75 g) organic granulated cane sugar

¼ cup (40 g) sweet white rice flour

¼ tsp fine sea salt

6 tbsp (85 g) unsalted butter, softened but cool

1 large egg

1 tsp vanilla extract

1 lb (450 g) ripe but firm plums (about 7 medium)

FOR FINISHING

1 tbsp (15 ml) milk or heavy cream, for brushing the dough

2 tbsp (25 g) organic granulated cane sugar, for sprinkling

2–4 tbsp (30–60 ml) honey, for drizzling

For the crust, make the dough, completing the fraisage and all the optional folds; this will make puff pastry–like layers. Chill the dough until cold as instructed.

To make the frangipane, position a rack in the lower third of the oven and preheat to 350ºF (175ºC). Spread the hazelnuts on a small, rimmed baking sheet and toast until the skins are loose, 10–12 minutes. Let cool completely, then rub off as much of the skins as you easily can. In the bowl of a food processor, combine the hazelnuts, sugar, rice flour and salt. Process until the nuts are very finely ground, 30–60 seconds. Add the softened butter, egg and vanilla extract and process to a paste, 30 seconds. Don't overprocess or the mixture could break and become greasy and separated.

Let the dough stand at room temperature until slightly softened, 5 minutes in a warm kitchen or 15 minutes in a cool kitchen. Sandwich the dough between 2 large pieces of parchment paper dusted lightly with teff flour, and gently begin pressing it flat, then roll it into a 12 by 16–inch (30 by 40–cm) rectangle. As you work, periodically peel back the top piece of parchment, dust the dough lightly with flour, replace the parchment, grasp the dough sandwich with both hands and flip the whole thing over. Peel off the new top piece of parchment, dust with flour and continue to roll. If the dough is uneven, cut off the long bits and press them onto the short bits, rolling to adhere. When your rectangle measures 12 by 16 inches (30 by 40 cm), trim the sides so that they're even and straight. If your dough becomes soft or sticky at any point, slip it onto a baking sheet, parchment and all, and chill it for 10–20 minutes to firm the butter.

Slide the dough onto a sheet pan, still on the parchment. Use a small offset spatula to gently spread the hazelnut paste over the dough in an even layer, leaving a 1-inch (2.5-cm) border all the way around. Gently fold over the edges to make a generous 1-inch (2.5-cm) crust. Chill the dough until firm, 30 minutes.

Prepare the plums. If they cling to the pit, cut the flesh off the pit in large pieces; otherwise, cut the plums into quarters and discard the pits. Slice the plums thinly, discarding the ends that are mostly skin. Keeping the plum slices together, fan them atop the chilled frangipane in 12–15 clumps; this makes the finished tart easier to cut. You may not need all of the plums, and it's better to err on the side of too little, as excess fruit will lead to a soggy crust. To finish, brush the edges of the tart with the milk. Sprinkle the sugar all over the plums and crust.

Bake the tart until the hazelnut paste is puffed and deeply bronzed and the bottom of the tart is crisp, 40–50 minutes, rotating the tart toward the end of the baking time. The crust will look dark because of the teff flour, but take care not to underbake it or the bottom will be soggy. Remove from the oven and let cool for at least 30 minutes and up to several hours. Just before serving, drizzle all over with the honey and cut into 12–15 rectangles.

FIG AND CHÈVRE BITES WITH HONEY AND THYME

{SWEET RICE, OAT, MILLET}

When I traveled to France's *très romantique* Loire Valley many years ago, I hoped to meet the man of my dreams. Instead, I met the cheese of my dreams: a log of goat cheese rolled in ash and aged until it formed a creamy, Brie-like exterior and dense, crumbly middle. I gladly eschewed dessert in favor of the cheese carts wheeled to the postprandial table. These little bites of flaky pastry topped with aged goat cheese, fresh figs and a sprinkle of honey, thyme and black pepper bring the cheese course into dessert—though they work equally well as a starter when accompanied by a glass of bubbly and will make you the star of any potluck. A bite of flaky crust against funky cheese, gooey fig and fresh thyme tastes like love. These are best served warm from the oven, but the dough rounds can be prepared, topped and chilled until serving time, up to one day ahead. That said, we brought cold, two-day-old leftovers to a party and they disappeared in seconds.

Look for a French-style aged goat cheese that looks a little bit like Brie on the outside, sometimes called a *crottin* and sometimes rolled in ash before being aged (such as Delice de Poitou). I've also baked these bites with several different types of Northern Californian cheeses and all work well: Cypress Grove's Humboldt Fog, Cowgirl Creamery's Mt. Tam and Laura Chenel's Goat Brie and Ash-Rinded Buchette. If aged chèvre isn't the cheese of your dreams, feel free to use a fresh chèvre or goat Brie instead. Do look for a cheese that isn't too soft, lest it run all over the place in the oven. Similarly, look for figs that are ripe but firm, such as Black Missions.

MAKES 14-16 (3-INCH [8-CM]) BITES

CRUST

1 batch Flaky Pie Dough (page 87)

GF oat flour, for dusting

FILLING

8 large figs, such as Black Mission (ripe but firm)

6 oz (175 g) aged chèvre (or other cheese, see headnote), cut into 14–16 slices

1 tbsp (3 g) fresh thyme leaves

Flaky sea salt, such as Maldon

Cracked black pepper

1–2 tbsp (15–30 ml) honey

For the crust, prepare the pie dough with the fraisage and 1–2 turns and chill as directed. If the pie dough is very firm, let it soften at room temperature until malleable, about 5 minutes. On a work surface dusted lightly with oat flour, roll out the chilled dough into a rough rectangle that measures ⅜-inch (1-cm) thick, rotating the dough frequently, dusting it with just enough flour to keep it from sticking and sweeping off excess flour with a pastry brush. When the dough has been rolled out, cut out 3-inch (7-cm) rounds with a fluted biscuit cutter or the top of a glass, cutting the rounds as close together as possible. (Note: If your figs are smaller, cut out smaller rounds of dough.) Stack the dough rounds on a plate, cover, and chill until firm, 30 minutes or up to 1 day. Optionally, press the dough scraps together, and repeat the chilling/rolling/cutting process once more.

Position a rack in the lower third of the oven and preheat to 375°F (190°C). Line a rimmed baking sheet with parchment paper.

For the filling, cut the stems off the figs and slice each one in half lengthwise. Place the chilled dough rounds 1–2 inches (2.5–5 cm) apart on the prepared baking sheet. Top each round with a slice of chèvre and a fig half placed cut side up, pressing the figs gently into the chèvre to keep them in place.

Bake the bites until the dough is golden, 22–27 minutes. Remove from the oven and place on a serving platter, allowing them to cool for a few minutes. Sprinkle with the thyme leaves, salt, pepper, and a drizzle of honey.

The bites are best served when still warm from the oven, but they will keep at room temperature for up to several hours or refrigerated for up to 2 days. Reheat before serving for best results.

MAPLE TEFF APPLE PIE WITH WALNUT CRUMBLE

{SWEET RICE, OAT, TEFF}

This was the first pie I baked with my flaky gluten-free pie dough, and I knew I'd finally struck gold when I literally forgot that the pie was gluten-free. The juicy apple filling is kissed with maple syrup and lemon, which keep the apples tasting bright and earthy. A maple sugar and teff crumb topping makes an attractive lid without the fuss of a top crust, and the slight bitterness of walnuts adds dimension (though pecans can take their place, too). Teff flour in the crust and crumble adds notes of caramel (or try the more vanilla version of this pie made with all oat flour, below).

MAKES ONE 9-INCH (23-CM) PIE, ABOUT 10 SERVINGS

CRUST
1 recipe Teff Pie Dough (page 90)

Teff flour, for dusting

FILLING
2¼ lb (1 kg) tart, firm baking apples, such as Granny Smith (6–8 medium apples)

½ cup (120 ml) maple syrup (preferably grade B)

Finely grated zest from ½ large lemon

2 tbsp (30 ml) strained lemon juice

1 tbsp (6 g) cornstarch

½ tsp ground cinnamon

⅛ tsp fine sea salt

CRUMBLE
¼ cup plus 2 tbsp (35 g) GF oat flour

2 tbsp (15 g) teff flour

¼ cup plus 2 tbsp (50 g) maple sugar (or packed organic light brown sugar)

¼ tsp ground cinnamon

¼ tsp freshly grated nutmeg

¼ tsp fine sea salt

5 tbsp (70 g) cold, unsalted butter

¾ cup (80 g) raw walnut halves

Vanilla Bean Ice Cream (page 227) or Maple Bourbon Whipped Cream (page 224) for serving

For the crust, prepare the dough, shape into a 9-inch (23-cm) crust as directed, and chill the unbaked crust until firm, at least 30 minutes.

For the filling, peel the apples, cut them off the core and slice them a scant ¼-inch (6-mm) thick. You should have 6 cups (900 g) total. Place the apple slices in a large bowl and gently toss with the maple syrup, lemon zest and juice, cornstarch, cinnamon and salt. Let sit while you prepare the crumble, 10–20 minutes, tossing a few times.

Meanwhile, position a rack in the lower third of the oven, place a baking stone on the rack if you have one and preheat to 350°F (175°C). If there are any holes in the pie crust, patch them with leftover dough scraps.

To make the crumble, in the bowl of a food processor, combine the oat and teff flours, maple sugar, cinnamon, nutmeg and salt. Pulse once or twice to combine, then pulse in the butter until the mixture looks like coarse meal, with no large butter chunks remaining. Add the walnuts and pulse several more times until the nuts are broken down a bit and the mixture begins to clump together; don't overmix. Cover and chill if not using right away.

Pour the apples and their liquid into the unbaked crust, and pack the apples snugly. Crumble the topping evenly over the apples, breaking it into some hazelnut-sized chunks and letting the rest be loose. Bake the pie until the top is golden and the juices are bubbling up thickly, 60–75 minutes. The topping and crust will look dark from the teff flour, but if it is getting too dark, reduce the oven temperature to 300°F (150°C). Let the pie cool most of the way, at least 2 and up to 8 hours to thicken the juices.

VARIATIONS

MAPLE OAT APPLE PIE WITH WALNUT CRUMBLE
For a more kid-friendly version of this pie, use the Flaky Pie Dough (page 87) in place of the teff crust, and make the topping with ½ cup (55 g) oat flour instead of the oat/teff blend.

MAPLE BOURBON APPLE PIE WITH WALNUT CRUMBLE
I like this grown-up version best with the milder, all-oat variation, above. Reduce the maple syrup to ⅓ cup (85 ml) and add ¼ cup (60 ml) GF bourbon to the apple mixture. Increase the cornstarch to 2 tablespoons (11 g) to help absorb the extra moisture.

BUCKWHEAT PEAR GALETTES WITH WALNUTS AND SALTY CARAMEL

{SWEET RICE, BUCKWHEAT, OAT}

Biting into one of these little tarts when warm from the oven is sheer ecstasy. Crisp crust shatters against tender pears, gooey caramel drips everywhere and nubs of walnuts add their roasty flavor to the mix. The crust sings with the bold flavor of buckwheat, which always reminds me of a blend of hazelnuts and cinnamon, with earthy notes that smack of coffee or chocolate. Here, the dark crust plays dramatically against the white flesh of ripe pears. Toasted walnuts absorb the pears' juices and keep the bottom crust crisp. I think my friend Erika, who tested this recipe, said it best: "I feel like I'm eating a fancy-ass pastry from Tartine, only I MADE IT."

MAKES EIGHT 3½-INCH (9-CM) GALETTES

CRUST
1 recipe Buckwheat Pie Dough (page 90)

Buckwheat flour, for dusting

FILLING
½ cup (55 g) raw walnut halves

4 medium ripe but firm pears, such as Bartlett (about 1½ lb [680 g])

1 tbsp (15 ml) lemon juice

2 tbsp (30 ml) cream or milk

3 tbsp (35 g) organic granulated cane sugar

½ cup (120 ml) Salty Caramel (any variation, page 231), at room temperature or warm enough to drizzle

Flaky sea salt, such as Maldon, for sprinkling (optional)

NOTE: Melon ballers aren't just for making fussy, 1970s-inspired fruit salads; they also make a handy tool for coring pears. Halve a pear lengthwise, then use the melon baller to scoop away the stem, seeds and blossom.

For the crust, prepare the buckwheat pie dough, preferably with the fraisage and 1–2 turns, and chill as directed. Place the chilled dough on a surface dusted lightly with buckwheat flour. Use a sharp chef's knife to divide the dough into 8 equal portions, and place 7 of the portions back in the refrigerator to keep cool. Use a rolling pin to roll out the first portion of dough into a 6-inch (15-cm) round a scant ⅛-inch (3-mm) thick, flipping and dusting the dough as you go to prevent it from sticking and sweeping away excess flour. Trim the edges to make an even round. Place the dough round on a plate and chill. Repeat with the remaining dough portions, stacking them on the plate and dusting with a bit of flour to prevent sticking. Cover and chill until firm, at least 30 minutes and up to 1 day.

Meanwhile, to make the filling, position racks in the upper and lower thirds of the oven and preheat to 350°F (175°C). Spread the walnuts on a small, rimmed baking sheet and toast on the upper rack until golden and fragrant, 8–10 minutes. Let cool, then chop fairly finely. Increase the oven temperature to 400°F (200°C).

Peel the pears, halve them lengthwise, and remove their cores, stems and blossoms. Place a half cut side down and, keeping the slices together, slice lengthwise ¼-inch (6-mm) thick. Repeat with the remaining pears. Drizzle the pear halves with the lemon juice to keep them from oxidizing while you work; this also adds a bit of brightness to the finished galettes.

Divide the dough rounds between 2 rimmed baking sheets lined with parchment paper for easy cleanup. Divide the chopped walnuts among the rounds, mounding them in the center. Keeping the slices together, use a small knife or offset spatula to transfer a pear half to the top of a tart, placing it over the nuts and fanning out the slices a bit. Gently fold up the dough around the fanned pear slices to create a 1-inch (2.5-cm) lip, creasing and pleating the dough as you go. If it cracks, don't worry—just press it back together. Use your palm to gently flatten down the galette slightly. If the dough has softened, place the galettes back in the refrigerator and chill until firm. Brush the dough lightly with the cream and sprinkle the pears and dough evenly with the sugar.

Bake the galettes until the pear juices bubble furiously and the dough is golden (you will have to look closely, as the dough will be dark and crusted in sugar), 30–40 minutes, rotating the pans front to back and top to bottom for even browning after the first 20 minutes.

Remove the galettes from the oven and let cool for at least 15 minutes or up to several hours. To serve, drizzle all over with the caramel sauce and top with a few flecks of flaky salt if desired. The galettes are best the day of baking but will keep at room temperature for 1 day or refrigerated airtight for up to 2 days.

PUMPKIN PIE WITH A BUCKWHEAT CRUST

{SWEET RICE, BUCKWHEAT, OAT}

My sweetie and I are obsessed with pumpkin pie, and would gladly eat it every day, all year round. And yet, I can understand where the world's pumpkin pie haters are coming from. Canned pumpkin can have a metallic, vegetal taste. The filling can be curdled and watery, or overly thick and starchy, plagued by too many heavy spices. To mitigate these pitfalls, I've taken a few tips from *Cook's Illustrated*, French patisserie and my own kitchen. First, I take the time to roast my own squash, which makes for a bright, fresh-tasting filling. Since most pumpkin puree actually comes from a squash in the butternut family, butternut is my go-to (though kabocha, carnival and red kuri squash also make excellent pie). Next, I add a bit of flour to the custard, a traditional French technique that helps absorb excess moisture. Finally, I give the squash puree a brief cook on the stove with the spices and sweeteners; this evaporates excess moisture and melds the flavors together. Maple syrup, fresh ginger and nutmeg and crème fraîche all make the filling sparkle, and all that pumpkin spice deliciousness is served up in a super flaky buckwheat crust that stays crisp longer than you'd guess.

For this pie, as for all custard-based pies and tarts, keep an eye on your oven temperature and be careful not to overbake the pie, lest the filling become grainy and watery. Watch the pie for visual cues of doneness, and be sure to allow 2 to 3 hours post-baking for cooling the pie; it will still be cooking from residual heat.

MAKES ONE 9-INCH (23-CM) PIE, ABOUT 10 SERVINGS

CRUST
1 recipe Buckwheat Pie Dough (page 90)

FILLING
¼ cup (50 g) organic granulated cane sugar

2 tbsp (17 g) sweet white rice flour

½ tsp ground cinnamon

¼ tsp freshly grated nutmeg

⅛ tsp ground allspice

½ tsp fine sea salt

2 cups (460 g) roasted squash puree (see Note) or canned pumpkin puree

¼ cup plus 2 tbsp (90 ml) maple syrup (preferably grade B)

1 tsp packed finely grated fresh ginger

1 cup (235 ml) whole milk

3 large eggs

½ cup (120 ml) Crème Fraîche (page 223) or sour cream

1 tsp vanilla extract

FOR SERVING (OPTIONAL)
Maple Bourbon Whipped Cream (page 224)

For the crust, prepare and parbake the buckwheat pie crust as directed. Position a rack in the lower third of the oven and preheat to 400°F (200°C). If you have a baking stone, place it on the rack. Place your crust on a rimmed baking sheet lined with parchment for easy cleanup. If your crust has cooled, place it in the oven until hot just before pouring in the custard, 5–10 minutes.

To make the filling, in a large saucepan, whisk together the sugar, sweet rice flour, cinnamon, nutmeg, allspice and salt. Whisk in the squash puree, maple syrup and ginger. Place the pot over medium heat and stir frequently until the mixture comes to a sputtering simmer. Continue to cook, stirring constantly, until the mixture is thick and shiny, 5 more minutes. Remove from the heat. Whisk in the milk, then the eggs, crème fraîche and vanilla. Strain the custard through a medium-mesh strainer (fine-mesh will take forever and make you hate life); alternatively, puree with an immersion blender.

Pour the custard into the hot pie crust and very carefully transfer to the oven. Bake at 400°F (200°C) for 10 minutes, then lower the temperature to 300°F (150°C) and bake for 20–35 more minutes, or until the outer edges are set and slightly puffed and the center wobbles like Jell-O. Let the pie cool completely at room temperature, 2–3 hours; it is still cooking from residual heat. For the cleanest slices or if the pie is soft, chill until firmer, 1–2 hours. Slice into wedges and serve cool or at room temperature with whipped cream if you like. The pie is best the day of baking but will keep, refrigerated airtight, for up to 3 days.

NOTE: To make your own roasted squash puree, cut a large butternut squash in half lengthwise and leave the seeds in for now (they're easier to remove post-roasting). Place the halves with a cut side down on a lightly oiled, rimmed baking sheet and roast in a 375°F (190°C) oven until very tender and collapsing slightly, about 45 minutes. Let cool, scoop out and discard the seeds and strings, and scoop out and reserve the flesh, discarding the skin. Puree the flesh in a food processor until smooth. The puree will keep, refrigerated airtight, for up to 2 weeks.

MEYER LEMON AND VANILLA BEAN BUTTERMILK PIE

{SWEET RICE, OAT, MILLET}

This pie is one of my very favorite cures for the midwinter doldrums, bridging the gap between the spiced fruit pies of fall and the first of the strawberries and rhubarb of early spring. Meyer lemons, a lemon-mandarin hybrid common to California, have a sweet-tart flavor that reminds me of sunshine, flowers and brighter days to come. Here, thick buttermilk custard contrasts with shatteringly crisp pie crust. Flecks of vanilla bean bring out the floral notes in the lemons, and cream adds richness to round out the lemons' acidity. It needs no accompaniment, but slices are nice when dressed up with Honey Candied Kumquats (page 235), fresh berries or segments of blood orange or tangerine. This pie is best the day of baking, when the crust is at its crispest, but it will keep well, refrigerated airtight, for up to 3 days. If Meyers aren't about, make an extra-tangy pie with regular lemon zest and juice.

MAKES ONE 9-INCH (23-CM) PIE, ABOUT 10 SERVINGS

CRUST
1 recipe Flaky Pie Dough (page 87)

FILLING
¾ cup plus 2 tbsp (175 g) organic granulated cane sugar

Finely grated zest from 2 large (or 3 smaller) Meyer lemons (1 packed tbsp, or 10 g)

1 vanilla bean

¼ cup (40 g) sweet white rice flour

¼ tsp salt

2 large eggs

2 large egg yolks

1¼ cups (300 ml) fresh, well-shaken buttermilk

½ cup (120 ml) heavy cream

¼ cup (60 ml) strained Meyer lemon juice (from 1–2 lemons)

For the crust, prepare and parbake the pie crust as directed.

To make the filling, position a rack in the lower third of the oven, top with a baking stone if you've got one and preheat to 325ºF (165ºC).

Place the sugar in a medium bowl and add the lemon zest. Slit the vanilla bean down the center, use the back of the knife to scrape out the seeds and add them to the sugar, reserving the pod for another use (such as Vanilla Extract, page 220). Use your fingertips to rub the zest and vanilla seeds into the sugar until it feels damp and slightly clumpy.

Whisk the flour and salt into the sugar until combined, then whisk in the eggs and yolks until smooth, whisking gently to avoid incorporating excess air into the batter. Slowly whisk in the buttermilk, then the cream and lemon juice until smooth.

If your pie crust has cooled, return it to the oven for about 5 minutes to get it hot, patching any holes with leftover dough if necessary. Pour the filling into the hot crust and carefully transfer to the oven.

Bake the pie until mostly set with a slight, Jell-O-like wobble, 40–50 minutes. It will be puffed all over, and will barely wiggle when you give it a shake. Cool the pie completely, about 2 hours. The pie can be served at room temperature, where it will keep for up to 4 hours, or chilled, which will yield cleaner slices.

The pie is best the day of baking, when the crust is crisp, but extras will keep airtight in the refrigerator for up to 3 days.

NOTE: Since the custardy filling leaks easily here, be sure to save scraps of pie dough for patching any tiny holes in the parbaked crust. Be sure to use fresh, well-shaken buttermilk in the filling; older buttermilk can become thin and watery, leading to a broken filling. While the pie bakes, watch the oven temperature like a hawk (preferably with an oven thermometer or two); most ovens don't run true to temperature and a too-hot oven can cause the filling to crack and become grainy.

TARTS

I used to loathe baking tarts. Butter was softened only to be mixed into dough and chilled again. The delicate dough was rolled out, fitted into the pan and chilled again. Pie weights were needed to keep the dough aloft, which often slumped and squished down into the pan despite my best efforts. I finally discovered the secret to positive tart experiences in a lemon bar recipe that called for a shortbread-like dough that was simply pressed into the pan. I mixed up the dough, pressed it into a tart pan, and baked it sans pie weights, and voilà—easy-peasy perfect tart crust. I've tweaked the recipe many times over the years, and I've ditched the wheat flour and added almond, sweet rice and oat flours (plus some alternative variations). I use my stand mixer to work in the cold butter, which gets pressed into the pan straight away. After a quick freeze, into the oven it goes, staying resolutely upright, no weights necessary.

Almond and oat flours make an earthy base for both butterscotchy brown butter crème fraîche custard and peaches, as well as a floral grapefruit custard tart laced with elderflower liqueur. A deep, dark cocoa crust houses a naturally sweetened pecan pie filling bursting with fresh cranberries. Mesquite flour and brown sugar make a wildly flavorful shell for creamy pudding, bananas and salty caramel. Chestnut flour enhances a classic apple tart. And a vegan coconut flour crust adds crunch to Hawaiian-inspired coconut custard and fresh berries.

The tart recipes in this book are some of my favorites, and I hope they become as not-loathed in your kitchen as they have in mine.

NOTE: All tarts in this section should work interchangeably in tart pans of the following dimensions: one 9-inch (23-cm) round tart crust, one 12 by 4-inch (30 by 10-cm) rectangular tart crust or eight 4-inch (10-cm) round tartlet crusts. Adjust the baking time as needed.

VANILLA ALMOND TART CRUST

{ALMOND, SWEET RICE, OAT}

At a patisserie where I once worked, the owner was so committed to using 100 percent organic ingredients that, because blanched almonds weren't available organic, some days were spent blanching the nuts for hours at a time. I didn't mind the task, standing in place and slipping the loose skins off of nuts that had been briefly boiled. But what I did mind was that the majority of the almonds were ground into tart dough. As my preferred glutinous tart dough contains just butter, flour, sugar and salt, the addition of these precious almonds seemed superfluous.

I changed my mind when it came time to make a gluten-free sweet tart dough. Here the almond flour is the magic ingredient that helps the dough hold together with no gums and a minimum of starches. The tiny nubbles of almond give the dough the sandy consistency of fine shortbread, oat flour adds earthy flavor and judicious amounts of sugar and salt bring the taste into balance. Cold butter gets rubbed into the dough with the help of a stand mixer, and the crumbly dough gets pressed right into the pan, no chilling or rolling necessary. As an added bonus, after a brief stint in the freezer, the dough gets baked as is, no pastry weights needed to hold the dough up the sides of the pan. Don't forget to press the sides and bottom of the hot crust with the back of a spoon, otherwise the delicate crust will be difficult to slice (though still delicious).

MAKES ONE 9-INCH (23-CM) ROUND TART CRUST, ONE 12 BY 4-INCH (30 BY 10-CM) RECTANGULAR TART CRUST OR EIGHT 4-INCH (10-CM) ROUND TARTLET CRUSTS

½ cup (60 g) blanched almond flour (such as Bob's Red Mill)

½ cup (80 g) sweet white rice flour

½ cup (55 g) GF oat flour

2 tbsp (12 g) tapioca flour

¼ cup (50 g) organic granulated cane sugar

¼ plus ⅛ tsp fine sea salt

6 tbsp (85 g) cold, unsalted butter, diced into ½-inch (1.3-cm) cubes

1 tsp vanilla extract

Position a rack in the center of the oven and preheat to 375ºF (190ºC).

In the bowl of a stand mixer fitted with the paddle attachment, combine the almond, sweet rice and oat flours with the tapioca starch, sugar and salt. Scatter the butter pieces over the top and drizzle with the vanilla extract. Turn the mixer to medium-low and run until the dough comes together in clumps and the butter is worked through, 3–5 minutes.

Dump the crumbs into the desired tart pan(s) with removable bottom(s) and press the dough evenly into the pan, starting with the sides and then moving to the bottom, keeping the edges square. (It usually takes me about 10 minutes to make it look pretty.) Prick the bottom of the crust all over with the tines of a fork and freeze until firm, 15–30 minutes.

Place the tart pan on a rimmed baking sheet and bake until pale golden and firm to the touch (18–22 minutes) for a parbaked crust, or until golden all over (5–10 minutes longer) for a fully baked crust. (If making tartlets, decrease the overall baking time by 5–10 minutes.) Remove the crust from the oven and, while it's still hot, press the sides and bottom with the back of a spoon. This will help it hold together when cool.

(continued)

Work cold butter into the flour mixture to form a crumbly, clumpy dough.

Press the edges into the pan first,

then press the bottom into the pan to form an even layer.

Freeze, then parbake until golden.

VANILLA ALMOND TART CRUST (CONT.)

VARIATIONS

COCOA ALMOND

Use ½ cup (45 g) cocoa powder (preferably Dutch-process) in place of the oat flour and decrease the butter to 5 tablespoons (70 g). Since the dough is dark, it can be difficult to tell when the crust is done, so do set a timer and look closely for edges that are beginning to darken and pull away from the sides of the pan. If the chocolate begins to smell at all burnt, remove the crust immediately.

MUSCOVADO MESQUITE

Use ½ cup (60 g) mesquite flour (sifted after measuring to eradicate lumps) in place of the oat flour and ¼ cup (50 g) muscovado (or packed organic light or dark brown) sugar in place of the granulated sugar. Bake this variation at 350°F (175°C) since mesquite flour is more sensitive to temperature than other flours.

CHESTNUT

Use ½ cup (50 g) chestnut flour in place of the oat flour.

See page 120 for a vegan variation made with coconut oil.

A COUPLE OF KEY TECHNIQUES MAKE THIS TART CRUST SHINE

- Use a stand mixer fitted with the paddle attachment to rub cold butter into the dough. A food processor smooths out the almond flour too much and it loses its delicate texture. It takes a good 3–5 minutes for this to happen. Alternatively, use your fingertips to rub the butter into the dough.
- Take the time to press the dough evenly into the pan, starting with the sides and then moving to the bottom, keeping the edges square. In a 9-inch (23-cm) round pan, the dough will be about ¼-inch (6-mm) thick. You can use a flat-bottomed glass to press the bottom of the dough smooth.
- When the dough has finished baking and is still hot, use the back of a spoon to gently but firmly press the bottom and sides of the crust. This will help it hold together better.

COCONUT CREAM AND RASPBERRY TART {VEGAN}

{ALMOND, SWEET RICE, COCONUT}

This tart gets a triple dose of coconut: coconut flour and oil in the crust and coconut milk in the filling. Fresh raspberries perch atop a vanilla-flecked coconut milk custard, all nestled into a coconut flour crust that tastes like a cross between a macaroon and shortbread. A smear of chocolate keeps the crust crisp and pairs well with both the coconut and the berries. The whole thing is so satisfying in taste and texture that no one will ever suspect it of being both vegan and gluten-free. This crust is similar in method to the Vanilla Almond Tart Crust (page 117) but with a few differences. A bit of water is necessary to help the dough stick together when baked; without, it crumbles into oblivion. Also, a light coating of cooking spray or oil is needed to prevent the stickier dough from adhering to the pan. Feel free to use this crust for any of the tarts in this book. And if you can't find fresh raspberries, top the tart with sliced strawberries, other summer berries, or Honey Candied Kumquats (page 235) instead.

MAKES ONE 12 BY 4-INCH (30 BY 10-CM) RECTANGULAR TART OR ONE 9-INCH (23-CM) ROUND TART, 8-10 SERVINGS

CRUST

Vegetable oil spray or 1 tsp melted coconut oil, for the pan

½ cup (60 g) blanched almond flour

⅓ cup (50 g) sweet white rice flour

⅓ cup (40 g) coconut flour

¼ cup (45 g) organic granulated cane sugar

¼ plus ⅛ tsp fine sea salt

7 tbsp (80 g) coconut oil (at cool room temperature or lightly chilled)

1 tsp vanilla extract

2 tbsp (30 ml) cold water

2 oz (55 g) bittersweet chocolate, chopped (about ⅓ cup)

FILLING

1 (13.5-oz [400-ml]) can full-fat coconut milk

½ vanilla bean, split lengthwise and scraped

3 tbsp (35 g) organic granulated cane sugar

3 tbsp (18 g) cornstarch

Pinch of fine sea salt

2 pints (340 g) fresh raspberries, or enough to cover the top of the tart in a single layer

To make the crust, position a rack in the center of the oven and preheat to 350°F (175°C). Lightly spray a 12 by 4-inch (30 by 10-cm) rectangular tart pan or a 9-inch (23-cm) round tart pan with a removable bottom with cooking spray or brush it with a teaspoon of melted coconut oil.

In the bowl of a stand mixer fitted with the paddle attachment, combine the almond, sweet rice and coconut flours with the sugar and salt. Scatter the coconut oil in clumps over the top and drizzle with the vanilla extract. Beat on medium-low speed until the coconut oil is evenly incorporated and the dough looks clumpy, 2–3 minutes. With the mixer running, slowly drizzle in the cold water, mixing until the dough comes together in large clumps. Dump the crumbly dough into the prepared tart pan and press the dough evenly into the pan, starting with the sides and then moving to the bottom, keeping the edges square. Prick the bottom of the crust all over with the tines of a fork and freeze until firm, 15–30 minutes.

Place the tart pan on a rimmed baking sheet and bake until golden all over, 20–25 minutes. Remove the crust from the oven and, while it's still hot, scatter the chopped chocolate over the bottom of the crust. Let the chocolate melt, 1 minute, then use the back of a small spoon to spread the melted chocolate over the bottom and up the sides of the crust. Let cool to room temperature, then chill until the chocolate is set, 10–20 minutes.

To make the filling, combine the coconut milk and vanilla pod and scrapings in a medium-sized, heavy-bottomed saucepan. Heat over medium heat, stirring occasionally, until the milk is hot and steamy (don't let it boil or it may scorch or separate). Remove from the heat, cover and let steep for 10 minutes or up to 1 hour to infuse with the vanilla.

Meanwhile, whisk together the sugar, cornstarch and salt in a small bowl. When the coconut milk has steeped, whisk a few tablespoons of the coconut milk into the cornstarch mixture to make a slurry, then whisk the slurry into the warm coconut milk. Cook the pudding over medium heat, whisking constantly and making sure to scrape the bottom and corners of the pot, until it comes to a low boil. Still stirring, boil for 1–2 minutes; it should be the texture of yogurt. Immediately strain the pudding through a mesh sieve and into a heatproof measuring pitcher. Pour the hot coconut cream into the chocolate-lined tart shell, spreading it evenly and taking care not to disturb the melty chocolate. Chill until set, 2 hours.

When ready to serve, release the sides from the pan by pushing the tart bottom upward, and slide the tart onto a large cutting board. Top the tart with the raspberries. Cut into pieces and serve.

PEACH BROWN BUTTER CRÈME FRAÎCHE TART

{ALMOND, SWEET RICE, OAT}

My sweetie and I were once taken to a ritzy San Francisco restaurant where one prix-fixe meal costs more than we spend on groceries in a month. Expecting an evening full of cozy decadence, we were disappointed when the first dish brought to us was a bowl of torn fish stomach served on a gelée made from the unfortunate fish's own juices and topped with its roe. After a dozen courses, each making us squirm more than the last, we staggered home, pondering whether foodies are so jaded, so weary of pork belly and truffles and hand-rolled pasta, that they need to be served fish innards for a gustatory thrill.

This tart is pretty much the opposite. It's as comfy as a slice of peach pie topped with vanilla ice cream, only reconfigured and fancied up a bit. A cookie-like crust crumbles against tangy, butterscotch-flavored custard that envelops tender peaches. Eating a slice warm from the oven is a little like slipping on a pair of sweats after sitting in a fancy restaurant for five hours in a tight dress eating fish innards. But nice sweats. Designer yoga pants, say. This tart is a crowd-pleaser, but with enough little twists to hold the interest of even the most jaded foodie.

MAKES ONE 9-INCH (23-CM) TART, 8-10 SERVINGS

CRUST
One 9-inch (23-cm) Vanilla Almond Tart Crust (page 117), parbaked

FILLING
6 tbsp (85 g) unsalted butter

1 vanilla bean, split lengthwise and scraped

1 lb (450 g) ripe but firm peaches (3–4 medium)

¼ cup (50 g) organic granulated cane sugar, plus 1 tbsp (10 g) for sprinkling

2 tbsp (17 g) sweet white rice flour

¼ tsp fine sea salt

1 large egg

½ cup (120 ml) Crème Fraîche (page 223) or sour cream

Powdered sugar (optional, for dusting)

For the crust, prepare and parbake the crust as directed.

Position a rack in the center of the oven and preheat to 350ºF (175ºC). Place the parbaked tart crust on a rimmed baking sheet lined with parchment paper for easy cleanup.

To make the filling, place the butter and vanilla pod and scrapings in a medium, heavy-bottomed saucepan and cook over medium-low heat, swirling occasionally. After about 3–5 minutes, the butter will foam up, turn golden and smell nutty, with brown flecks mingling with black vanilla bean seeds on the bottom of the pan. At this point, remove the pan from the heat. Pour the butter into a heatproof measuring cup to stop the cooking, and let cool for 5 minutes. Remove the vanilla bean and discard.

Meanwhile, halve the peaches and remove the pits. Cut each half into 6 wedges; you should have about 3 cups of sliced peaches.

In a medium bowl, whisk together the ¼ cup (50 g) sugar, rice flour and salt. Whisk in the egg until smooth, then the crème fraîche. Whisking constantly, slowly drizzle in the browned butter. Pour the custard into the crust. Arrange the peach wedges over the custard in concentric circles and sprinkle with the remaining 1 tablespoon (10 g) sugar.

Bake the tart until the custard is gently puffed and pale golden around the edges, and mostly set when you give the pan a shuffle, 30–40 minutes. Remove from the oven and let cool completely, at least 1 hour and up to several hours. Remove the sides of the tart pan by placing it on a large can or small inverted bowl and gently loosening. Dust with powdered sugar, if desired. Place the tart on a cutting board, cut into wedges and serve. The tart is best within the first 2 days of baking when the crust is crisp, but it will keep, refrigerated airtight, for up to 3 days.

NOTE: If you're new to browning butter, see how it's done on page 219.

CARAMELIZED FIG AND WHIPPED HONEY YOGURT TARTLETS

{ALMOND, SWEET RICE, OAT}

These tarts carry the Mediterranean flavors of almond, orange blossom, honey and fresh figs. Dusting the figs with sugar and torching the tops mellows their bite just a bit, adds a touch of smoky sweetness and brings the tart components together into one luscious late-summer dessert. Buttery tart shells contrast cool and tangy whipped yogurt kissed with honey and orange blossom water, all nestled up against juicy figs. These must be assembled to order, lest the crust and burnt sugar soften prematurely, but guests will love watching the sugar sizzle as you torch the fruit.

MAKES EIGHT 4-INCH (10-CM) INDIVIDUAL TARTLETS OR ONE 9-INCH (23-CM) TART, 8-10 SERVINGS

CRUST
8 (4-inch [10-cm]) fully baked Vanilla Almond Tartlet Crusts (page 117), cooled

FILLING
¾ cup (180 g) plain whole-milk Greek yogurt (such as Straus Family Creamery) or skyr (such as Siggi's)

¾ cup (180 ml) heavy cream

3 tbsp (45 ml) honey

¾ tsp orange blossom water, or more to taste (optional)

16 medium-small ripe but firm figs (about 1 lb [450 g])

8 tsp (32 g) organic granulated cane sugar (for caramelizing the figs)

For the crust, prepare and bake the tartlet shells as directed. When cool, remove the tart crusts from their pans and place on a large cutting board.

To make the filling, in the bowl of a stand mixer fitted with the whip attachment, combine the yogurt, cream, honey and orange blossom water. Whip on medium-high speed until the mixture holds firm peaks. (Alternatively, beat with a sturdy wire whisk or hand beater in a large bowl.) Cover and chill until needed, up to several hours. Re-whip if the mixture has separated.

Divide the whipped yogurt among the baked, cooled tartlet crusts, filling them nearly to the top and spreading the yogurt into an even layer.

Slice the figs lengthwise ⅛-inch (3-mm) thick, discarding the round ends and keeping the slices together. Fan the slices over the yogurt-filled tart crust, curving the slices with the tart sides to form a ring of overlapping slices. Sprinkle the figs on each tart with 1 teaspoon sugar. Use a kitchen torch to burn the sugar, holding it straight down and several inches away from the figs, until the sugar is golden and bubbling. As you work, wave the torch in small circles. If the sugar blackens, hold the torch farther away.

Repeat with the remaining tartlets and serve right away (or chill for up to 30 minutes).

NOTE: If you don't have a kitchen torch, don't despair: place the fig slices in an even layer on a baking sheet, sprinkle with the sugar and place under the broiler until the sugar has caramelized, a minute or two. Scrape the figs off the pan and over the tarts for a messier—though still tasty—presentation. Or skip the sugar altogether and top the fresh figs with a drizzle of honey.

APPLE CHESTNUT TART WITH SALTY CARAMEL

{ALMOND, SWEET RICE, CHESTNUT}

The classic apple tart is the soul of simplicity, epitomizing French baking at its finest. I learned to make it while working at an organic French-style bakery in San Francisco. Thinly sliced apples are nestled into an unbaked tart shell, topped with a bit of butter and sugar, and given a long bake. The juices from the apples mix with the butter and sugar, and the submerged apples bake into a chunky jamlike texture while the tips caramelize and retain a bit of bite.

Against a crumbly crust warm from earthy chestnut flour and topped with gooey caramel, this updated version makes a sensational dessert for fall and winter months, especially when served warm from the oven with Whipped Crème Fraîche (page 224) or Vanilla Bean Ice Cream (page 227). Store leftovers airtight in the refrigerator for up to 2 days. If you're short on time or crave a more traditional finish, skip the caramel and brush the tart with a few tablespoons of apricot jam loosened with a few drops of water, heated and strained.

MAKES ONE 9-INCH (23-CM) TART, 8-10 SERVINGS

CRUST
One 9-inch (23-cm) Chestnut Tart Crust (page 119), unbaked and frozen

FILLING
5 medium-sized tart, firm baking apples, such as Granny Smith or Belle de Boskoop (1¾ lb [800 g])

¼ cup (50 g) organic granulated cane sugar

3 tbsp (42 g) unsalted butter, in small pieces

½ cup (120 ml) Salty Caramel (any variation, page 231), at room temperature or warm enough to drizzle

For the crust, prepare and freeze the tart crust as directed.

Position a rack in the center of the oven and preheat to 350ºF (175ºC). Place the frozen, unbaked tart crust on a rimmed baking sheet lined with parchment paper for easy cleanup.

To make the filling, use a T-shaped vegetable peeler to peel the apples. Cut the flesh off the core in large chunks, cutting close to the core (alternatively, halve and core the apples). Cut each chunk or half into slices as thin as possible, about ⅛-inch (3-mm) thick, keeping the slices together and discarding the rounded edges. Fan the slices out lengthwise slightly and place them, cut side facing the center of the tart, around the outside of the shell, tucking the last apple under the first to make a continuous loop. Repeat with a second layer just inside the first, reversing the fan if you like, and continue until you've filled the tart, tucking in as many of the extra pieces as you can; the apples will reduce a lot as they cook. Sprinkle all over with the sugar and dot with the butter.

Bake the tart until the tips of the apples are bronzed and the fruit is bubbling furiously, 65–75 minutes. There's a fine line between cooking the apples all the way and burning the crust, so keep an eye on that as well and remove the tart early if the crust becomes too dark.

Let the tart cool most of the way, 1 hour, then drizzle all over with the caramel and serve warm or at room temperature. The tart is best the day of baking and will keep at room temperature for up to 1 day. Store leftovers, refrigerated airtight, for up to 2 days.

NOTE: A T-shaped vegetable peeler is my favorite tool for peeling apples. And rather than halving the apples and cutting out their core, I like to simply hold the apple stem side up on a cutting board and cut off large chunks, cutting as close to the core as possible, cutting around the apple until all the flesh is removed.

CHOCOLATE CRANBERRY PECAN TART

{ALMOND, SWEET RICE}

Pecan pie is a tricky dessert. The filling, a custard made from eggs, butter, sugar and corn syrup, can be toothachingly sweet and unhealthy to boot. I trade out the refined sugars for muscovado and maple syrup, both of which, in addition to containing trace minerals that refined sugars lack, add depth of flavor that kicks corn syrup to the curb. Shards of dark chocolate work with a salt-kissed cocoa crust to deliver a punch of flavor, and cranberries provide the perfect bright counterpoint to the richness of chocolate and nuts, bursting brightly like fresh raspberries. (In fact, raspberries make a fine stand-in when cranberries aren't around.) This tart gained cult status among my followers, which included people who "find chocolate desserts boring" and others who "don't have a sweet tooth." These people fought over slices. When you try a wedge of buttery crust, gooey pecans and tart cranberries topped with a plume of Maple Bourbon Whipped Cream (page 224), you'll see why.

MAKES ONE 9-INCH (23-CM) ROUND TART, 10-12 SERVINGS

CRUST
One 9-inch (23-cm) Cocoa Almond Tart Crust (page 119), parbaked and hot

FILLING
1 cup (100 g) raw pecan halves

2 tbsp (15 g) sweet white rice flour

¼ cup plus 2 tbsp (75 g) packed dark muscovado sugar or packed organic dark brown sugar

¼ tsp fine sea salt

2 large eggs

¼ cup (60 ml) maple syrup

1 tsp vanilla extract

4 tbsp (56 g) unsalted butter, melted

½ cup (85 g) roughly chopped bittersweet chocolate (preferably 70% cacao mass)

1 cup (90 g) fresh or frozen cranberries, halved

Maple Bourbon Whipped Cream (page 224), for serving

For the crust, prepare and parbake the tart crust as directed.

To make the filling, position a rack in the lower third of the oven and preheat to 325°F (165°C).

Spread the pecans on a small, rimmed baking sheet and toast until darkened slightly and fragrant, 10–12 minutes. Cool completely, then use your fingers to break the pecan halves into quarters and eighths.

In a large bowl, whisk together the sweet rice flour, muscovado sugar and salt. Whisk in the eggs, whisking until smooth, then add the maple syrup and vanilla, taking care not to incorporate too much air into the custard. Whisk in the melted butter, then fold in the toasted, cooled pecans.

Sprinkle the chopped chocolate over the bottom of the crust, then the cranberries, and carefully pour in the filling, distributing the nuts evenly.

Bake the tart until the sides are gently puffed and center is wobbly like Jell-O under the nuts and fruit (which will float to the top), 20–30 minutes.

Let cool completely, then cut into slender wedges and serve. Alternatively, chill the tart before cutting into wedges for the cleanest slices, dipping the knife in hot water and wiping it clean between cuts. Serve the tart at room temperature, with a dollop of the whipped cream. The tart is best the day of baking when the crust is crisp, but extras keep well, refrigerated airtight, for up to 4 days.

NOTE: Breaking up the pecans with your fingers rather than chopping creates less dust and keeps the filling pretty and clear.

SALTY CARAMEL BANANA CREAM TART WITH MESQUITE CRUST

{ALMOND, SWEET RICE, MESQUITE}

Muscovado sugar and mesquite flour create an earthy base against which creamy custard, ripe bananas and a deep, dark caramel sauce flecked with vanilla bean play. Painting the tart shell with a thin layer of chocolate creates a barrier between the custard and keeps the crust crisp for a day or two. Top slices with an extra pinch or two of flaky salt.

MAKES ONE 9-INCH (23-CM) TART, 8-10 SERVINGS

CRUST
One 9-inch (23-cm) fully baked Muscovado Mesquite Tart Crust (page 119), hot

¼ cup (45 g) finely chopped bittersweet chocolate

FILLING
⅓ cup (65 g) organic granulated cane sugar

3½ tbsp (30 g) cornstarch

¼ tsp fine sea salt

½ vanilla bean, split lengthwise and scraped

1½ cups (350 ml) whole milk

½ cup (120 ml) heavy cream

4 tbsp (56 g) unsalted butter, in several pieces

3 large ripe but firm bananas (about 1 lb [450 g])

1 recipe Salty Vanilla Bean Caramel Sauce (page 231), at room temperature

Flaky salt (such as Maldon), for serving

TOPPING
1 cup (235 ml) heavy whipping cream

1 tbsp (10 g) organic granulated cane sugar (to taste)

1 tsp vanilla extract

NOTE: Chocophiles can make this in the Cocoa Almond Tart Crust (page 119), if preferred.

For the crust, prepare and bake the crust as directed. While still hot, scatter the chocolate pieces over the bottom and let sit for 1 minute to melt the chocolate. Use a small offset spatula or the back of a spoon to spread the chocolate into an even layer all over the bottom and sides of the crust. Let cool until set. The crust can be made up to 1 day ahead and stored airtight at room temperature. When ready to assemble, remove the sides from the pan and place the tart shell on a large plate or serving platter.

To make the filling, in a small saucepan, whisk together the sugar, cornstarch, salt and vanilla pod and seeds. Whisk in the milk and cream. Bring the mixture to a slow boil over medium-high heat, whisking constantly, making sure to scrape the bottom and corners of the pan with the whisk. Once the mixture comes to a boil, continue cooking and whisking for 1–2 minutes. You'll have to stop whisking for a few seconds to verify that the pudding is boiling, which you'll know by the big bubbles that pop gloopily. Remove from the heat and whisk in the butter; it should be the consistency of creamy yogurt.

Strain the pudding through a mesh sieve and into a bowl. Press plastic wrap right onto the surface of the pudding, and let cool at room temperature until warm, 30–45 minutes.

When the pudding has cooled, spread half of it into the chocolate-lined tart shell. Slice the bananas ¼-inch (6-mm) thick and layer them evenly over the top, drizzle with 6 tablespoons (90 ml) of the caramel sauce and cover with the remaining pudding. Cover with plastic wrap pressed to the surface of the pudding. Chill until set, at least 2 hours and up to 1 day.

To make the topping, use a handheld or stand mixer fitted with the whisk attachment to whip the cream with the sugar and vanilla until it holds firm peaks; the whipped cream should be on the firmer side to make the tart easier to slice. If you take the cream too far and it becomes lumpy, you can rescue it by folding in additional heavy cream until it loosens up again.

Remove the plastic wrap from the tart and spread the cream evenly over the top. Chill the tart for 30 more minutes to set the cream. Place the tart on a cutting board, and use a sharp chef's knife to slice the tart into wedges, wiping the knife clean between each cut. Drizzle slices generously with more caramel and sprinkle with a pinch or two of flaky salt.

The tart is best on the day of baking, but it will keep, refrigerated airtight, for 2 or 3 days.

CHOCOLATE BERGAMOT TRUFFLE TART WITH OLIVE OIL AND FLAKY SALT

{ALMOND, SWEET RICE}

I don't like to play favorites, but this tart was a clear winner around our place. My sweetie, who doesn't have much in the way of a sweet tooth, forbade me from giving any away, and he hoarded the last slice in the fridge for a week before finally polishing it off. I couldn't really blame him—this tart is pretty one-of-a-kind. A buttery cocoa shortbread crust contrasts the silkiest chocolate truffle filling, and fresh bergamot zest makes the whole thing sing with citrusy floral notes. If you want to gild the lily, top the tart with a drizzle of flavorful olive oil and a few pinches of flaky salt, and serve slender wedges with a billow of softly whipped cream. The complexity of the olive oil plays up the bergamot, the salt adds an addicting crunch and the cream smooths out any rough edges. This tart is all about the chocolate, so use a high-quality brand that you like the taste of on its own. It's best to buy bars of chocolate and chop them up rather than using chocolate chips, which generally have less flavor and more lecithin to keep them from melting in cookies—not what we want here. If fresh bergamot eludes you, leave it out altogether or try the Earl Grey variation, below.

MAKES ONE 12 BY 4-INCH (30 BY 10-CM) RECTANGULAR TART OR ONE 9-INCH (23-CM) ROUND TART, 10-12 SERVINGS

CRUST
1 parbaked 12 by 4-inch (30 by 10-cm) OR 9-inch (23-cm) round Cocoa Almond Tart Crust (page 119)

FILLING
1¼ cups (295 ml) heavy cream

3 tbsp (45 ml) honey

Finely grated zest from 1 medium bergamot (1 packed tsp)

⅛ tsp fine sea salt

6 oz (170 g) bittersweet chocolate (60–70% cacao mass), roughly chopped (1¼ cups)

1 large egg

FOR FINISHING
¾ cup (180 ml) heavy whipping cream

Really good olive oil

Flaky sea salt (such as Maldon)

For the crust, prepare and parbake the crust as directed. Position a rack in the center of the oven and preheat to 300ºF (150ºC).

To make the filling, in a small, heavy-bottomed saucepan set over a medium flame, heat the cream with the honey, bergamot zest and salt, swirling occasionally, until hot and steamy. Remove from the heat, cover and let steep for 10 minutes.

Place the chocolate in a medium-sized bowl. When the cream has steeped, heat it again until hot and steamy and pour over the chocolate. Let sit for 1 minute, then whisk gently until very smooth. Whisk in the egg, then strain the mixture through a sieve and into a large measuring pitcher. Pour the filling into the hot crust and carefully transfer to the oven. Bake the tart until the filling quivers gently in the center when you give it a jostle and the edges are just set, 10–20 minutes. Let the tart cool completely, then chill until firm, 1–2 hours and up to 1 day.

To serve, use a large, sharp chef's knife to cut the tart into slender slices, dipping the knife in hot water and wiping it clean between slices for the cleanest cuts. To finish, whip the cream to soft peaks and serve slices of tart with a dollop of cream, a drizzle of olive oil and a pinch of flaky salt. The tart is best on the day of baking when the crust is crisp, but extras keep well, refrigerated airtight, for up to 5 days.

VARIATION: EARL GREY CHOCOLATE TART

Black tea adds its malty flavor here while conveying the floral notes of bergamot.

Omit the bergamot, steeping 2 tablespoons (6 g) top-quality Earl Grey tea leaves with the hot cream and honey for 10–20 minutes, or until the cream turns beige. Strain the cream into the chocolate, pressing on the tea to extract all of the flavor, and proceed with the recipe.

FROMAGE BLANC TARTLETS WITH HONEYED KUMQUATS

{ALMOND, SWEET RICE, OAT}

These sunny tartlets make a bright treat for late winter when other citrus and pomes have petered out and rhubarb and berries haven't yet emerged. Thick honey-kumquat syrup sweetens a cheesecake-like filling and rounds of kumquat flecked with vanilla bean crown the tops. Fromage blanc, also called farmer cheese, tastes a bit like goat cheese without the funk, and it keeps the filling airy and not-too-rich. That said, mascarpone will work in its place. Packaged in buttery almond-flour crusts, these will make you the star of any dinner party. To ease the day-of prep, make the kumquats and prepare and freeze the tartlet crusts up to 1 week ahead. Feel free to bake this in a single 9-inch (23-cm) round tart or pie pan, increasing the bake time as needed.

MAKES EIGHT 4-INCH (10-CM) TARTLETS OR ONE 9-INCH (23-CM) TART, 8-10 SERVINGS

CRUST
Eight 4-inch (10-cm) or one 9-inch (23-cm) Vanilla Almond Tart Crusts (page 117), parbaked

FILLING
1 recipe Honey Candied Kumquats (page 235)

1 cup (8 oz [225 g]) fromage blanc or mascarpone

Finely grated zest from 1 medium lemon (preferably Meyer)

1 large egg

1 large egg yolk

2 tbsp (30 ml) candied kumquat syrup (page 235)

2 tbsp (30 ml) honey

¾ cup (180 ml) heavy cream

For the crust, prepare and parbake the tart crusts as directed. Place on a baking sheet lined with parchment for easy cleanup.

For the filling, prepare the Honey Candied Kumquats and chill until ready to use.

Position a rack in the lower third of the oven and preheat to 325ºF (165ºC).

In a large bowl, whisk together the fromage blanc, lemon zest, egg and egg yolk. Whisk in the kumquat syrup and honey, then the cream, whisking until smooth. Divide the filling among the tart crusts, filling them to the top and giving them a gentle shake to even out the custard. (Extra custard can be baked in a small ramekin alongside the tarts.)

Bake the tarts until the filling puffs slightly around the edges and is mostly set when you give the pan a shake, 18–25 minutes (30–35 minutes for a large tart). Remove the tarts from the oven and let cool to room temperature. Carefully remove the rings and bottoms, place the tarts on a small baking sheet and chill until cold, 1 hour.

To serve, place the tarts on plates, spoon over some of the chilled, honeyed kumquats and devour immediately.

The tarts are best the day of baking when the crust is crisp, but they will keep, refrigerated airtight, for up to 3 days.

VARIATION: BERRY FROMAGE BLANC TARTLETS
No kumquats? No worries! Make the filling with 4 tablespoons (60 ml) honey and top the tartlets with fresh summer berries.

GRAPEFRUIT AND ELDERFLOWER CURD TART

{ALMOND, SWEET RICE, OAT}

When you're a baker or a cook, you tend to learn about people's tastes. You learn that Nancy hates rhubarb, or that Joe is allergic to tree nuts. A surprising fact that I recently learned is that several people I know are obsessed with grapefruit. Grapefruit! I love the juice in mimosas, but I never expected people to go so crazy for grapefruit desserts.

Grapefruits, particularly the pale pink variety, come into season in midwinter and remain sweet and delicious through the spring. Their flavor is a complex mix of bitter and astringent, floral and sweet. This tart celebrates grapefruit's zest and juice with a buttery curd that bursts with intense flavor. Elderflower, here in the form of St-Germain liqueur, makes grapefruit taste even more like itself—like flowers and champagne and old fancy hats in your grandmother's closet (in a good way). Against a buttery shortbread crust flavored with almond and vanilla, this magical curd will convert the staunchest grapefruit haters, and make its fans supremely happy.

Blood orange juice, if you've got it, turns the curd a pretty shade of pink; alternatively, just use more grapefruit juice. This tart needs no accompaniment, but you can gussy up slices with pink grapefruit supremes or a dollop of Whipped Crème Fraîche (page 224) sprinkled with a few crushed lavender buds, as one of my testers did so prettily.

MAKES ONE 9-INCH (23-CM) TART, 8–10 SERVINGS

One 9-inch (23-cm) Vanilla Almond Tart Crust (page 117), parbaked

2 tsp (5 g) packed finely grated pink grapefruit zest (from 1 large or 2 small grapefruit)

¾ cup (180 ml) strained pink grapefruit juice (from 2 medium grapefruit)

¼ cup (60 ml) strained blood orange juice (from 1–2 small blood oranges)

¾ cup (150 g) organic granulated cane sugar

¼ tsp fine sea salt

3 large eggs

2 large egg yolks

8 tbsp (113 g) cold, unsalted butter, in ½-inch (1.3-cm) dice

¼ cup (60 ml) St-Germain elderflower liqueur

Position a rack in the lower third of the oven and preheat to 325°F (165°C). Place the parbaked tart crust on a rimmed baking sheet, and if it has cooled, place in the oven to heat for 5–10 minutes before you add the curd; this will help keep the crust crisp.

To make the curd, set a mesh strainer over a heatproof bowl or large measuring cup and set aside.

In a medium, heavy-bottomed saucepan, whisk together the zest, grapefruit and blood orange juices, sugar, salt, eggs and egg yolks to combine. Place the pot over medium-low heat, and cook, stirring constantly with a heatproof silicone spatula, until the mixture thickens slightly and reaches 170°F (77°C) on an instant-read thermometer, about 10 minutes. As you stir, be sure to scrape the entire bottom of the pan and into the corners, so that the mixture heats as evenly as possible. Immediately strain the mixture through the strainer and into the bowl. Stir in the butter pieces until melted, then the liqueur. Cool the curd for 10 minutes.

Pour the slightly cooled curd into the warm tart shell and very carefully transfer it into the oven; it will be very full! Bake the tart until the sides are barely puffed and the tart wobbles like Jell-O when you give it a gentle shake, 18–25 minutes. It should not be wet or watery (underbaked), nor should it be puffed in the center or cracking (overbaked).

Remove the tart from the oven and let cool to room temperature, about 1 hour. Remove the tart sides by placing the tart atop a large can or small, inverted bowl and gently easing the sides from the tart. Chill the tart until firm, at least 2 hours and up to 1 day. Cut into wedges and serve. The tart is best within the first 2 days of baking, but keeps well, refrigerated airtight, for up to 3 days.

RUSTIC FRUIT DESSERTS

The first time I baked a pandowdy—an apple rhubarb recipe from a favorite Deborah Madison cookbook—I brought it to a friend's house along with a pint of ice cream. We dished up bowls of fragrant, warm apples and tart rhubarb coated in spices and lidded with flaky pie dough, ice cream melting into puddles against the hot fruit, and tucked in. Jay broke the silence, proclaiming the dessert well worth the calories, and our friend's eyes widened at the mention of the word. "But, this is FRUIT!" she declared. I thought back to the stick of butter I'd worked into the pastry dough, to the cup of sugar that went into taming the tart apples and rhubarb, and the pint of ice cream we'd demolished. "Yes," I agreed. "It is fruit."

This is why I love rustic fruit desserts. Though topped with buttery-sweet biscuits, cobbles, crumbles and batters, they are indeed made up in large proportion by good-for-you fruit. If you use peak-of-season fruit that bursts with sweetness and flavor, you needn't do much to turn it into a wildly delicious dessert. A warm bowl of peach cobbler or blackberry crisp accompanied by a scoop of drippy ice cream, crisp pastry breaking against gooey fruit and silky custard: this is my happy place.

Here, alternative grains and flours add their unique tastes and textures to a variety of old-fashioned, fruit-based sweets. Buckwheat pairs up with winey blackberries for deep, dark crisps accented with lemon and spice. Marzipan and oat flour create a crunchy crumble topping to crown a pan of tender stone fruit screaming with almond flavor. Teff flour adds earthy sweetness to fluffy cobbler biscuits perched atop thick slices of bourbon-roasted peaches. A trio of alternative flours makes the flakiest pie dough to lid persimmon cranberry and apricot raspberry pandowdies. And millet lends buttery tenderness to ricotta biscuits for a twist on strawberry shortcake.

These desserts are all about the fruit, so use the ripest, most flavorful, locally grown versions you can find. And do have a pint or two of ice cream handy to top those warm, gooey fruit desserts; ice cream melting over tender pastry and mingling with thickened fruit is one of life's greatest pleasures. After all, it's fruit.

STRAWBERRY RHUBARB COBBLER WITH GINGER-AMARANTH BISCUITS

{SWEET RICE, AMARANTH, OAT}

There are many different cobblers in the world, with toppings ranging from cut biscuits to drop biscuits to a cakelike batter. I went through topping after topping trying to find a biscuit that baked up light and tender while standing up to juicy fruit. It wasn't until my friend and recipe tester Caterina found an old recipe from *Gourmet* with 491 positive reviews (!) that employed the bizarre technique of adding boiling water to the biscuit dough, which gives the baking powder a head start before hitting the heat of the oven. We warmed the dairy, gave the dough the gentlest of handlings and voilà: cobbler perfection. Caterina also discovered that a combination of yogurt and heavy cream produces the fluffiest, most meltingly tender biscuits. This cobbler combines three of my favorite flavors in one gooey dessert: strawberry, rhubarb and ginger.

MAKES 6 SERVINGS

FILLING

1 lb (450 g) trimmed rhubarb, sliced ½-inch (1.3-cm) thick on the diagonal (about 4 cups)

¾ lb (340 g) strawberries, hulled, quartered if large, halved if small (about 3 cups)

⅓ cup (70 g) organic granulated cane sugar

1 tbsp (7 g) cornstarch

⅛ tsp fine sea salt

BISCUITS

2 tbsp (25 g) organic granulated cane sugar, plus 2 tsp (8 g) for sprinkling the biscuits

2 tbsp (25 g) lightly packed finely chopped crystallized ginger

⅓ cup (50 g) sweet white rice flour

⅓ cup (35 g) amaranth flour

⅓ cup (35 g) GF oat flour

1 tsp baking powder

¼ tsp fine sea salt

4 tbsp (56 g) cold, unsalted butter, in ¼-inch (6-mm) dice

¼ cup (60 ml) plain, whole-milk yogurt

3 tbsp (45 ml) heavy cream, plus 1 tbsp (15 ml) for brushing the biscuits

Vanilla Bean Ice Cream (page 227) or Whipped Cream (page 224), for serving

Position a rack in the center of the oven and preheat to 425°F (220°C).

To make the filling, combine the rhubarb, strawberries, sugar, cornstarch and salt in a large bowl, and toss until combined. Scrape the fruit and any juices into a 9-inch (23-cm) square or 10-inch (25-cm) round baking dish or the equivalent, and place the dish on a rimmed baking sheet to catch any drips. Bake for 20 minutes, until the juices bubble thickly.

While the filling bakes, make the biscuits. In a large bowl, combine the 2 tablespoons (25 g) sugar and finely chopped ginger, rubbing it between your fingers until the sugar is moistened. Add the sweet rice, amaranth and oat flours, baking powder and salt. Add the butter and work in with a pastry blender or your fingertips until broken down into the size of small peas. Chill until needed, about 10 minutes.

When the fruit is nearly done, combine the yogurt and 3 tablespoons (45 ml) cream in a small saucepan. Place over a medium flame and heat, stirring frequently, until the mixture is hot and steamy, 1–2 minutes (don't let it boil or it might separate). Quickly but gently stir the hot dairy into the butter/flour mixture, stirring just until combined, evenly moistened and no floury bits remain; do not overstir. Remove the fruit from the oven, give it a gentle stir to redistribute, then use a tablespoon to drop the batter onto the fruit, creating 10–12 rough mounds. Immediately dab and brush the tops with the remaining 1 tablespoon (15 ml) cream and sprinkle with the remaining 2 teaspoons (8 g) sugar.

Bake the cobbler until the biscuits are golden on top and the fruit is bubbling thickly, 18–25 more minutes. Let the cobbler cool for at least 10 minutes to allow the fruit to thicken up and the biscuits to finish baking from residual heat. Scoop into bowls and serve warm, topped with scoops of vanilla ice cream, or at room temperature with whipped cream. The cobbler is best within a few hours of baking, but leftovers can be refrigerated airtight for up to 2 days. Reheat before serving.

NOTE: Do be sure to trim away any rhubarb leaves, which can be toxic in large quantities. And if you don't have access to fresh rhubarb, this works equally well with frozen; just let it thaw slightly beforehand and give the fruit a little extra cooking time.

STRAWBERRY RICOTTA SHORTCAKES WITH HONEY AND TARRAGON

{OAT, MILLET}

The key ingredient to this twist on a classic springtime treat is a good-quality whole-milk ricotta. Rich and creamy, with large, soft curds, this thick cheese is a far cry from the bland, grainy supermarket variety. First the ricotta creates a tender biscuit, then it gets whipped with heavy cream for a pillow on which to rest sliced strawberries coated in a nap of honey and fresh tarragon leaves. Despite the surprising taste of tarragon and ricotta, a bite of this dessert will still conjure up memories of classic strawberry shortcake. Basil or mint can stand in for the tarragon if none is to be found, or trade the strawberries for nectarines, plums or peaches.

MAKES 6 SERVINGS

6 Lemon Ricotta Biscuits (page 19)

2 cups (230 g) sliced ripe strawberries

2 tbsp (30 ml) honey, plus extra for drizzling

1 tbsp (3 g) loosely packed torn tarragon leaves, plus some pretty sprigs for garnish

½ cup (120 ml) heavy cream

⅓ cup (80 ml) whole-milk ricotta

2 tsp (8 g) organic granulated cane sugar

Prepare and bake the biscuits. Let cool completely.

Toss the sliced berries with the honey and tarragon and let sit for 10 minutes to macerate and draw out the juices.

In a large bowl with a whisk, or in the bowl of a stand mixer fitted with the whip attachment, whip together the cream, ricotta and sugar until the mixture forms soft peaks.

Use a serrated knife to slice the biscuits in half horizontally. Place the bottom halves on plates, top each with a large dollop of ricotta cream and place a mess of honeyed berries on top, letting some fall off onto the plate. Top with the biscuit lid, garnish with a drizzle of honey and a tarragon sprig or two, and serve.

VARIATION: BLACKBERRY RICOTTA SHORTCAKES WITH HONEY AND THYME

In place of the strawberries, use 2 cups (230 g) blackberries, halved if large. In place of the tarragon, use 1 tablespoon (3 g) loosely packed thyme leaves (preferably lemon thyme).

APRICOT RASPBERRY PANDOWDY

{SWEET RICE, OAT, MILLET}

This springy combination of apricots and raspberries topped with cutouts of pie dough and sprinkled with coarse sugar makes a sublime alternative to pie when you're pressed for time. I especially like this pandowdy served barely warm and topped with a bit of crème fraîche. Do use apricots that are ripe and fragrant; Blenheims are the gold standard among apricots, but any small, flavorful variety will do the trick. If your apricots are on the tart side, increase the sugar to ½ cup (100 g).

MAKES 6-8 SERVINGS

TOPPING

½ recipe Pie Dough for Pandowdies (page 93)

GF oat flour, for dusting

1 tbsp (15 ml) milk or cream (for brushing the dough)

1 tbsp (10 g) coarse sugar (turbinado or demerara)

FILLING

1½ lb (680 g) apricots, pitted and quartered (about 5 cups)

2 cups (225 g) raspberries

¼ cup plus 2 tbsp (75 g) organic granulated cane sugar

1 tbsp (15 ml) lemon juice

1½ tbsp (12 g) cornstarch

⅛ tsp salt

Vanilla Bean Ice Cream (page 227) or Crème Fraîche (page 223), for serving

To make the topping, prepare and chill the dough as directed. On a surface dusted lightly with oat flour, roll out the dough into a round roughly ¼-inch (6-mm) thick. Use a 2-inch (5-cm) fluted biscuit cutter to cut out rounds of dough, placed close together. Stack the dough pieces on a plate and chill until cold.

Position a rack in the upper third of the oven and preheat to 375ºF (190ºC).

To make the filling, in a large bowl, toss together the quartered apricots, raspberries, sugar, lemon juice, cornstarch and salt until well combined. Scrape the mixture into a 10-inch (25-cm) skillet or ceramic tart pan, a 9-inch (23-cm) deep-dish pie pan or a 9-inch (23-cm) square baking dish. Lay the chilled squares of dough over the fruit, overlapping them slightly and leaving some gaps for steam to escape. Brush the dough with the milk and sprinkle with the sugar. Place the pan on a rimmed baking sheet to catch any drips.

Bake the pandowdy until the crust is golden and the fruit is bubbling, 45–55 minutes. Let cool for at least 10 minutes. Serve warm with vanilla ice cream or crème fraîche.

The pandowdy is best freshly baked when the crust is crisp. It will keep for up to 1 day at room temperature, or up to 3 days refrigerated airtight. Reheat in a 375ºF (190ºC) oven before serving.

APRICOT, ALMOND AND BROWN BUTTER BUCKLE

{ALMOND, SWEET RICE, OAT}

Buckles are one of those nebulous, old-fashioned desserts, like cobblers, crisps and crumbles, that can take on many different forms. Recipes range from a spoonable dessert of fruit and batter to a more sliceable coffee cake of sorts topped with a generous amount of fruit. As either type of buckle bakes, the fruit sinks into the cake and the batter buckles up through it, hence the name. This version features a sturdy cake loaded with almond flour to drink up moisture from ripe apricots, which bake into creamy pockets in the heat of the oven, and the whole cake sings with the butterscotch taste of vanilla bean, brown butter and dark brown sugar. The texture lies somewhere between a coffee cake and a financier (page 64), moist and dense from the almond flour. Sweet rice and oat flours create a fine crumb and add structure, and a smattering of sliced almonds and sugar make a crisp topping.

Apricots are unique in that they become more tart as they cook, so use the ripest, sweetest ones you can find here. All stone fruits play well with almonds and brown butter, so feel free to give this a go with cherries, peaches or nectarines, or try the buckwheat plum variation below. For tips on browning butter, see page 219.

MAKES ONE 9-INCH (23-CM) CAKE, 8 SERVINGS

8 tbsp (113 g) unsalted butter, plus 1 tsp for the pan

1 vanilla bean, split lengthwise and scraped

½ cup plus 2 tbsp (130 g) packed organic light brown sugar

2 large eggs

1 cup (120 g) blanched almond flour

½ cup (75 g) sweet white rice flour

¼ cup (25 g) GF oat flour

1 tsp baking powder

½ tsp fine sea salt

12 oz (340 g) ripe apricots (about 8 medium), pitted and halved

¼ cup (25 g) unblanched sliced almonds

1½ tbsp (15 g) organic granulated cane sugar

VARIATION: BUCKWHEAT, PLUM AND ALMOND BROWN BUTTER BUCKLE

Omit the apricots and use 4–5 medium-sized plums (¾ pound [340 g]). Cut the plums off the pits and slice into large wedges. Omit the oat flour and use ¼ cup (35 g) buckwheat flour. Top the batter with the plums placed with a cut side down in concentric circles over the batter and press into the batter slightly. Proceed with the recipe.

Position a rack in the upper third of the oven and preheat to 350°F (175°C). Grease a 9-inch (23-cm) round springform pan with the 1 teaspoon butter. Place the pan on a rimmed baking sheet to catch any drips and set aside.

Place the remaining 8 tablespoons (113 g) butter and vanilla pod and scrapings in a medium, heavy-bottomed saucepan and cook over medium heat, swirling occasionally. After 3–5 minutes, the butter will foam up, turn golden and smell nutty, with brown flecks mingling with black vanilla bean seeds on the bottom of the pan. At this point, remove the pan from the heat. Pour the butter into a large heatproof bowl to stop the cooking, and let cool for 10 minutes. Remove the vanilla bean and discard.

Add the brown sugar to the browned butter, stir to combine, then beat in the eggs one at a time. Set a strainer over the bowl and add the almond, sweet rice and oat flours with the baking powder and salt. Sift the dry ingredients into the butter mixture, pushing through what you can and adding back any almond bits into the bowl. Stir to combine.

Scrape the batter into the prepared pan; it will seem like too thin of a layer but will rise as it bakes. Place the apricots, cut side up, over the batter in concentric circles and press them into the batter slightly. Sprinkle with the almonds, then the sugar.

Bake the buckle until the top is golden and a toothpick inserted near the center comes out clean, 45–60 minutes. Be careful not to underbake: the cake has a lot of moisture to absorb from the juicy fruit. Remove from the oven and let cool until warm, then release the sides from the springform pan and let cool completely.

The cake is best the day of baking but will keep at room temperature for up to 1 day, or refrigerated airtight for up to 3 days. Bring to room temperature before enjoying.

SWEET CHERRY CACAO NIB CRISP

{OAT, SWEET RICE}

My friend and dance crony Steve once brought a bag of cacao nibs to a dance rehearsal because the packaging advertised them as a "superfood." Before I could stop him, he shoved a handful in his mouth, and his face contorted with horror. Cacao nibs are simply cacao beans that have been roasted and broken up. They have bitter chocolate notes but aren't sweet at all, so eating them plain is a little like chewing on coffee beans. I explained to Steve that the nibs were at their best when combined with other sweets, such as baked into cookies. Steve's response was to hand me the bag. And that's how I ended up with a boatload of cacao nibs.

Here, they fleck an earthy brown sugar and oat flour streusel that lids fresh cherries, gently sweetened and baked until jammy but still holding their shape. The topping turns crisp and toothsome in the heat of the oven and the place where streusel meets fruit stays a little gooey. Like all crisps, this is best slightly warm and topped with a scoop of vanilla ice cream, though, as with all crisps, I'm not above eating spoonfuls straight from the fridge at all hours of the day.

MAKES 6-8 SERVINGS

FILLING

1½ lb (680 g) fresh sweet cherries, stemmed and pitted (about 4½ cups)

1 tsp cornstarch

2 tbsp (25 g) packed organic light brown sugar

⅛ tsp fine sea salt

TOPPING

½ cup plus 1 tbsp (65 g) oat flour

¼ cup plus 2 tbsp (55 g) sweet white rice flour

2 tbsp (12 g) tapioca flour

½ cup (50 g) GF old-fashioned rolled oats

½ cup (100 g) packed organic light or dark brown sugar

½ tsp fine sea salt

3 tbsp (20 g) cacao nibs, chopped

6 tbsp (85 g) cold, unsalted butter, cut into small pieces

1 tsp vanilla extract

1 tsp coarse sugar, such as demerara or turbinado, for sprinkling (optional)

Vanilla Bean Ice Cream (page 227), for serving

Position a rack in the upper third of the oven and preheat to 375ºF (190ºC). Place a 9-inch (23-cm) round or square pan on a rimmed baking sheet lined with parchment for easy cleanup.

To make the filling, in a large bowl, stir together the cherries, cornstarch, brown sugar and salt to combine. Let sit, tossing once or twice while you make the topping.

To make the topping, combine the oat, rice and tapioca flours with the oats, brown sugar, salt and cacao nibs in the bowl of a stand mixer fitted with the paddle attachment. Scatter the butter pieces over the top, sprinkle with the vanilla and mix on medium-low speed until the butter is incorporated and the mixture forms large clumps, 2–3 minutes. (Alternatively, use your fingers to work the topping together in a large bowl.)

Scrape the cherries and their juices into the prepared pan and sprinkle the topping over, squeezing some of it into hazelnut-sized clumps and letting the rest be loose. Sprinkle with the coarse sugar. Bake the crisp until the filling is bubbling thickly and the topping is golden, 35–45 minutes. Remove from the oven and let cool for at least 10 minutes or to room temperature. Serve warm or at room temperature with vanilla ice cream. The crisp is best on the day of baking but leftovers will keep, refrigerated airtight, for up to 3 days.

MAPLE BOURBON PEACH COBBLER WITH CINNAMON TEFF BISCUITS

{SWEET RICE, TEFF, OAT}

This cobbler is full of earthy flavors that contrast bright peaches: maple syrup, bourbon whiskey and biscuits redolent with teff flour and cinnamon sugar. Malty teff is the dominant flavor in these biscuits, and its slightly coarse texture stands up well to the juicy fruit. Adding hot yogurt and cream to the biscuit mixture right before it goes into the oven gives the dough an instant lift, baking it into craggy biscuits that positively melt in your mouth.

I like to leave the skins on the peaches not only because I'm lazy but also because they add color, help the fruit hold together, and soften into buttery tenderness in the heat of the oven. Serve this cobbler warm with a scoop of ice cream or at room temperature with whipped cream (sweetened or not). Be sure to source a certified GF whiskey if your cobbler eaters are highly sensitive to trace amounts of gluten; otherwise I like Bulleit bourbon here.

MAKES 6 SERVINGS

FILLING
2 lb (905 g) ripe but firm peaches (about 6 medium-large peaches, 6 cups sliced)

¼ cup plus 1 tbsp (75 ml) GF whiskey (such as Queen Jennie) or bourbon

¼ cup plus 1 tbsp (75 ml) maple syrup

1 tbsp (6 g) cornstarch

¼ tsp fine sea salt

BISCUITS
⅓ cup (50 g) sweet white rice flour

⅓ cup (50 g) teff flour

⅓ cup (35 g) GF oat flour

2 tbsp (25 g) organic granulated cane sugar, plus 2 tsp (8 g) for sprinkling the biscuits

1 tsp baking powder

¼ tsp fine sea salt

¼ tsp ground cinnamon, plus ⅛ tsp for sprinkling the biscuits

4 tbsp (56 g) cold, unsalted butter, in ¼-inch (6-mm) dice

3 tbsp (45 ml) heavy cream, plus 1 tbsp (15 ml) for brushing the biscuits

¼ cup (60 ml) plain, whole-milk yogurt

Vanilla Bean Ice Cream (page 227) or Whipped Cream (page 224), for serving

Position a rack in the center of the oven and preheat to 425°F (220°C).

To make the filling, rinse the peaches and rub off the fuzz. Cut the peaches in half, then cut each half into 4–6 wedges. Place the wedges in a large bowl and drizzle with the bourbon, maple syrup, cornstarch and salt. Gently toss to coat the peaches evenly, then transfer to a 9-inch (23-cm) or (preferably) 10-inch (25-cm) ovenproof skillet or 9-inch (23-cm) square pan. Place in the oven and bake for 20 minutes, until the juices bubble thickly.

To make the biscuits, in a large bowl, combine the sweet rice, teff and oat flours with the 2 tablespoons (25 g) sugar, baking powder, salt and ¼ teaspoon cinnamon. Add the butter and work in with a pastry blender or your fingertips until broken down into the size of small peas. Chill until needed, about 10 minutes.

In a small bowl, stir together the remaining 2 teaspoons (8 g) sugar with the remaining ⅛ teaspoon cinnamon. Place the 1 tablespoon (15 ml) cream in a second small bowl and have a pastry brush (or scrunched-up paper towel) nearby.

When the fruit is nearly done, combine the yogurt and remaining 3 tablespoons (45 ml) cream in a small saucepan. Place over a medium flame and heat, stirring frequently, until the mixture is hot and steamy, 1–2 minutes (don't let it boil or it might separate). Quickly but gently stir the hot dairy into the butter/flour mixture, stirring just until combined, evenly moistened and no floury bits remain; do not overstir. Remove the fruit from the oven, give it a gentle stir to redistribute, then use a tablespoon to drop the batter onto the fruit, creating 10–12 rough mounds. Immediately dab and brush the tops with the cream and sprinkle with the cinnamon sugar.

Bake the cobbler until the biscuits are golden on top and the fruit is bubbling thickly, 18–25 more minutes. Let the cobbler cool for at least 10 minutes to allow the fruit to thicken up and the biscuits to finish baking from residual heat. Scoop into bowls and serve warm, topped with scoops of vanilla ice cream, or at room temperature with whipped cream. The cobbler is best within a few hours of baking, but leftovers can be refrigerated airtight for up to 2 days. Reheat before serving.

SUMMER STONE FRUIT AND MARZIPAN CRUMBLE

{SWEET RICE, OAT}

Almond paste can be a divisive ingredient, with people either loving or loathing its intense flavor laced with bitter almond notes. I'm adamantly on the pro side; once I open a package I can't resist breaking off nubs to eat straight. Sometimes called marzipan (though marzipan is actually a sweeter version designed to be shaped into edible decorations for cakes and the like), it pairs beautifully with stone fruit, which reside in the same family as almonds. When my countertop becomes overwhelmed with apricots, cherries, peaches and plums in the peak of summer, this catchall crisp turns them into an easy dessert. The almond paste keeps the topping extra crisp and gives it a bold almond flavor reminiscent of amaretti cookies. Do feel free to make this with any combination of stone fruit you like—you'll need 6 cups (1 kg) of prepared fruit. And don't miss the summer berry variation below.

MAKES 6-8 SERVINGS

TOPPING

6 oz (170 g) almond paste, crumbled (scant 1½ cups)

¼ cup (35 g) sweet white rice flour

¼ cup (25 g) GF oat flour

¼ cup (50 g) packed organic light brown sugar

½ tsp fine sea salt

4 tbsp (56 g) cold, unsalted butter, cubed

½ cup (55 g) sliced almonds

FRUIT

8 oz (225 g) cherries

8 oz (225 g) apricots

8 oz (225 g) plums

8 oz (225 g) peaches or nectarines

1½ tbsp (12 g) cornstarch

¼ cup (50 g) packed organic light brown sugar

¼ tsp fine sea salt

Vanilla Bean, Fresh Ginger or Crème Fraîche Ice Cream (pages 227–228), for serving

Position a rack in the center of the oven and preheat to 375ºF (190ºC). Place a 10-inch (25-cm) ceramic tart pan or 9-inch (23-cm) pie or cake pan on a rimmed baking sheet.

To make the topping, combine the almond paste, sweet rice and oat flours, brown sugar and salt in the bowl of a stand mixer fitted with the paddle attachment. Beat on low speed, increasing to medium speed, until the almond paste is broken down into pea-sized bits, 3 minutes. Add the butter and continue to beat until the crumble clumps together and the butter is mostly incorporated, 2–3 minutes. Stir in the almonds just until combined. (Alternatively, in a food processor, pulse together the almond paste, flours, brown sugar and salt until the almond paste is broken into pea-sized bits, about ten 1-second pulses. Add the butter and pulse until the mixture begins to clump together, 15–20 pulses. Add the almonds and pulse just to combine, 1 or 2 short pulses.) Cover and chill until needed. (Can be made up to 2 days ahead.)

To prepare the fruit, pit the cherries. Halve the apricots, plums and peaches, remove their pits and cut them into large slices. You should have 6 cups of fruit. Toss the fruit with the cornstarch, brown sugar and salt until combined, and spread in the pan. Bake the fruit for 20 minutes; it will be hot and beginning to soften.

Scatter the chilled topping over the hot fruit. Bake the crisp until the topping is golden and cooked through and the fruit is bubbling vigorously, 30–40 more minutes. Let cool slightly, then serve warm with scoops of ice cream. The crisp is best shortly after baking, but will keep at room temperature for up to 1 day and refrigerated airtight for up to 3 days.

VARIATION: INDIVIDUAL BERRY MARZIPAN CRUMBLES

This variation pairs especially well with tangy Vanilla Bean Frozen Yogurt (page 228). Omit the stone fruit, using instead 6 cups (800 g) mixed summer berries (strawberries, raspberries, blueberries, blackberries, huckleberries). Hull the strawberries and halve or quarter. Halve large blackberries. Add 1 tablespoon (15 ml) lemon juice to the fruit mixture. If your berries are very ripe and sweet, reduce the brown sugar to 2 tablespoons (25 g). Divide the fruit among eight 8-ounce (225-g) ramekins or canning jars placed on a rimmed baking sheet to catch any drips. Bake the fruit for 15–20 minutes, then add the topping and bake for 20–25 more minutes. Pictured on pages 216 and 226.

BLUEBERRY PLUM COBBLER WITH CORN FLOUR BISCUITS

{SWEET RICE, CORN, OAT}

This cobbler carries the sunny flavor of corn flour in light, buttery biscuits perched atop indigo blueberry-plum compote. Adding hot yogurt and cream to the biscuit dough may seem like an odd instruction, but it's the key to fluffy biscuits that bake up light, craggy and full of flavor. The biscuits taste like very moist, tender cornbread, the perfect foil for tart-sweet summer fruit. I especially like this cobbler at room temperature with a scoop of yogurt or whipped cream. Feel free to trade the plums for peaches, or the blueberries for black- or raspberries; all are lovely with stone fruit and corn.

MAKES 6 SERVINGS

FILLING

1¼ lb (580 g) plums or pluots (about 8 medium, or 4½ cups sliced)

9 oz (255 g) fresh blueberries (2 cups)

⅓ cup (70 g) organic granulated cane sugar

1 tbsp (7 g) cornstarch

⅛ tsp fine sea salt

DROP BISCUITS

⅓ cup (50 g) sweet white rice flour

⅓ cup (40 g) corn flour

⅓ cup (35 g) GF oat flour

2 tbsp (25 g) organic granulated cane sugar, plus 2 tsp (8 g) for sprinkling the biscuits

1 tsp baking powder

¼ tsp fine sea salt

4 tbsp (56 g) cold, unsalted butter, in ¼-inch (6-mm) dice

¼ cup (60 ml) plain, whole-milk yogurt

3 tbsp (45 ml) heavy cream, plus 1 tbsp (15 ml) for brushing the biscuits

Vanilla Bean Ice Cream (page 227) or Whipped Cream (page 224), for serving

Position a rack in the center of the oven and preheat to 425°F (220°C).

To make the filling, halve the plums (or if they cling to the pit, cut them off of the pit) and cut them into ½-inch (1.3-cm) wedges. Rinse the blueberries and drain well. Combine the sliced plums, blueberries, sugar, cornstarch and salt in a large bowl, and toss to combine. Scrape the fruit and any juices into a 9-inch (23-cm) square or 10-inch (25-cm) round baking dish or the equivalent, and place the dish on a rimmed baking sheet to catch any drips. Place in the oven and bake for 20 minutes, until the juices bubble thickly.

While the filling bakes, make the biscuits. In a large bowl, combine the sweet rice, corn and oat flours with the 2 tablespoons (25 g) sugar, baking powder and salt. Add the butter, and rub with your fingertips or cut in with a pastry blender until the butter is somewhat worked in with lots of little pea-sized butter bits. Chill this mixture until needed, about 10 minutes.

When the fruit is nearly done, combine the yogurt and 3 tablespoons (45 ml) cream in a small saucepan. Place over a medium flame and heat, stirring frequently, until the mixture is hot and steamy, 1–2 minutes (don't let it boil or it might separate). Quickly but gently stir the hot dairy into the butter/flour mixture, stirring just until combined, evenly moistened and no floury bits remain; do not overstir. Remove the fruit from the oven, give it a gentle stir to redistribute, then use a tablespoon to drop the batter onto the fruit, creating 10–12 rough mounds. Immediately dab and brush the tops with the remaining 1 tablespoon (15 ml) cream and sprinkle with the remaining 2 teaspoons (8 g) sugar.

Bake the cobbler until the biscuits are golden on top and the fruit is bubbling thickly, 18–25 more minutes. Let the cobbler cool for at least 10 minutes to allow the fruit to thicken up and the biscuits to finish baking from residual heat. Scoop into bowls and serve warm, topped with scoops of vanilla ice cream, or at room temperature with whipped cream. The cobbler is best within a few hours of baking, but leftovers can be refrigerated airtight for up to 2 days. Reheat before serving.

BLACKBERRY BUCKWHEAT CRISPS

{BUCKWHEAT, SWEET RICE, OAT}

Blackberries always strike me as the most precious fruit. They are usually the last summer berry to come into season (besides huckles), and always command a high price. The fragile fruits don't travel well, thus the ones you find in the market are often underripe and painfully tart. But venture into the Northern Californian woods come high summer, and you may well find thick tangles of brambles flocked with clusters of deep purple fruit. When left to ripen in the sun, the berries turn as sweet as candy.

Whether made with hand-foraged fruit or the store-bought variety (or even frozen berries), these crisps highlight blackberries' untamed flavor. Bright lemon sets off inky fruit lidded with pebbles of rich, spicy streusel full of buckwheat's earthy flavor. The buckwheat makes for a softer topping than most crisps, but I find the deep, dark flavor worth it. Topped with a scoop of Vanilla Bean or Crème Fraîche Ice Cream (pages 227–228), they make a sumptuous late summer treat. And if you can't find this many blackberries, try the Individual Berry Marzipan Crumbles (page 152); the topping stands up better to berries with a higher water content than sturdy blackberries.

MAKES 6 SERVINGS

FILLING

4 cups (1 lb [450 g]) blackberries, rinsed and drained

¼ cup plus 2 tbsp (75 g) packed organic light or dark brown sugar

2 tsp (5 g) cornstarch

Finely grated zest from ½ medium lemon

2 tbsp (30 ml) lemon juice

⅛ tsp fine sea salt

CRUMBLE

¼ cup plus 2 tbsp (45 g) buckwheat flour

2 tbsp (15 g) sweet white rice flour

1 tbsp (6 g) tapioca flour/starch

½ cup (50 g) GF old-fashioned rolled oats

¼ cup (50 g) packed organic light or dark brown sugar

½ tsp ground cinnamon

¼ plus ⅛ tsp fine sea salt

4 tbsp (56 g) cold, unsalted butter, cut into small pieces

Vanilla Bean or Crème Fraîche Ice Cream (page 227 or 228), for serving (optional)

Position a rack in the center of the oven and preheat to 350ºF (175ºC). Place six 4-ounce (112-ml) ovenproof ramekins or canning jars on a rimmed baking sheet.

To make the filling, in a large bowl, toss the blackberries with the brown sugar, cornstarch, lemon zest, lemon juice and salt until well combined. Divide the fruit among the ramekins. Bake until bubbling, 20–25 minutes.

Meanwhile, make the crumble. In the bowl of a stand mixer fitted with the paddle attachment, combine the buckwheat, sweet rice and tapioca flours with the oats, brown sugar, cinnamon, salt and butter. Beat on medium-low speed until the mixture forms large, moist clumps, about 3 minutes. (Alternatively, combine the ingredients in a large bowl and rub the butter in with your fingertips.)

When the fruit has baked, crumble the topping over, squeezing some into roughly hazelnut-sized chunks and leaving the rest loose—don't pack it down. Bake the crisps until the topping is golden and the fruit is bubbling furiously, 20–30 minutes. Remove from the oven and let cool for at least 10 minutes. Serve the crisps warm or at room temperature, topped with ice cream if desired.

The crisps are best when freshly baked, but extras will keep, refrigerated airtight, for up to 3 days.

APPLE CRANBERRY POMEGRANATE CRISPS WITH BROWN SUGAR TEFF STREUSEL

{TEFF, SWEET RICE, OATS}

Crisps and tiny canning jars are a match made in heaven, particularly where dinner parties and potlucks are concerned. They're easy to store and reheat, and having an individual portion just for you always feels a little bit special. Here, apples, cranberries and pomegranate arils form a sweet-tart base for crumbly streusel redolent with the flavors of earthy teff flour, molasses and a whiff of cinnamon. Roasting the fruit in the jars until bubbling lets the apples cook through, releasing steam in order to keep the topping crisp. The pomegranates add a bit of pop and, along with the berries, turn the filling a vibrant crimson. Teff flour forms the base for a delicate, richly flavored topping bound together with sweet rice and tapioca flours, and rolled oats add heft. Top with a scoop of ice cream and you'll have yourself a cozy dessert, though these are equally good with a bit of plain yogurt for breakfast.

You'll need 6–8 small 4-ounce (112-ml) canning jars to make these dainty servings, or you can make 4 larger servings in 8-ounce (224-ml) jars or ramekins. To feed a crowd, double the filling and streusel and bake in a 10-inch (25-cm) ovenproof skillet or 9-inch (23-cm) square pan, increasing the fruit baking time to 40–50 minutes, giving the fruit a stir, then adding the topping and baking for 20–25 more minutes.

MAKES 6-8 DAINTY SERVINGS

FILLING
1 lb (450 g) tart baking apples, such as Granny Smith (about 3 large)

½ cup (55 g) coarsely chopped fresh or frozen cranberries

½ cup (65 g) fresh or frozen pomegranate arils

2 tbsp (30 g) organic granulated cane sugar

1 tbsp (15 ml) fresh lemon juice

1 tsp cornstarch

STREUSEL
¼ cup (35 g) teff flour

2 tbsp (15 g) sweet white rice flour

1 tbsp (6 g) tapioca flour

½ cup (50 g) GF old-fashioned rolled oats

¼ cup (50 g) packed organic dark brown sugar

½ tsp fine sea salt

¼ tsp ground cinnamon

4 tbsp (56 g) cold, unsalted butter, cut into small pieces

Vanilla Bean Ice Cream (page 227), for serving

Position a rack in the center of the oven and preheat to 350ºF (175ºC).

To make the filling, peel the apples, cut the flesh off the core and cut into ½-inch (1.3-cm) chunks. You should have about 3 cups.

In a large bowl, toss together the apple chunks, chopped cranberries, pomegranate arils, sugar, lemon juice and cornstarch until evenly combined. Pack the mixture into 6–8 small 4-ounce (112-ml) heatproof jars (such as canning jars), filling the jars to the top. Use your hands to really pack the fruit down; it will reduce as it cooks.

Place the jars on a rimmed baking sheet and cover loosely with a piece of foil. Bake until the fruit is bubbling vigorously, 25–35 minutes. Remove from the oven and uncover.

To make the streusel, in a medium-sized bowl, stir together the teff, sweet rice and tapioca flours with the oats, brown sugar, salt and cinnamon. Add the butter pieces and rub them into the flour mixture with your fingertips until the butter is blended in and the mixture forms large clumps. (You can also do this in the bowl of a stand mixer fitted with the paddle attachment.)

When the fruit has cooked, divide the streusel evenly among the ramekins, pinching some of it into chunks the size of hazelnuts and leaving the rest loose—don't pack it down. Bake the crisps until the streusel is golden, 18–22 more minutes.

Let the crisps cool slightly, then serve warm topped with scoops of vanilla ice cream. They are best shortly after baking when the streusel is crisp, but will keep at room temperature for up to a day, or chilled for up to 3 days. Reheat in a 350ºF (175ºC) oven before serving.

GINGERED PERSIMMON AND CRANBERRY PANDOWDY

{SWEET RICE, OAT, MILLET}

Fuyu persimmons are one of my favorite fruits. They're mild and sweet, with a buttery-crisp texture that you can eat like an apple. The first Fuyus to come into the market each fall tend to be bland and underripe. After a couple of weeks, though, they begin to turn a deep orange and, when ripened until crisp-tender, they're juicy and full of flavor. I usually eat at least one a day for the whole of fall, until they peter out in January. We toss them into salads, bake them into desserts and sprinkle them over yogurt and granola for breakfasts. Here, wedges of mild Fuyus complement tangy, astringent cranberries, whose strong personality they help to mellow, all laced with a bit of ginger and lemon zest for zip and lidded with cutouts of flaky pie dough. Scoop this into bowls and serve warm with vanilla or ginger ice cream for a dessert worthy of any fall festivity. Look for Fuyus that are bright orange and feel heavy for their size, and let them ripen at room temperature until they have just a hint of give, usually a few days in cool weather.

MAKES 6–8 SERVINGS

TOPPING
GF oat flour, for dusting

½ recipe Pie Dough for Pandowdies (page 93)

1 tbsp (15 ml) milk or cream, for brushing the dough

1 tbsp (10 g) coarse sugar (turbinado or demerara)

FILLING
5 large or 7–8 smaller Fuyu persimmons (800 g [5 cups] sliced)

1 cup (100 g) fresh or frozen cranberries (halved if large)

¼ cup plus 2 tbsp (75 g) organic granulated cane sugar

Finely grated zest from 1 small or ½ large lemon

2 tbsp (30 ml) lemon juice

2 tbsp (25 g) lightly packed finely chopped crystallized ginger

⅛ tsp fine sea salt

1 tbsp (8 g) cornstarch

Vanilla Bean or Fresh Ginger Ice Cream (pages 227–228), for serving

To make the topping, on a surface dusted lightly with oat flour, roll out the dough into a round roughly ¼-inch (6-mm) thick. Cut into 2-inch (5-cm) squares (or use a 2-inch [5-cm] fluted biscuit cutter to cut out rounds of dough, placed close together). Stack the dough pieces on a plate and chill until cold.

Position a rack in the upper third of the oven and preheat to 375ºF (190ºC).

To make the filling, cut the tops off the persimmons, cut each one in half, and cut each half into 6–8 wedges, removing the seeds if there are any. You should have about 5 cups. In a large bowl, toss together the persimmon wedges, cranberries, sugar, lemon zest and juice, candied ginger, salt and cornstarch until well combined. Scrape the mixture into a 10-inch (25-cm) skillet or ceramic tart pan, a 9-inch (23-cm) deep-dish pie pan or a 9-inch (23-cm) square baking dish. Lay the chilled squares of dough over the fruit, overlapping them slightly and leaving some gaps for steam to escape. Brush the dough with the cream and sprinkle with the coarse sugar. Place the pan on a rimmed baking sheet to catch any drips.

Bake the pandowdy until the crust is golden and the fruit is bubbling, 45–55 minutes. Let cool for at least 10 minutes. Serve warm with vanilla ice cream. The pandowdy is best freshly baked when the crust is crisp. It will keep for up to 1 day at room temperature, or up to 3 days refrigerated airtight. Reheat in a 375ºF (190ºC) oven before serving.

VARIATIONS

GINGERED PEAR AND CRANBERRY PANDOWDY
When persimmons are nowhere to be found, trade them out for an equal amount of ripe but firm pears, peeled, cored, and cut into wedges.

APPLE, PEAR AND QUINCE PANDOWDY
Omit the persimmons, cranberries and ginger, and make the filling with 2–3 large, firm-ripe pears (300 g), 2 large tart baking apples (300 g), and 4 halves poached quinces (300 g, page 73), all peeled, cored, and cut into ½-inch (1.3-cm) thick wedges (6 cups prepared fruit). Add ½ teaspoon ground cardamom (or cinnamon) to the filling.

CUSTARDS, PUDDINGS AND SPOON DESSERTS

I've always had a penchant for cool, creamy sweets, whether it was cracking the lid on a crème brûlée, savoring a pot of yogurt or devouring a cup of ice cream. Spoonable desserts are as much about texture as they are flavor. Here, alternative grains and flours add their unique qualities to custardy desserts while maintaining the delicate consistencies that we crave.

Tres leches cake made with coconut flour turns light and delicate with an open crumb that soaks in coconut cream spiked with rum and covered in ripe chunks of mango. Clafoutis made with almond, rice and oat flours is especially delicate. Ice cream and roasted berries find an earthy home layered with chestnut brownies, and teff flour adds malty richness to a baked chocolate mousse of sorts studded with bourbon-soaked cherries. Mesquite flour adds a warm, wild flavor to gingersnaps that form a base for banana pudding, cheesecake and ice cream sandwiches. Dive into a trifle loaded with citrus layered over Lillet-soaked chiffon cake and sabayon—it's like an edible ray of sunshine in the depths of winter.

CHESTNUT BROWNIE ICE CREAM SUNDAES WITH PORT-ROASTED STRAWBERRIES

{CHESTNUT}

The first red strawberries of the season, which show up in late February or early March in Northern California, always bring much excitement after an (admittedly short) winter of brown and orange foods. But what the berries have in color they often lack in sweetness and flavor. In a technique I learned in the pastry kitchen of San Francisco's Farallon restaurant, roasting these subpar berries with sugar draws out their jammy flavor and makes them meltingly tender. Though if you make this with ripe strawberries at the peak of their season, the compote will be extra delicious. A splash of ruby port gives an extra boost of color, adding a bit of gravitas to the sweet compote.

Roasted berries keep well for up to a week or two, so feel free to double or triple the recipe as you see fit. The cooled berries can be used anywhere you would a chunky compote, i.e., spooned over crackers topped with goat cheese, enjoyed with yogurt and granola for breakfast or, my favorite, layered with ice cream and Chestnut Brownies (page 205) for a grown-up sundae. The warmth of the chestnut flour plays well with the inky port in the berries, all softened with mild vanilla ice cream. If you don't have ice cream on hand, try this layered with Whipped Crème Fraîche (page 224) for brownie berry trifles.

MAKES 2-3 SUNDAES

ROASTED STRAWBERRIES
1 pint (225 g) strawberries, hulled and halved

1 tbsp (12 g) organic granulated cane sugar

3 tbsp (45 ml) ruby port (more as needed)

SUNDAES
3–4 Chestnut Brownies (page 205), crumbled or cut into chunks

4–6 scoops Vanilla Bean Ice Cream (page 227), slightly softened (or use store-bought)

To make the roasted strawberries, position a rack in the center of the oven and preheat to 400°F (200°C). Spread the prepared berries on a small, rimmed baking sheet and sprinkle with the sugar and port. Roast the berries until collapsed and surrounded by a thick syrup, 35–50 minutes, gently flipping the berries over toward the end of the baking time and adding more port if the berries look dry. While still warm, scrape the berries and their syrup into a heatproof jar or container. Use warm or let cool to room temperature and chill. The berries will keep, refrigerated airtight, for up to a week or two.

To make the sundaes, place a layer of brownie crumbles or chunks in a glass. Top with a scoop of ice cream and a spoonful of berries. Repeat with 1–2 more layers and serve immediately.

APRICOT CLAFOUTIS WITH HONEY AND CARDAMOM

{ALMOND, SWEET RICE, OAT}

I didn't fully appreciate apricots until one spring day many years ago, when Jay's mom inherited property that came with an apricot tree. The small, heirloom-variety fruits were nothing like the underripe, pale, watery specimens found in grocery stores, and the tree was heavy with blushing fruit no bigger than a walnut in its shell. Breaking one open, still warm from the sun and bursting with flavor, I fell instantly in love with apricots.

Sadly for my taste buds, the tree was not long for this world and met its maker the following year. But now I know to look out for the dainty heirloom apricots that crowd the markets each June. Here I pair them with honey and cardamom in a baked custard laced with vanilla that lets the apricots star. Apricots are unique in that they become more tart as they bake, so be sure to use the sweetest, ripest ones you can find. If you don't have apricots on hand, give this a try with sliced peaches or brandy-soaked cherries in their place.

MAKES 6-8 SERVINGS

3 tbsp (42 g) unsalted butter, plus 1 tsp softened butter for greasing the pan

3 tbsp (45 ml) honey, plus 2–4 tbsp (30–60 ml) for drizzling over the top

½ vanilla bean, split lengthwise and scraped

3 large eggs

¼ cup plus 2 tbsp (45 g) blanched almond flour

¼ cup (35 g) sweet white rice flour

¼ cup (25 g) oat flour

¾ tsp ground cardamom

¼ tsp fine sea salt

¾ cup (180 ml) whole milk

¼ cup (60 ml) heavy cream

1 lb (450 g) ripe but firm apricots (about 12 medium), halved and pitted

Position a rack in the center of the oven and preheat to 400ºF (200ºC). Grease a 10-inch (25-cm) solid tart pan or a 9-inch (23-cm) pie or cake pan with the 1 teaspoon butter and place on a rimmed baking sheet.

In a small pot set over a medium flame, melt the remaining 3 tablespoons (42 g) butter and 3 tablespoons (45 ml) honey with the vanilla pod and scrapings until simmering. Remove from the heat and let steep for 10 minutes. Remove the vanilla pod (you can rinse it, let it dry and save it for making Vanilla Extract, page 220).

In a large bowl, whisk the eggs until smooth. Push the almond, oat and rice flours and the cardamom and salt through a strainer directly into the egg mixture, adding back any bits that get caught in the strainer. Whisk until very smooth, then whisk in the melted butter and vanilla seed mixture. Gradually whisk in the milk and heavy cream. The consistency will be that of a thick crepe batter. (The batter can be made a day ahead and chilled overnight. If it separates, whisk it to recombine.)

Pour the batter into the pan and arrange the apricot halves, cut side up, over the batter. Bake the clafoutis until puffed and golden and a toothpick inserted near the center comes out clean, 30–35 minutes. Remove and let cool for at least 20 minutes, then drizzle with the remaining 2–4 tablespoons (30–60 ml) honey. Serve warm or at room temperature. Leftovers can be refrigerated airtight for up to several days; reheat prior to serving if you like.

LEMON RICOTTA BISCUIT BREAD PUDDING WITH BERRIES AND HONEY

{OAT, MILLET}

I came up with this dessert as a way to use extra ricotta biscuits while testing out the recipe, though now I dare say I often bake a batch of biscuits for the sole purpose of turning them into this pudding. Toasted biscuits soak up a tangy custard laced with crème fraîche, nutmeg, vanilla and lemon. Topped with blistered blueberries and a drizzle of honey, the whole thing tastes a bit like ricotta cheesecake.

MAKES 6 SERVINGS

1 tsp softened butter, for the pan

4 Lemon Ricotta Biscuits (page 19), preferably day old, cut into 1-inch (2.5-cm) chunks to equal about 3 cups (200 g)

2 tbsp (25 g) organic granulated cane sugar

Seeds from ½ vanilla bean (or ½ tsp vanilla extract)

Finely grated zest from ½ large lemon

⅛ tsp fine sea salt

⅛ tsp freshly grated nutmeg

2 large eggs

½ cup (120 ml) Crème Fraîche (page 223) or heavy cream

1 cup (235 ml) whole milk

1 cup (120 g) fresh or frozen blueberries

2 tbsp (30 ml) honey, for drizzling

Position a rack in the center of the oven and preheat to 325ºF (165ºC). Lightly grease a 10 by 7–inch (25 by 18–cm) oval gratin dish or 8-inch (20-cm) round or square baking pan with the softened butter.

Spread the biscuit pieces on a rimmed baking sheet and toast in the oven until golden and dry, 10–15 minutes. Let cool. Spread the toasted biscuits evenly in the buttered baking dish.

Place the sugar in a medium-sized bowl, add the vanilla seeds and lemon zest and rub with your fingers until the sugar is moistened. Whisk in the salt and nutmeg, then whisk in the eggs one at a time until smooth. Whisk in the crème fraîche, then the milk. Pour the custard over the biscuits in the pan and scatter the berries over the top.

Bake the pudding in the center of the oven until puffed and golden all over, 35–45 minutes. There should be no wet liquid if you peek into the center with the tip of a knife. Let the pudding cool to warm or room temperature, at least 20 minutes and up to 1 hour. Serve warm or at room temperature, drizzled with the honey. Leftover pudding can be refrigerated airtight for up to 3 days; rewarm before serving.

CREAMY BAKED GRITS WITH SWEET CORN AND BERRIES

{CORN}

My dad used to make us Cream of Wheat cereal for breakfast every morning, and these baked grits satisfy in a similar way. Creamy, flecked with bits of grain, this turns out a handsome golden porridge from yellow corn polenta and crunchy kernels of sweet corn. Starting the grits on the stove then giving them a long bake in the oven means less hands-on time stirring, stirring, stirring. The top and edges get a bit caramelized and the grits thicken as they cool. These make a cozy early summer breakfast when doused with a splash of cream, a drizzle of honey and fresh berries. And don't miss the savory variation topped with cheese and a turn of black pepper—it's also highly addictive.

MAKES 6-8 SERVINGS

2 tbsp (28 g) unsalted butter, plus 1 tsp for greasing the pan

2 large ears sweet corn

2½ cups (590 ml) water

2½ cups (590 ml) whole milk

¾ tsp fine sea salt

1 cup (160 g) uncooked yellow corn grits or polenta

3 tbsp (45 ml) mild honey, plus extra for drizzling

Cream or milk, for serving

2–4 cups (230–460 g) mixed summer berries, for serving

Position a rack in the upper third of the oven and preheat to 350ºF (175ºC). Rub a 2-quart (2-L) gratin dish, 10-inch (25-cm) ovenproof skillet or 9-inch (23-cm) square baking pan with the 1 teaspoon butter.

Shuck the corn and remove the silk. Hold a cob upright in a shallow bowl and, with a downward sawing motion, use a small serrated knife to carefully slice off the top half of the kernels. Reverse the knife and use the back of the blade to scrape the remaining milk from the cob and into the bowl with the kernels. Repeat with the remaining cob. You should have about 1½ cups (217 g) kernels and scrapings.

In a medium, heavy-bottomed saucepan, heat the water, milk and salt over a medium-high flame until it comes to a simmer, stirring occasionally to prevent the milk from scorching and taking care not to let the pot boil over. Whisking constantly, slowly sprinkle in the grits, and cook, still whisking, until the grits have swollen into a thin porridge, about 10 minutes, decreasing the heat as needed to maintain a bare simmer. Remove from the heat and whisk in the corn kernels and scrapings, the 3 tablespoons (45 ml) honey and the remaining 2 tablespoons (28 g) butter.

Pour the grits into the greased pan and place the pan on a rimmed baking sheet to catch any drips. Place in the oven and bake until the edges and top are golden and the grits have thickened, 60–70 minutes. The grits will soufflé up in the oven, but will settle back down when cool. Let the grits cool for 15 minutes—they will thicken considerably—then spoon into bowls and serve warm topped with a splash of cream, a drizzle of honey and a mess of fresh berries. The grits will continue to thicken and firm as they cool. Leftovers can be chilled, cut into squares and seared in a hot, buttery skillet to reheat. They will keep, refrigerated airtight, for up to 3 days.

VARIATION: CHEESY SWEET CORN BAKED GRITS

Honey and corn give this dish a nice savory/sweet contrast that's well suited to breakfast. Omit the honey altogether if you prefer a strictly savory dish.

Omit the berries and cream topping. Make the grits as directed on the stove top, pour them into the greased pan and sprinkle the top all over with 1½ cups (150 g) grated sharp cheddar or other flavorful melting cheese. Top with plenty of coarsely ground black pepper and proceed with the recipe.

BOOZY CHOCOLATE CHERRY TEFF POTS

{TEFF}

These little pots of chocolate cherry goodness fall somewhere between a baked mousse and a flourless cake in taste and texture. Whipping the whole eggs with sugar makes for a fluffy batter that, while rich in flavor from chocolate and teff flour, still tastes feather-light on the palate. Infusing the cherries with bourbon adds another layer of flavor, though you can leave it out if you prefer.

Individual jars make these particularly well suited to dinner parties and potlucks, though you could also bake the batter in a 2-quart (2-L) baking dish, increasing the baking time as needed and spooning the baked pudding into bowls. I like these best when still slightly warm from the oven, but they can be made ahead and rewarmed to order. To play up the boozy factor, pass a bowl of maple bourbon whipped cream at the table; a scoop of vanilla ice cream melting over the top makes a fine accompaniment as well. Teff flour creates a silky smooth base, but another soft flour (buckwheat, chestnut or sweet rice) could easily stand in.

MAKES 8 SERVINGS

1¼ lb (560 g) fresh sweet cherries, stemmed, pitted and halved (about 3 cups)

¼ cup (60 ml) bourbon or GF whiskey (such as Queen Jennie)

4 tbsp (56 g) unsalted butter

5 oz (145 g) bittersweet chocolate (60–70% cacao mass), coarsely chopped (1 cup)

3 large eggs

½ cup (100 g) organic granulated cane sugar

½ tsp fine sea salt

5 tbsp (40 g) teff flour

½ cup (120 ml) heavy cream

1 tsp vanilla extract

Powdered sugar, for dusting

Whipped Cream, Maple Bourbon Whipped Cream (page 224) or Vanilla Bean Ice Cream (page 227), for serving (optional)

Position a rack in the center of the oven and preheat to 325°F (165°C). Place eight 8-ounce (225-ml) ramekins or canning jars on a rimmed baking sheet.

Combine the prepared cherries and the bourbon in a bowl and let macerate, tossing occasionally, while you prepare the filling, at least 20 minutes and up to several hours.

Meanwhile, combine the butter and chocolate in a small saucepan and place over the lowest possible flame, stirring constantly until the mixture is melted and smooth, about 5 minutes. Set aside to cool slightly.

In the bowl of a stand mixer fitted with the paddle attachment, combine the eggs, sugar and salt. Whip on high speed until the mixture has tripled in volume, 5–10 minutes. Reduce the speed to low and slowly sprinkle in the teff flour, mixing until just combined. Pour the melted chocolate mixture into the bowl, mixing until just combined, then add the cream and vanilla. Drain the cherries, reserving their bourbony juices, and add the juices to the filling mixture. Remove from the mixer and fold with a flexible silicone spatula to make sure it is homogenous.

Place the soaked cherries in the bottom of the ramekins and pour the filling over the top, dividing it evenly. Bake the pots until puffed and cracked and a toothpick inserted into the center comes out with wet crumbs, or until an instant-read thermometer reaches 170°F (75°C), 30–35 minutes.

Let cool for at least 30 minutes. Dust with powdered sugar and serve warm or at room temperature, passing whipped cream at the table. The pots are best when freshly baked but will keep for a few hours at room temperature or up to 3 days refrigerated airtight. Rewarm in a 325°F (165°C) oven until warmed through, 10–15 minutes, before serving.

NOTES
- If you don't have a cherry pitter, these can be made with pitted frozen cherries.
- If you or your guests are highly sensitive to gluten, be sure to source a certified GF whiskey such as Queen Jennie, or substitute a GF brandy. Otherwise, I like spicy Bulleit bourbon in these pots.

BLACKBERRY CRISP FROZEN YOGURT

{SWEET RICE, OAT}

This frozen yogurt is just the thing for summer days when you crave a warm, gooey crisp but in a more cooling form. The ultra-creamy Vanilla Bean Frozen Yogurt on page 228 makes an easy-peasy base for thick blackberry compote flecked with nubs of cinnamon oat crumble that tastes a bit like berry cheesecake. The crumble stays toothsome for up to a few days and you'll have enough left over to sprinkle on top of individual scoops, too. Roasting the berries with sugar until jammy releases moisture and keeps them from freezing into icy chunks. If you lack an ice cream maker, never fear; layer the compote and crisp into jars or glasses with some gently sweetened Greek yogurt for blackberry crisp yogurt parfaits.

MAKES ABOUT 5 CUPS (1.2 L), 10 SERVINGS

ROASTED BERRIES

2 cups (250 g) blackberries

¼ cup (50 g) organic granulated cane sugar

Finely grated zest from 1 medium lemon

1 tbsp (15 ml) lemon juice, or more as needed

CRISP

¼ cup (35 g) sweet white rice flour

2 tbsp (10 g) oat flour

1 tbsp (5 g) tapioca flour

½ cup (50 g) GF old-fashioned rolled oats

¼ cup (50 g) packed organic light or dark brown sugar

¼ plus ⅛ tsp fine sea salt

¼ plus ⅛ tsp ground cinnamon

3 tbsp (42 g) cold, unsalted butter, cut into small pieces

1 recipe Vanilla Bean Frozen Yogurt (page 228)

Position a rack in the center of the oven and preheat to 375ºF (190ºC).

To make the roasted berries, combine the blackberries, sugar and lemon zest in a small baking dish. Bake, stirring and mashing the mixture occasionally, until the berries are bubbling thickly, 30–40 minutes. Remove from the oven and stir in the lemon juice, then scrape into a heatproof container and chill until cold, at least 1 hour and up to 2 days.

To make the crisp, in the bowl of a stand mixer fitted with the paddle attachment, combine the sweet rice, oat and tapioca flours with the oats, brown sugar, salt, cinnamon and butter. Mix on low speed, increasing to medium speed, until the butter is worked in and the crisp begins to clump together, about 3 minutes. (Alternatively, combine the crisp ingredients in a large bowl and rub the butter with your fingertips until the mixture begins to clump together.) Spread the crumble on a small, rimmed baking sheet lined with parchment paper and bake until golden and fragrant, 15–20 minutes, gently stirring the crisp once or twice to bring the outer edges in, and breaking up any large clumps bigger than the size of a hazelnut. Let the crisp cool completely. Place 1 cup (100 g) in the freezer to layer into the frozen yogurt and reserve the rest for garnish, airtight at room temperature.

Place a large loaf pan in the freezer. Make and churn the frozen yogurt and while it's still soft, spread one-third of it in the frozen loaf pan. Dollop with one-third of the berries and one-third of the frozen crisp. Repeat with 2 more layers, giving the top layer a swirl with the tip of a knife or chopstick to make it pretty. Chill the frozen yogurt until firm, at least 2 hours and up to several weeks. Let soften for 5–10 minutes, then serve scoops sprinkled with the extra crisp.

The frozen yogurt is best within a day or two, when the crisp is crunchy, but it will keep for up to several weeks. For longer storage, press a piece of parchment paper directly onto the top of the frozen yogurt to discourage ice crystallization and wrap or cover airtight.

VARIATION: BLUEBERRY CRISP FROZEN YOGURT
Omit the blackberries, using 2 cups (250 g) blueberries in their place (as pictured on page 162).

NECTARINE CHEESECAKES IN JARS WITH MESQUITE GINGERSNAP CRUSTS

{SWEET RICE, MESQUITE}

Jars make easy work of cheesecakes for a variety of reasons: 1) They can easily bake in a water bath, which keeps the custard extra creamy; 2) they bake and cool in a fraction of the time a larger cheesecake would, meaning cheesecake in your face sooner; and 3) they are adorable. Here, relatively thin layers of crust and custard leave room on top for a rosette of nectarine slices and a good fruit-to-custard ratio. The rosettes look harder to make than they really are, requiring merely wrapping thin slices of the fruit around themselves in layers. If you're pressed for time, you can simply toss slices or chunks of the fruit with a bit of lemon juice and honey and pile them on top. The deep, dark flavor of the mesquite gingersnaps sets off the mild custard and summer fruit.

The 6-ounce (180-ml) jars from Weck, measuring 3½ inches (9 cm) in diameter, are an ideal vessel for these custards, leaving ample room for the fruit topping. Alternatively, make 4 larger servings in 8-ounce (235-ml) jars or ramekins.

MAKES 6 INDIVIDUAL 6-OUNCE (180-ML) CHEESECAKES

2 cups (110 g) broken-up Mesquite Gingersnaps (page 198), or store-bought gingersnaps

2 tbsp (28 g) unsalted butter, melted

8 oz (225 g) cream cheese, at room temperature

¼ cup (50 g) organic granulated cane sugar

⅛ tsp fine sea salt

1 large egg, at room temperature

1 tsp vanilla extract

¼ cup (60 ml) Crème Fraîche (page 223) or sour cream

3–4 medium ripe but firm nectarines

Lemon juice, for drizzling over the nectarines

Honey, for drizzling over the nectarines

NOTE: When making cheesecake, always have your cream cheese and eggs at room temperature; otherwise, you may end up with lumpy custard. To warm it up quickly, cut the cream cheese into small cubes, place them in the bowl of your mixer, and set them in a warm spot (such as on top of the oven) while you make the crust. It should be soft within 20–30 minutes.

Position a rack in the center of the oven and preheat to 350ºF (175ºC). Place six 6-ounce (180-ml) canning jars in a roasting pan.

Process the gingersnaps in a food processer until finely ground. Add the melted butter and pulse until evenly moistened. Divide the crust mixture among the jars and use the back of a spoon or small, silicone spatula to pack it in firmly. Bake the crusts for 10 minutes. Remove from the oven and let cool slightly.

Decrease the oven temperature to 300ºF (150ºC). Bring a kettle of water to a boil.

In the bowl of a stand mixer fitted with the paddle attachment (or in a large bowl with a handheld mixer or wooden spoon), beat together the softened cream cheese, sugar and salt on medium-low speed until smooth, 2–3 minutes, scraping down the paddle and sides of the bowl a few times. Add the egg and beat until smooth, scrape the paddle and bowl, then beat in the vanilla and crème fraîche. Give the batter a final stir by hand to make sure it's homogenous. Scrape the batter into a liquid measuring pitcher and divide it evenly among the jars. Rap each jar on the counter a few times to pop any large air bubbles. Pour enough boiling water into the roasting pan to come halfway up the sides of the jars, and carefully transfer to the oven.

Bake the cheesecakes until set when you give them a shake, 15–35 minutes (the bake time will vary greatly with the size and shape of the baking vessels). Remove from the oven and use oven mitts to carefully lift the jars out of the water. Let cool to room temperature, about 1 hour. Serve at room temperature or cover and chill until cold, 1 hour or up to 2 days.

To make the nectarine rosettes, slice the fruit off of the pit. Place a cut side down and use a sharp knife to cut it into very thin slices, a scant ⅛-inch (3-mm) thick. Squeeze a little lemon juice over the slices; this will keep then from oxidizing. Starting with the smallest slices, hold a slice on your work surface and gently roll into a circle with overlapping ends; this will be the innermost "petal." Wrap slices around the first slice, overlapping as you go. When you can no longer hold the rosette closed on your work surface, use a butter knife or small offset spatula to transfer it to the center of the cheesecake. Continue wrapping slices around the rosette until the jar is full. Repeat with the remaining cheesecakes. Drizzle a bit of honey over the top of each and serve immediately.

PEAR AND POMEGRANATE CLAFOUTIS WITH VANILLA, SAFFRON AND PISTACHIOS

{ALMOND, SWEET RICE, OAT}

Similar to an oven pancake or Dutch baby, clafoutis traditionally involves boozy cherries roasted in a crepelike batter until gently puffed. This fall version uses ripe pears and pomegranate arils kissed with vanilla, saffron and pistachios for an Eastern take on the traditional French dessert. Use pears that are ripe and fragrant but firm enough to hold their shape, such as Bartlett or Anjou. The pomegranate seeds keep their shape as they bake, and, along with the pistachios, add a pleasant pop of color as well as texture. Soft pears, tart pomegranate, floral vanilla and exotic saffron all come together to make a beguiling dessert with flavors emerging one after another as you chew. A trio of flours—almond, sweet rice and oat—creates a smooth batter that puffs gently as it cooks, just like the real deal. The batter can be made a day ahead to ease preparations on the day you plan to serve it.

If you prefer, feel free to use all half-and-half in place of the milk and cream in the custard. A little precious saffron goes a long way, so don't overdo it. Its flavor continues to emerge the longer the baked dessert sits. I wouldn't hesitate to eat leftovers for breakfast the next morning with a scoop of plain yogurt.

MAKES 6 SERVINGS

3 tbsp (42 g) unsalted butter, plus 1 tsp softened butter for greasing the pan

½ vanilla bean, split lengthwise and scraped

A pinch of saffron threads (1⁄16 tsp), crumbled

3 large eggs

¼ cup (50 g) organic granulated cane sugar, plus 1 tbsp (12 g) for sprinkling over the top

¼ tsp fine sea salt

¼ cup plus 2 tbsp (45 g) blanched almond flour

¼ cup (35 g) sweet white rice flour

¼ cup (25 g) oat flour

¾ cup (180 ml) whole milk

¼ cup (60 ml) heavy cream

3 medium ripe but firm pears (1 lb [450 g]), peeled, cut off the core and sliced lengthwise ¼-inch (6-mm) thick

½ cup (65 g) pomegranate arils

¼ cup (30 g) raw, shelled pistachios, roughly chopped

Position a rack in the center of the oven and preheat to 400ºF (200ºC). Rub the bottom and sides of a 10-inch (25-cm) round solid-bottom tart, pie or cake pan or skillet (or the equivalent) with the 1 teaspoon softened butter.

In a small pot set over a medium flame, melt the remaining 3 tablespoons (42 g) butter with the vanilla pod and scrapings and the saffron until simmering. Remove from the heat and let steep for 10 minutes. Remove the vanilla pod (you can rinse it, let it dry and save it for making Vanilla Extract, page 220).

In a large bowl, whisk together the eggs, ¼ cup (50 g) sugar and salt. Push the almond, rice and oat flours through a strainer directly into the egg mixture, adding back any bits that get caught in the strainer. Whisk until very smooth, then whisk in the flavored butter and any good stuff hanging out on the bottom of the pan. Gradually whisk in the milk and heavy cream. The consistency will be that of a thick crepe batter. (The batter can be made a day ahead and chilled overnight. If the batter separates, whisk it to recombine.)

Pour the batter into the buttered pan. Arrange the pears over the batter and sprinkle with half of the pomegranate arils and half of the pistachios, reserving the rest for garnish, then sprinkle with the remaining 1 tablespoon (12 g) sugar.

Bake the clafoutis until puffed and golden and a toothpick inserted near the center comes out clean, 25–35 minutes. Remove and let cool for at least 20 minutes. Garnish with the remaining pomegranate arils and pistachios and serve warm or at room temperature. Leftovers can be refrigerated airtight for up to several days; reheat prior to serving if you like.

NOCINO TIRAMISÙ

{SWEET RICE, MILLET, OAT}

In Italy, caffè corretto, espresso fortified with a shot of booze, is a classic hangover cure. My favorite spirit with which to correct my coffee (and occasionally myself) is nocino, a fortified brandy or grappa made by steeping unripe green summer walnuts with spices and sugar. After several months, the tannins in the walnuts turn the spirit a deep chestnut brown, and the spices create a fall-flavored beverage perfect for holiday imbibing. Nocino della Cristina, made in the Napa Valley of California, is a favorite brand, with notes of sweet, bitter and spice melded together into one heavenly digestivo.

Here, I've added nocino to the classic Italian treat tiramisù (literally, "pick me up") usually made with ladyfingers soaked in boozy coffee and smothered in zabaglione and whipped mascarpone. Chiffon cake stands in for the ladyfingers here, and its richer taste makes it fine to omit the zabaglione for a less fussy, and still very boozy, dessert. The result is a spoonable mouthful of moistened cake, a bit of salty tang from the mascarpone and lots of deep, dark nocino and coffee. This is a snap to put together once the cake is made, which, along with the other components, can be done up to 2 days ahead and refrigerated airtight. Additionally, the whole tiramisù can also be assembled up to 1 day ahead; it just gets better as it sits.

MAKES 9 LARGE OR 12 SMALLER SERVINGS

1 Vanilla Chiffon Cake (page 49), cooled

COFFEE SYRUP
1¼ cups (300 ml) strong-brewed coffee, hot or warm

¼ cup plus 2 tbsp (90 ml) nocino liqueur

2 tbsp (25 g) organic granulated cane sugar

WHIPPED MASCARPONE
8 oz (225 g) mascarpone

1¼ cups (300 ml) heavy cream

Seeds from ½ vanilla bean (or ½ tsp vanilla extract)

¼ cup (50 g) organic granulated cane sugar

⅛ tsp fine sea salt

2- or 3-oz (56- or 85-g) bar semisweet or bittersweet chocolate, for grating

Prepare the cake as directed and let cool completely.

To make the coffee syrup, stir together the coffee, nocino and sugar until the sugar is dissolved. Set aside.

To make the whipped mascarpone, in the bowl of a stand mixer fitted with the whip attachment (or in a large bowl with a balloon whisk or hand beater), whip together the mascarpone, cream, vanilla seeds, sugar and salt until the mixture holds firm peaks. Cover and chill until needed.

Cut the cake in half, then cut crosswise into ½-inch (1.3-cm) thick slices. Lay 1 layer of cake slices cut side up in an 8- or 9-inch (20- or 23-cm) square pan or the equivalent, cutting the pieces as needed to make them fit. Drizzle with half of the coffee syrup; it should be enough to moisten the cake through, but not so much that it pools in the bottom. Spread the soaked cake with half of the whipped mascarpone and grate a good layer of chocolate directly over the cream, about 1 ounce (28 g); a small handheld grater works well. Repeat the layering process once more, ending with the grated chocolate. Serve right away with a spoon if you just can't wait; otherwise, chill the tiramisù for 1–2 hours until set, or up to 1 day, and cut into slices to serve. Tiramisù keeps well, refrigerated airtight, for up to 3 days.

VARIATION: RUM TIRAMISÙ
Omit the nocino. Make the coffee syrup with dark or spiced rum (such as The Kraken) and 3 tablespoons (40 g) sugar. Proceed with the recipe.

NOTE: Nocino is traditionally made with grappa or brandy and is usually free from trace amounts of gluten. If you or your tiramisù eaters are highly sensitive, check with individual retailers before imbibing. Alternatively, try the rum variation, above.

PUMPKIN ICE CREAM SANDWICHES WITH MESQUITE GINGER MOLASSES COOKIES

{SWEET RICE, MESQUITE}

San Francisco is known for its wonky seasons, as noted by Mark Twain one summer long ago. We get our summer in the fall, when the rest of the country is cozied up in scarves and mittens sipping hot cider and baking pumpkin spice everything. Meanwhile, I can usually be found sweltering in our apartment, drinking icy cocktails and trying to concoct desserts full of warming spices that still manage to refresh. Enter these ice cream sandwiches. The chewy version of the mesquite gingersnaps on page 198 makes a spicy vessel for ice cream that tastes like frozen pumpkin pie, delivering a fall flavor fix inside even when it's still Indian summer out there.

MAKES ABOUT FOURTEEN 3-INCH (7-CM) SANDWICHES

PUMPKIN ICE CREAM

1 cup (235 ml) whole milk

¼ cup (50 g) organic granulated cane sugar

4 cinnamon sticks (3 inches [7.5 cm] each), crushed

1 generous tbsp (8 g) coarsely chopped fresh ginger

½ vanilla bean, split lengthwise and scraped

⅛ tsp salt

4 large egg yolks

1¼ cups (300 ml) heavy cream

1 cup (235 ml) roasted squash puree (see Note on page 111) or unsweetened canned pumpkin puree

¼ cup plus 2 tbsp (75 g) packed organic light brown sugar

½ tsp freshly grated nutmeg

1 recipe Chewy Double-Ginger Molasses Cookies (page 198), baked and cooled

NOTE: Save the egg whites for making Chestnut Plum Financiers (page 64) or Vanilla Chiffon Cake (page 49).

To make the ice cream, in a medium, heavy-bottomed saucepan, heat the milk with the sugar, crushed cinnamon sticks, ginger, vanilla pod and seeds and salt, swirling occasionally until the mixture begins to steam and small bubbles appear around the sides of the pot. Turn off the heat, cover and let steep for 30 minutes.

When the milk mixture has steeped, place the egg yolks in a medium bowl and place the bowl on a damp towel to stabilize it. Rewarm the milk mixture to steaming, and drizzle the hot dairy into the egg yolks, whisking constantly. This is called "tempering," and it prevents the yolks from scrambling.

Return the custard to the pot, and cook over medium-low heat, stirring constantly with a heatproof silicone spatula, scraping the bottom and sides of the pot, just until the mixture begins to "stick" (forms a thin film) to the bottom of the pot, and/or registers 170°F (77°C) on an instant-read thermometer. Immediately remove the pot from the heat, and whisk in the cream, squash puree, brown sugar and nutmeg.

Pour the ice cream base through a fine-mesh strainer, working the mixture through with a silicone spatula. Cover the mixture and chill until very cold, at least 4 hours and up to 2 days.

Process the ice cream in an ice cream maker according to the manufacturer's instructions. Scrape the ice cream into a container, cover and freeze until firm enough to scoop, at least 2 hours and up to several weeks.

To make the sandwiches, let the ice cream soften slightly, 5 minutes or so. Place a small baking sheet in the freezer. Working quickly, place a ¼ cup (60 ml) scoop of ice cream on the flat side of a cookie, and top with a second cookie, flat side down, pressing the cookie to flatten the ice cream slightly. Transfer the sandwich to the pan in the freezer. Continue until you've used up all the cookies or all the ice cream. For long-term storage, place the sandwiches in a large storage container or wrap individually. They will keep for up to 1 month. For best results, let soften at room temperature for 5 minutes before devouring.

BANANA BUTTERSCOTCH PUDDING WITH MESQUITE GINGERSNAPS

{SWEET RICE, MESQUITE}

My friend Michelle, who was a rock star recipe tester for this book, turned me on to banana pudding when we baked together one summer at a music camp in Mendocino, California. She made the famous pudding from Magnolia Bakery in New York, which, despite being comprised of boxed cookies, instant vanilla pudding mix and sweetened condensed milk, all layered together with bananas and whipped cream and allowed to chill for several hours until melded, tasted like it had descended from heaven. After a few (hundred) mouthfuls, I developed a Pavlovian response to Michelle, dreaming of pudding each time I saw her.

Here is a marginally healthier version, gussied up with mesquite gingersnaps, homemade butterscotch pudding and a whiff of bourbon. Eat it fresh and the cookies will be crisp, or let it chill for up to 24 hours and the pudding will meld into one deliciously spoonable dessert. The pudding portion is adapted lightly from a *Gourmet* recipe that's a snap to make and gets the ratios just right.

MAKES 6 SERVINGS

PUDDING
2 tbsp (28 g) unsalted butter, in several pieces

2 tbsp plus 2 tsp (18 g) cornstarch

¼ tsp fine sea salt

½ cup (110 g) packed organic dark brown sugar

1½ cups (355 ml) whole milk

½ cup (120 ml) heavy whipping cream

½ vanilla bean, split lengthwise and scraped (or ½ tsp vanilla extract)

WHIPPED CREAM
¾ cup (175 ml) heavy whipping cream

2 tsp (8 g) organic granulated cane sugar

1 tbsp (15 ml) bourbon or GF whiskey (such as Queen Jennie)

½ tsp vanilla extract

FOR FINISHING
2 cups (110 g) Mesquite Gingersnaps (page 198), crumbled

3–4 large ripe but firm bananas

To make the pudding, have the butter measured out and close at hand. Place a strainer over a medium heatproof bowl or large measuring pitcher and set aside.

In a medium saucepan, whisk together the cornstarch, salt and brown sugar. Add the milk, cream and vanilla bean and scrapings and bring to a boil over medium heat, whisking frequently (you will have to stop whisking to verify that it is boiling; there will be fat bubbles that pop gloopily). While you whisk, be sure to scrape the entire bottom of the pot, including the corners. When you see the gloopy bubbles, reduce the heat to medium-low to maintain a simmer and continue cooking and whisking for an additional 1–2 minutes; the pudding should be the texture of a loose yogurt. Turn off the heat and whisk in the butter.

Scrape the pudding through the strainer and into the bowl. Let cool to room temperature, then cover and chill until cool but still spoonable, 30–60 minutes.

To make the whipped cream, in the bowl of a stand mixer fitted with the whip attachment (or in a large bowl with a sturdy wire whisk or hand mixer), whip the cream with the sugar until soft peaks form. Beat in the bourbon and vanilla. Cover and chill until needed.

In six 6- to 8-ounce (175- to 235-ml) glasses, ramekins or jars, crumble in a shallow layer of gingersnaps. Top with a layer of butterscotch pudding. Peel the bananas and cut them into ¼-inch (6-mm) slices. Fan a layer of bananas over the pudding, and top with a layer of whipped cream. Repeat with a second layer of each component, ending with a dollop of whipped cream. Garnish with a crumble of gingersnaps. Serve immediately, or cover the puddings and chill for up to 2 days. The cookies will be crisp at first but will soften up after an hour or two.

NOTE: If you or your dessert eaters are highly sensitive to gluten, be sure to use a GF whiskey here, such as Queen Jennie. Otherwise, I like Bulleit's bitey bourbon.

CITRUS TRIFLE WITH LILLET SABAYON

{SWEET RICE, MILLET, OAT}

Sabayon is a workout. Ten minutes of vigorous whisking is required to produce the frothy custard, a mixture of eggs, sugar and booze cooked over a hot water bath until light and airy. You'll feel the burn, but hey, no pain no gain, right? Here, the sabayon is chilled and folded together with whipped cream to form layer upon layer of spoonable dessert, which beats the heck out of a recovery shake. Lillet Blanc, a GF wine–based aperitif, has notes of floral honey, ripe apricots and bittersweet citrus. Here, I use it in place of the usual vermouth to make a fluffy sabayon, which captures its beautiful flavors. More Lillet soaks slices of citrus-kissed chiffon cake, and the whole thing gets layered in a glass vessel for a sunny presentation that will gussy up any winter soirée. Spoon trifle into individual dessert glasses or bowls, or construct individual portions in glass mason jars. You'll likely have a bit of cake left over to enjoy with a cup of tea (or glass of Lillet) while you wait for guests to arrive. You'll need some of the leftover egg whites from the sabayon for the chiffon cake; save the rest for making financiers (page 64). In the summer, try this trifle with berries in place of the citrus.

MAKES 10-12 SERVINGS

SABAYON

8 large egg yolks

½ cup (100 g) organic granulated cane sugar

⅛ tsp fine sea salt

¾ cup (180 ml) Lillet Blanc (or other sweet, white wine–based aperitif)

1 cup (235 ml) heavy whipping cream

CITRUS

1 large Cara Cara or navel orange

2 medium pink or ruby grapefruits

2 medium blood oranges

3 medium tangerines

CAKE

One 8-inch (20-cm) round Citrus Chiffon Cake (page 50)

½ cup (120 ml) Lillet Blanc

Honey, for drizzling

To make the sabayon, prepare an ice bath by combining ice cubes and cool water in a large bowl. Set aside. In a large, stainless steel or copper bowl, whisk together the egg yolks, sugar, salt and ¾ cup (180 ml) Lillet. Place the bowl over a pot of barely simmering water and whisk the dickens out of it constantly for 5–10 minutes. The mixture will froth up, then begin to thicken and eventually form a ribbon when you lift the whisk and let the sabayon drip back into the bowl. As you whisk, be sure to swipe every inch of the bowl's walls to prevent the eggs from scrambling, and adjust the heat under the pot as needed to maintain a gentle simmer. You may want to hold the bowl with one oven-mitted hand and use the other to whisk. When the sabayon reaches the ribbon stage, quickly remove the bowl from the pot, taking care not to burn yourself on the steam, and place the bowl in the ice bath. Stir occasionally to chill the sabayon.

Meanwhile, in a stand mixer fitted with the whip attachment or in a large bowl with a hand blender, whip the cream until it just holds firm peaks. When the sabayon is chilled, gently fold in the whipped cream until no streaks remain. Cover and chill the sabayon until needed; it will hold for a couple of hours.

To prepare the citrus, cut the outer ends off of the fruits to reveal the flesh. Squeeze the ends into a pitcher to save any precious juice; you'll use it to moisten the cake. With a cut side down, use a sharp paring knife to cut away the skin and pith, following the curve of the fruit. Slice the fruit crosswise into ¼-inch (6-mm) thick rounds, removing any seeds. Reserve any juices from the citrus and add it to the pitcher with the juice. You should have ¼–½ cup (60–120 ml).

To assemble the trifle, cut the cake into ½-inch (1.3-cm) thick slices, and cut each slice into a 2-inch (5-cm) rectangle. Stir together the ½ cup (120 ml) Lillet and reserved citrus juice. In a large glass bowl or other vessel, make a layer of cake pieces, overlapping them slightly. Drizzle with a few tablespoons of the Lillet/juice mixture to moisten the cake slightly. Make a layer of overlapping citrus rounds atop the cake, and top with generous dollops of the sabayon. Repeat the layering process until you've filled your vessel, or used up your ingredients, ending with a layer of citrus.

Cover and chill the trifle until ready to serve, preferably 1–6 hours to meld the flavors. When ready to serve, drizzle a little honey over the top of the citrus to give it a pretty shine, and scoop portions into serving bowls. Leftover trifle keeps well, refrigerated airtight, for up to 3 days.

TRIPLE COCONUT "TRES LECHES" CAKE WITH MANGO AND LIME {DAIRY-FREE}

{SWEET RICE, COCONUT, MILLET}

If you find regular cakes overly dry, tres leches is the cake for you. A sponge cake traditionally soaked with a mixture of sweetened condensed milk, evaporated milk and heavy cream, the luscious Mexican sweet falls somewhere between cake and custard. This dairy-free version is made with gently sweetened coconut milk kissed with rum and vanilla bean. With coconut flour in the cake and toasted coconut shreds on top, it's more of a tres cocos cake (but who's counting?). Ripe chunks of mango threaded with lime zest provide a bright counterpoint, though I've found this equally lovely when topped with fresh raspberries or sliced strawberries tossed with a bit of sugar. A splash of dark rum adds an extra layer of flavor to the milks, but you can leave it off if need be. Be sure to source one that is gluten-free if you or your cake eaters are extra-sensitive.

MAKES 9 SERVINGS

1 recipe Coconut Flour Chiffon Cake
(page 50), warm

MILK MIXTURE
3 tbsp (30 g) organic granulated cane sugar

½ vanilla bean, split lengthwise and scraped

2½ cups (590 ml) full-fat, well-shaken canned coconut milk

Big pinch of fine sea salt

3 tbsp (45 ml) dark or spiced rum
(gluten-free such as The Kraken)

FOR FINISHING
1 cup (30 g) unsweetened coconut flakes
(chips)

2 medium mangos, ripe and fragrant but firm
(1½ lb [680 g])

1 lime

NOTE: To make individual round cakes as pictured, bake the cake in an 8- or 9-inch (20- or 23-cm) square pan and use a plain biscuit cutter to cut 9 equal rounds out of the cake. Bonus: You'll have plenty of scraps to nibble on while you wait for the cakes to chill. Alternatively, cut the cake into 9 squares, or bake a round cake and cut it into wedges.

Prepare the cake in an 8- or 9-inch (20- or 23-cm) square pan as directed (see Note).

To make the milk mixture, place the sugar in a medium saucepan and add the vanilla pod and scrapings. Use your fingertips to rub the seeds into the sugar to distribute them evenly. Stir in the coconut milk and salt. Bring to a bare simmer over medium heat, stirring frequently, then remove from the heat, cover and let steep for 10–20 minutes to infuse with the vanilla. Strain the mixture through a fine-mesh sieve and into a heatproof bowl or jar. Let cool to warm, stirring occasionally to prevent a skin from forming, then stir in the rum.

When the cake has cooled to warm, cut it into 9 rounds or squares, leaving the cake in the pan, and poke it all over with a slender chopstick or skewer. Slowly pour over 1½ cups (355 ml) of the milk mixture, letting it absorb into the cake. Let cool completely at room temperature, adding more of the milk mixture if you want it creamier. Use a small, offset spatula or butter knife to pry up the cake rounds/slices and peel away any scraps (save these for snacking!), placing the cakes on a platter or sheet pan lined with a clean sheet of parchment paper. Cover the cakes loosely with plastic wrap, and chill both the cakes and the extra milk mixture until cold, at least an hour and up to a day or two.

To finish, preheat the oven to 325°F (165°C). Spread the coconut flakes on a small baking sheet and toast until golden, 5–10 minutes.

To prepare the mango, use a T-shaped vegetable peeler to pare away the peel. Cut the mango off the core, and cut the flesh into a medium dice, placing it in a medium bowl. Repeat with the second mango. Use the vegetable peeler to pare away 3–4 thin strips of lime zest, then cut the strips into whisper-thin strands. Add them to the mango, and add a tablespoon (15 ml) of lime juice, folding it through evenly. Taste, adding more lime or a bit of sugar if you feel the fruit needs it.

Serve the cake rounds in shallow bowls splashed with some of the chilled coconut milk mixture, spoon the mango over and top with a small handful of coconut chips.

COOKIES
AND BARS

My first attempt at gluten-free cookies was an epic fail. Not knowing any better, I simply traded the wheat flour for brown rice flour in a classic recipe. The cookies looked fine when they baked up. Ha! I thought. That was easy. I slipped the cookies into a container and brought them to a party, where I proffered them to the hostess. She eagerly dug into the container to lift up a cookie, and her face fell as it crumbled into a million particles. Since then, I've learned a thing or two about alternative flour cookies. Namely, they need something sticky to hold them together. Sweet white rice flour helps a lot, as does tapioca flour for chewiness. The plus side is that the doughs can't be overworked the way that wheat doughs can, meaning that you'll always have tender cookies (though hopefully not quite so tender as my very first batch).

Here, alternative flours add tastes and textures of their own. Soft chestnut flour makes for the most melt-in-your-mouth brownies imaginable, and it bakes into insanely tasty chocolate chip cookies loaded with browned butter, dark milk chocolate and tart cherries. Buckwheat adds earth and spice to double chocolate cookies, contrasting a whiff of fresh bergamot zest and keeping them extra tender. Teff adds malty depth to classic oatmeal cookies, and coconut flour gives blondies extra chew. Pistachio meal adds its elusive flavor to a shortbread-like base for cheesecake squares, and what would madeleines be without nubby almond flour to keep them moist and light?

Though these recipes are some of the simplest in the book, many are sensitive to slight changes in temperature and measurements. For instance, the oatmeal cookies on page 194 took me ten tries to get just right! When making drop cookies, here are some tips for success:

- Measure accurately. Use dry measuring cups and spoons for dry ingredients, and use the dip and sweep method (see page 15). Better yet, invest in a small digital kitchen scale and use weight measurements.

- If possible, use the brands of flour suggested (see "Alternative Grains and Flours," pages 236–249). Different grinds of grains can have dramatic effects on a cookie's ability to absorb moisture, spread and bake properly.

- Make sure your oven is accurate to the best of your knowledge. (See page 15.)

- Bake off a test cookie to check the spread and bake time. This way if something needs adjusting, you have only one imperfect cookie instead of a whole tray. And if you've accidentally left out an essential ingredient—say, the leavening or salt—you'll be able to add it to the rest of the dough. If the cookie doesn't spread enough, decrease the oven temperature by 25–50ºF (5–10ºC) and try again. And if it spreads too much, increase the temperature that amount.

- If your cookies get close to overbaking, remove them from the sheet pan immediately to stop the cooking. This is extra-easy to do if you bake the cookies on a rimless cookie sheet lined with parchment paper—just slide the whole thing, parchment and all, onto a cooling rack.

- Always cool your cookies completely before storing, lest they steam themselves and become brittle or stale.

CHERRY CHESTNUT CHOCOLATE CHIP COOKIES

{CHESTNUT}

These cookies get loads of flavor from vanilla bean brown butter, toasted pecans and plenty of salt, and they bake up with crispy edges and chewy middles that stay soft for days. One tester described them perfectly: "These are SO delicious! I thought they'd taste more like chestnut, but really they just have this incredibly nutty, toasty je ne sais quoi about them that's enhanced by the pecans and perfectly offset by the tartness of the cherries." Do feel free to swap out the cherries for dried cranberries, the pecans for walnuts. If you can't find dark milk chocolate, use a good semisweet or bittersweet bar instead; do be warned that the bitterness of the chocolate will exaggerate the assertive taste of the chestnut flour. Be sure to pull these from the oven when they still seem underbaked; they will continue cooking from residual heat. For fresh-baked cookies on the fly, cover and chill the dough for up to 1 week. When ready to bake, let the dough soften at room temperature for an hour or so, then scoop and bake. Cookies from dough that has chilled bake up extra thick and chewy, while baking the dough freshly made results in thinner cookies with crispier edges. See tips for browning butter on page 219.

MAKES ABOUT FOURTEEN 3-INCH (7.5-CM) COOKIES

½ cup (55 g) raw pecan halves

8 tbsp (113 g) unsalted butter

½ vanilla bean, split lengthwise and scraped

½ cup (110 g) packed organic light brown sugar

¼ cup (50 g) organic granulated cane sugar

¾ cup (80 g) chestnut flour

¼ cup (30 g) tapioca flour

½ tsp baking soda

½ tsp fine sea salt

1 large egg

6 oz (170 g) dark milk chocolate (35–40% cacao mass), coarsely chopped (1¼ cups)

½ cup (55 g) dried tart cherries

NOTE: These cookies were tested with Calleris chestnut flour, which is darker in color and has an assertive, smoky flavor. If making these with lighter-hued chestnut flour from Ladd Hill Orchards, increase the chestnut flour to 1 cup (105 g). If you find the cookies made with dark chestnut flour too spready, add 2 tablespoons (12 g) oat flour to the dough, and/or chill the dough until firmer, 30 minutes or up to 1 week, before baking.

Position racks in the upper and lower thirds of the oven and preheat to 375°F (190°C). Line 2 rimless cookie sheets with parchment paper.

Spread the pecans on a small, rimmed baking sheet and toast until fragrant and slightly darkened in color, 8–10 minutes. Remove and let cool completely, then break into rough quarters.

Meanwhile, melt the butter and vanilla bean and scrapings together in a small, heavy-bottomed saucepan over medium heat. Continue to cook, swirling occasionally, until the butter turns golden and smells nutty, 3–5 minutes.

Place the sugars in a large bowl and when the butter has browned, scrape it and any browned bits into the sugar immediately to stop the cooking. Let cool, stirring occasionally, 10 minutes. Remove the vanilla pod and discard (or save for making Vanilla Extract, page 220).

Meanwhile, sift together the chestnut and tapioca flours, baking soda and salt into a medium-sized bowl. Set aside.

When the sugar mixture has cooled to warm, beat in the egg until well combined. Use a sturdy wooden spoon to stir the flour mixture into the sugar mixture, stirring until well combined, then continue to stir vigorously for a few more seconds; the mixture will firm up slightly. Stir in the cooled pecans, chopped chocolate and cherries until evenly distributed. If the dough is soft, let it sit at room temperature or in the refrigerator to firm up a bit, 15–30 minutes (or chill for up to 1 week).

Scoop the dough into 1½-inch (4-cm) diameter balls (about 3 tablespoons; a size 24 or 30 spring-loaded ice cream scoop makes this a snap) and place them on the prepared cookie sheets, spacing them 2–3 inches (5–7.5 cm) apart.

Bake the cookies until the edges are golden and set and the tops are pale golden but still soft and underbaked, 10–14 minutes, rotating the pans back to front and top to bottom after 8 minutes for even baking.

Remove the cookies from the oven, let cool on the pans for a minute, then pull them, parchment and all, onto cooling racks to stop the cooking. They will be very soft and fragile at first, but will firm up when cool. Let cool to warm, at least 10 minutes, before devouring. Cooled cookies can be stored airtight for up to 3 days.

TEFF OATMEAL COOKIES WITH WHISKEY CURRANTS

{TEFF, OATS}

Cookies are one of the simplest sweets you can make, but sometimes they're the hardest to get just right. These particular cookies took me ten tries! Each time when I was about to give up, I'd take a bite of a failed cookie. Tasting the combination of malty teff, peppery nutmeg and whiskey-kissed currants gave me the inspiration (and sugar high) I needed to soldier on. Luckily, even the failed batches were easy to get rid of. Jay turned into a cookie monster, wandering around the house bellowing, "Mee want cooookie" when there was a lull in production. These cookies bake up thick and chunky with moist middles and a bit of heft from chewy oats and currants. This makes a relatively small batch, so be sure to double the amounts if you need to appease any cookie monsters in your life. Do give yourself an extra 3–4 hours for soaking the currants when making these, or soak them for up to a week ahead of time. If you're in a hurry, bring the whiskey to a simmer in a small saucepan (being careful not to ignite it if using an open flame), add the currants, cover the pot and let steep for an hour or two until the whiskey is absorbed.

MAKES ABOUT FIFTEEN 2½-INCH (6-CM) COOKIES

½ cup (75 g) currants

2 tbsp (30 ml) bourbon or GF whiskey (such as Queen Jennie)

¾ cup (90 g) walnuts

8 tbsp (113 g) unsalted butter

¼ cup plus 2 tbsp (80 g) packed organic light brown sugar

¼ cup (50 g) organic granulated cane sugar

1 large egg

½ tsp vanilla extract

¾ cup (100 g) teff flour (I use Bob's Red Mill)

¼ cup (27 g) tapioca flour

¾ tsp fine sea salt

¼ tsp baking soda

1 tsp lightly packed freshly grated nutmeg

1 cup (90 g) GF old-fashioned rolled oats

NOTE: Freshly grated nutmeg tastes infinitely more nuanced and delicious than the pre-ground stuff, which loses volatile oils as it sits.

Combine the currants and bourbon in a jar and let sit to absorb the bourbon, at least 3 hours and up to several days, shaking the jar occasionally.

Position a rack in the upper third of the oven and preheat to 350°F (175°C). Line 2 rimless cookie sheets with parchment paper. Spread the walnuts on a small sheet pan and toast in the oven until golden and fragrant, 8–10 minutes. Let cool completely, then chop roughly.

Place the butter in a small saucepan and set over low heat to melt, swirling occasionally. Place the sugars in a large bowl and stir in the melted butter. Let cool slightly, 5 minutes, then whisk in the egg and vanilla. Place a strainer over the bowl and add the teff flour, tapioca flour, salt, baking soda and nutmeg. Sift the flour mixture into the butter mixture, then stir vigorously to combine thoroughly. Drain the currants of any excess whiskey (no need to squeeze them dry) and stir them into the dough along with the oats and nuts. If the dough is soft, let it stand at room temperature to firm up, at least 15 minutes or up to 2 hours. The dough can also be chilled for up to several days; bring back to room temperature before proceeding to the next step.

Scoop the dough into 1½-inch (4-cm) diameter balls (about 3 tablespoons; a size 24 or 30 spring-loaded ice cream scoop makes this a snap) and place them on the prepared cookie sheets, spacing them 2–3 inches (5–7.5 cm) apart. Bake the cookies one pan at a time on the upper rack until the edges of the cookies are golden and set and the tops are pale golden but still soft, 10–15 minutes.

Remove the cookies from the oven and let them cool on the pans. They will be very soft and fragile at first, but will firm up as they cool. These are best the day of baking when the edges are crisp and the centers moist. Cooled cookies can be stored airtight for up to 3 days; they will soften slightly and become more fragile as they sit.

VARIATION: TEFF OATMEAL CHOCOLATE CHIP COOKIES
Omit the currants, whiskey and nutmeg, folding in 6 ounces (168 g) coarsely chopped bittersweet chocolate (1¼ cups) along with the nuts.

BUCKWHEAT BERGAMOT DOUBLE CHOCOLATE COOKIES

{BUCKWHEAT}

These little chocolate pillows are essentially brownies masquerading as cookies, packed with the flavors of citrusy fresh bergamot, nutty buckwheat flour and crunchy flakes of Maldon salt. Whipping the eggs with the sugar lends an airy texture, and plenty of warm butter and chocolate give the tops a pretty, glazed crackle. The trick to the crackly tops is to have the melted chocolate/butter mixture hot enough to partially dissolve the sugar but not so hot as to cook the eggs or melt the chocolate chunks once added. The mixture should feel pleasantly warm, but not scalding hot, to the touch.

If you don't have access to fresh bergamots, use orange zest in its place. Or you can leave out the citrus altogether and you'll still have the most divine chocolate cookies imaginable.

MAKES ABOUT THIRTY 2-INCH (5-CM) COOKIES

6 tbsp (85 g) unsalted butter

12 oz (345 g) bittersweet chocolate (60–70% cacao mass), chopped (about 2¼ cups), plus several chunks for the tops of the cookies

1½ tsp (1 g) packed finely grated zest from 1 medium bergamot (or orange)

½ cup (65 g) buckwheat flour

2 tbsp (15 g) tapioca flour

¾ tsp baking powder

2 large eggs, at room temperature

½ cup plus 2 tbsp (130 g) organic granulated cane sugar

½ tsp fine sea salt

1 tsp vanilla extract

Flaky salt such as Maldon, for the tops

Position racks in the upper and lower thirds of the oven and preheat to 350ºF (175ºC). Line 2 rimless cookie sheets with parchment paper.

Place the butter in a small, heavy-bottomed saucepan set over the lowest possible heat. Add 8 ounces (230 g) of the chocolate and the bergamot zest, and melt together, stirring frequently to prevent the chocolate from scorching. Continue cooking until the mixture is pleasantly warm, but not super hot, to the touch. Remove from the heat and keep warm. Sift the buckwheat flour, tapioca flour and baking powder into a small bowl and set aside.

Meanwhile, place the eggs, sugar and salt in the bowl of a stand mixer fitted with the paddle attachment and whip on medium-high speed until the mixture is very light and fluffy, 5 minutes. Turn the mixer to low and stir in the vanilla until just combined, then the warm chocolate butter mixture. Add the flour mixture and beat on low speed until combined. Remove the bowl from the mixer and use a flexible silicone spatula to fold in the remaining 4 ounces (115 g) chopped chocolate.

If the batter is very runny, let it cool for a few minutes until it firms to the consistency of a thick brownie batter. Use a #40 spring-loaded ice cream scoop or 2 spoons to drop heaping tablespoons of batter onto the prepared baking sheets, spacing them at least 2 inches (5 cm) apart. Top each cookie with a few chunks of chocolate and a few flecks of flaky salt.

Bake the cookies until puffed and cracked and the edges are set, 8–12 minutes, rotating the pans front to back and top to bottom halfway through baking. Let cool on the pans. Enjoy warm or at room temperature. The cookies are best the day of baking but will keep, airtight at room temperature, for up to 3 days.

MESQUITE GINGERSNAPS OR GINGER CATS

{SWEET RICE, MESQUITE}

The bright, spicy flavors of cinnamon and ginger complement earthy mesquite flour beautifully, so I shoved them all into these buttery cookies, which can take on many shapes. Chill the dough and cut them into gingersnaps, gingerbread guys and gals or (my personal favorite) ginger cats! I scored my cat cutters from the originator of ginger cat cookies, fellow orange tabby mom and gluten-free food blogger Sarah Menanix of SnixyKitchen.com. These thin, crisp cookies can be crumbled into Banana Butterscotch Pudding (page 184) or crushed into a crust for Nectarine Cheesecakes (page 196). The chewy version below makes killer ice cream sandwiches (page 183).

MAKES ABOUT 36 COOKIES

12 tbsp (170 g) unsalted butter, softened but cool

⅔ cup (130 g) organic granulated cane sugar

¼ cup (60 ml) unsulfured blackstrap molasses

1 large egg

1 cup (155 g) sweet white rice flour, plus extra for rolling the cookies

1 cup (125 g) mesquite flour

¼ cup (25 g) cornstarch

¾ tsp baking soda

1 tsp powdered ginger

½ tsp ground cinnamon

½ tsp fine sea salt

VARIATION: CHEWY DOUBLE-GINGER MOLASSES COOKIES

Make the dough as directed, stirring ½ cup (70 g) finely chopped crystallized ginger into the finished dough. Cover and chill the dough until firm, 1 hour and up to 3 days prior to baking. Place ½ cup (100 g) organic granulated cane sugar in a shallow bowl. Scoop the dough into 1-inch (2.5-cm) diameter balls, roll in the sugar and place on sheet pans spaced 2–3 inches (5–7.5 cm) apart. Bake the cookies one pan at a time until the edges are golden and the centers are soft and cracked, 10–14 minutes.

In the bowl of a stand mixer fitted with the paddle attachment (or in a large bowl with a wooden spoon), beat the butter and sugar together until light and fluffy, 2–3 minutes. Add the molasses, then the egg, beating to combine after each. Place a mesh strainer over the bowl and sift in the sweet rice and mesquite flours with the cornstarch, baking soda, ginger, cinnamon and salt. Return to the mixer and beat on low speed until well combined, then give the bowl a final scrape on the bottom and sides with a flexible spatula to make sure the dough is homogenous. (If making Chewy Double-Ginger Molasses Cookies, skip to the directions in the variation, below.)

For gingersnaps, divide the dough in half and place each half on a large piece of plastic wrap. Flatten into disks roughly ½-inch (1.3-cm) thick, and wrap and chill until firm, at least 1–2 hours and up to 3 days.

When ready to bake, position a rack in the upper third of the oven and preheat to 325ºF (165ºC). Line 2–3 cookie sheets with parchment paper. Unwrap 1 portion of dough and place it between 2 pieces of parchment paper dusted lightly with rice flour. Use a rolling pin to roll the dough to ¼-inch (6-mm) thick, dusting with flour as needed to keep the dough from sticking, turning and flipping the dough and parchment paper as you work and dusting off excess flour with a pastry brush. Slide the whole thing onto a baking sheet and chill again until firm, 15–30 minutes. Repeat with the other half of the dough.

Peel away the top piece of parchment, make sure the dough isn't sticking to the bottom piece and use cookie cutters to cut out shapes as close together as possible, placing the cookies on the prepared cookie sheets spaced 1 inch (2.5 cm) apart. If the cookies are soft after cutting, chill them again until firm; this will help them hold their shape. Press dough scraps together and repeat the rolling/chilling/cutting process until you've used up all the dough.

Bake the cookies one sheet at a time until fairly set and beginning to color around the edges, 8–12 minutes. They will still be soft and slightly puffed, but will settle down and crisp up when cool. Watch closely, as these go from baked to burnt in no time. If your cookies are still soft after cooling, return them to the oven for a few more minutes to crisp them up. Let cool, then store airtight at room temperature for up to 3 days.

VARIATION: BUCKWHEAT GINGERSNAPS

Omit the mesquite flour, using ½ cup (70 g) buckwheat flour and ¼ cup (25 g) oat flour. Follow directions for either the gingersnaps or the Chewy Double-Ginger Molasses Cookies.

PISTACHIO LIME AND MATCHA SNOWBALLS

{ALMOND, OAT}

I have my sweetie's mother, Mary, to thank for showing me the way to perfect snowballs. Also known as polvorones or Russian tea cakes, these orbs of nutty dough encased in powdered sugar are some of my favorite cookies both to make and to eat. There's something meditative about shaping the dough into balls and rolling them—twice—in powdered sugar. As the sugar absorbs moisture from the baked cookies, it transforms into an icing of sorts, giving way to a sandy shortbread full of nuts and gently sweetened.

These snowballs get a verdant update from green pistachios, lime zest and matcha green tea powder, which, along with a generous dose of salt, create layers of flavor. A trio of flours—almond, oat and tapioca—create a neutral backdrop and a melt-in-the-mouth texture that will leave you hungry for more. These cookies store well, making them ideal for holiday gift-giving, but good luck making them last that long …

MAKES ABOUT THIRTY-TWO 1½-INCH (3.8-CM) COOKIES

½ cup (100 g) organic granulated cane sugar

Zest from 3 large limes (about 4 packed tsp [8 g])

1 cup (125 g) blanched almond flour

½ cup (55 g) oat flour

¼ cup (30 g) tapioca flour/starch

1 tbsp (4 g) culinary-grade matcha, plus extra for sprinkling

½ tsp fine sea salt (not table salt)

1 cup (125 g) raw pistachios, chopped semi-fine into ⅛–¼-inch (3–6-mm) pieces

8 tbsp (113 g) cold, unsalted butter, diced

¾ cup (90 g) powdered sugar

Position a rack in the center of the oven and preheat to 350ºF (175ºC). Line a rimmed baking sheet with parchment paper.

Place the sugar in the bowl of a stand mixer fitted with the paddle attachment and add the lime zest. Mix on low speed until the sugar is moistened, 1–2 minutes. Add the almond, oat and tapioca flours, matcha powder, salt and chopped pistachios and mix on low speed to combine, 30 seconds. Scatter the butter pieces over the top and mix on medium-low speed until the butter is completely incorporated and the dough comes together in large clumps, 3–5 minutes.

Sift the powdered sugar into a shallow bowl. Form tablespoon-sized 1-inch (2.5-cm) balls of dough and roll them in the powdered sugar, knocking off any large clumps. Place the balls on the baking sheet, spacing them at least 1 inch (2.5 cm) apart. Bake the cookies until puffed, cracked and slightly golden, 15–20 minutes. The cookies will be soft at first but will crisp up when cool.

Let the cookies cool completely on the pan, then roll each one a second time in the powdered sugar. Dust the tops with a bit of matcha pushed through a small strainer. They will keep, airtight at room temperature, for up to 1 week.

TANGERINE VANILLA BEAN MADELEINES

{ALMOND, MILLET, SWEET RICE}

Madeleines intimidated me for many years, and the madeleine pan I impulse-bought once at a cookware store sat neglected at the bottom of the cupboard for years. I may have made one batch in the beginning and, finding them bland and high-maintenance, gave up. Then one day in my food readings, I learned that madeleines can be flavored with brown butter and ground almonds, similar to financiers (page 64)—which are neither bland nor high-maintenance—and my curiosity was piqued. Using a gluten-free recipe from one of my favorite sites, London Bakes, as a springboard, thus began my Proustian love affair with the elusive cookies.

Unlike my first madeleine trial of yore, these get a kick of flavor from tangerine zest and butter browned with vanilla, and the batter comes together easily with one bowl and a whisk. Madeleines are undeniably adorable to look at and, when coated in a thin glaze kissed with vanilla bean and tangerine juice, they take on the appearance of pretty shells found by the sea. I keep the cookies on the less-sweet side to complement the glaze, but you can also finish them with a light dusting of powdered sugar if you prefer. Unlike most madeleines, these keep well for up to several days, the glaze and almond flour locking in moisture. Do let the batter rest in the fridge for at least an hour to firm up the melted butter, and be sure to use a pastry brush dipped in room-temperature butter to paint the crevices of the madeleine molds. My madeleine pan has 12 molds, so I make these in two rounds. If you lack madeleine molds, give these a try in mini muffin pans for tiny fairy cakelets.

MAKES 18 MADELEINES

MADELEINES
7 tbsp (100 g) unsalted butter, plus 1–2 tbsp (14–28 g) very soft (not melted) unsalted butter, for the pan

½ vanilla bean, split lengthwise and scraped

¼ cup plus 2 tbsp (75 g) organic granulated cane sugar

2 tsp (10 g) finely grated tangerine zest (from 3–4 tangerines)

2 large eggs

¼ tsp fine sea salt

½ cup (60 g) almond flour

¼ cup plus 3 tbsp (60 g) millet flour

¼ cup plus 1 tbsp (50 g) sweet white rice flour

1 tsp (5 g) baking powder

GLAZE
1 cup (110 g) powdered sugar

Seeds from ½ vanilla bean

2–3 tbsp (30–45 ml) strained fresh tangerine juice (as needed to make a runny glaze)

To make the madeleines, in a small, heavy-bottomed saucepan, melt the 7 tablespoons (100 g) butter with the vanilla pod and scrapings over medium heat, swirling occasionally. After 3–5 minutes, the butter will foam up, then turn golden and smell nutty. Watch it closely at this point so it doesn't burn. When the butter has browned, remove from the heat and let cool slightly. Remove the vanilla pod and discard.

Place the sugar and tangerine zest in a large bowl and use your fingertips to rub the zest into the sugar until moistened; this helps draw out the citrus oils. Whisk in the eggs and salt. Place a strainer over the top of the bowl and add the almond, millet and sweet rice flours and baking powder. Sift in the dry ingredients, adding back any bits left in the strainer. Stir the flour into the egg mixture until well combined, then whisk in the slightly cooled brown butter and any good stuff hanging out on the bottom of the pan. Cover the dough and chill until firm, 1 hour or up to overnight.

When ready to bake, position a rack in the center of the oven and preheat to 375ºF (190ºC). Use a pastry brush to coat the molds of a madeleine pan generously with some of the remaining 1–2 tablespoons (14–28 g) softened butter. Fill the molds three-quarters full with the batter; it will be rather firm. I find it easiest to place a scant scoop of batter from a spring-loaded #40 ice cream scoop in the molds and flatten the batter out with my fingers; a small spoon or a piping bag fitted with a large, plain tip are other good options.

Bake the madeleines until they spring back to the touch, 8–12 minutes. Let cool slightly, then carefully loosen from their molds (a small offset spatula can help) and place, pretty side up, on a rack to cool. Wipe the madeleine pan clean and repeat the buttering/battering/baking process to make the rest of the cookies.

To make the glaze, in a small bowl, whisk together the powdered sugar, vanilla seeds and enough tangerine juice to make a glaze that's the consistency of heavy cream. While the madeleines are still slightly warm, dip the shell-shaped side in the glaze, coating it completely and letting the excess drip back into the bowl. Place glaze side up on the rack and let set until firm, 20 minutes. The madeleines are best the day of baking but will keep, airtight at room temperature, for up to 3 days.

CHESTNUT BROWNIES

{CHESTNUT}

It's always a win when an alternative flour doesn't just match its glutinous counterpart but actually bests it. Such is the case with these brownies, which are adapted from a favorite Alice Medrich recipe. Chestnut flour gives the middles a velvety texture that wheat-based brownies only dream of, and it adds its own earthy sweetness, blending seamlessly with copious amounts of butter and chocolate. If you make these, I warn you that you may be hard-pressed to ever use a more mundane flour in brownies again. That said, buckwheat and teff flours both complement chocolate and can likely take the place of the harder to find chestnut flour here. Like the double chocolate cookies on page 197, whipping the eggs with sugar adds lightness to the batter, making leavening unnecessary. The trick to the pretty tops is to have the chocolate-butter mixture fairly warm when you add it to the eggs. These keep well for up to several days. Turn them into a grown-up ice cream sundae topped with port-roasted strawberries and ice cream (page 164).

MAKES 16 SMALL BUT RICH BROWNIES

6 tbsp (85 g) unsalted butter

8 oz (230 g) bittersweet chocolate (60–70% cacao mass), chopped (about 1½ cups)

½ cup (50 g) chestnut flour

2 tbsp (15 g) tapioca flour

3 large eggs, at room temperature

¾ cup (150 g) organic granulated cane sugar

½ tsp fine sea salt

1 tsp vanilla extract

Position a rack in the center of the oven and preheat to 350°F (175°C). Line an 8-inch (20-cm) square baking pan with 2 crisscrossed pieces of parchment paper cut to fit widthwise, leaving an overhang on each side. This will make the brownies easy to remove from the pan.

Place the butter in a small, heavy-bottomed saucepan set over the lowest possible heat. Add the chocolate and let melt together, stirring frequently to prevent the chocolate from scorching. Continue cooking until the mixture is pleasantly warm, but not super hot, to the touch. Remove from the heat and keep warm. Sift the chestnut and tapioca flours into a small bowl and set aside (chestnut flour tends to clump, so don't skip this step).

Meanwhile, place the eggs, sugar and salt in the bowl of a stand mixer fitted with the paddle attachment and whip on medium-high speed until the mixture is very light and fluffy, 5 minutes. Turn the mixer to low and stir in the vanilla until just combined, then the warm chocolate-butter mixture. Add the flour mixture and mix on low until combined. Remove the bowl from the mixer and use a flexible silicone spatula to give the batter a final stir by hand, scraping the bottom of the bowl and making sure all the flour is incorporated.

Scrape the batter into the prepared pan and smooth into an even layer. Bake the brownies until the top is puffed and a toothpick inserted into the center comes out with moist crumbs, 24–30 minutes, taking care not to overbake. Let the brownies cool completely, then use the parchment handles to lift them out of the pan and onto a cutting board. Use a sharp chef's knife dipped in hot water and wiped clean between each cut to slice the brownies into 16 squares.

The brownies keep well, airtight at room temperature, for up to 3 days, or refrigerated for up to 5 days.

CASHEW LIME BLONDIES

{SWEET RICE, COCONUT}

One of my favorite childhood treats was a soft and chewy drop cookie flavored with plenty of brown sugar and packed with white chocolate and macadamia nuts. I have a distinct memory of nomming them on the way home from day camp one summer, purchased from Gelson's market in Los Angeles by my dad. Now that my taste buds are a bit more grown up, I like hefty doses of flaky salt and lime to cut the sweet richness of white chocolate, and I make sure to get the good stuff made with cacao butter and plenty of vanilla. Green & Black's is my preferred brand, which is organic and flecked with vanilla bean. Since macadamias can be difficult to find, I trade them out for toasted cashews. Coconut flour is the magic ingredient that makes these extra dense, moist and chewy, adding a tropical note without the bothersome texture of shredded coconut and setting off the brown sugar cookie bars beautifully. Organic dark brown sugar has the extra moisture and molasses that we want here, but light brown sugar should work in a pinch. I like these best the day after baking, when the flavor of the lime zest becomes more pronounced.

MAKES SIXTEEN 2-INCH (5-CM) BLONDIES

¾ cup (105 g) raw cashews

8 tbsp (113 g) unsalted butter

Finely grated zest from 2 medium limes

½ cup plus 2 tbsp (125 g) packed organic dark brown sugar

1 large egg

1 tsp vanilla extract

¼ cup plus 1 tbsp (45 g) sweet white rice flour

¼ cup (30 g) coconut flour

½ tsp baking powder

½ tsp fine sea salt

4 oz (120 g) good-quality white chocolate (such as Green & Black's), coarsely chopped (1 scant cup)

¼–½ tsp flaky salt (such as Maldon)

Position a rack in the center of the oven and preheat to 350ºF (175ºC). Line the bottom and sides of an 8-inch (20-cm) square baking pan with parchment paper.

Spread the cashews on a small, rimmed baking sheet and toast in the oven until golden, 5–7 minutes. Remove and let cool, then chop coarsely.

Meanwhile, place the butter in a small saucepan and set over low heat to melt. Zest the limes directly into the pot and cook for a few minutes to infuse the butter, swirling the pan occasionally. Place the brown sugar in a large bowl and stir in the melted butter mixture. Let the mixture cool to warm, 5 minutes, then stir in the egg and vanilla until combined. Set a strainer over the bowl and sift in the sweet rice and coconut flours along with the baking powder and sea salt. Stir vigorously until well combined, then stir in the chopped cashews and white chocolate.

Scrape the dough into the prepared pan and use a small offset spatula to spread it evenly. Sprinkle the top with the flaky salt. Bake the blondies until puffed, shiny and slightly cracked on top, and a toothpick inserted near the center comes out with a few large, wet crumbs clinging, 18–22 minutes. Let the blondies cool completely, then remove from the pan, peel away the parchment and use a large, sharp chef's knife to trim away the outer ¼ inch (6 mm) and cut into 16 bars. Store the blondies, airtight at room temperature, for up to 3 days.

BERRY CHÈVRE CHEESECAKE SQUARES WITH PISTACHIO SHORTBREAD CRUST

{SWEET RICE, MILLET}

I could pretty much live off of goat cheese at every meal, including and especially dessert! Here, fresh chèvre adds a touch of sophistication to a creamy cheesecake base wrapped around fresh summer berries, all perched atop a crumbly pistachio–millet flour crust. Bring these to a party and watch them disappear—they're a true crowd-pleaser. These bars come together easily, with both components being made in a food processor, and they are less fussy to bake than a large, round cheesecake, as cracking isn't an issue. They take about 1½ hours total to assemble and bake, plus an additional 4 hours to cool and chill, so plan accordingly. Most of this time is inactive, and the bars can be made a day or two ahead of time, a boon for dinner parties and potlucks. If you're not a goat cheese fan like I am, feel free to make this with 1 pound (450 g) of cream cheese. These bars also work well with huckleberries or wild blueberries. For thinner bars, bake these in a 9 by 12–inch (23 by 30–cm) pan, adjusting the bake times as needed.

MAKES 16 LARGE OR 24 SMALLER BARS

CRUST
¾ cup (100 g) shelled raw pistachios, plus extra for decorating

½ cup (80 g) sweet white rice flour

½ cup (75 g) millet flour

3 tbsp (20 g) tapioca flour

⅓ cup (65 g) organic granulated cane sugar

½ tsp fine sea salt

8 tbsp (113 g) cold, unsalted butter, cubed

1 tsp vanilla extract

FILLING
8 oz (230 g) fresh soft goat cheese, at room temperature

8 oz (230 g) cream cheese, at room temperature

¾ cup (165 g) organic granulated cane sugar

2 tbsp (15 g) sweet white rice flour

Seeds from 1 vanilla bean (or 1 tsp vanilla extract)

Finely grated zest from 1 small lemon

¼ tsp fine sea salt

3 large eggs, at room temperature

¼ cup (60 ml) heavy cream, sour cream or Crème Fraîche (page 223)

1 cup (130 g) raspberries, plus extra, halved, for decorating

1 cup (140 g) blueberries, plus extra for decorating

Position a rack in the lower third of the oven and preheat to 350ºF (175ºC). Line the bottom and sides of a 9-inch (23-cm) square baking pan with 2 crisscrossed pieces of parchment paper or aluminum foil, leaving an overhang on each side. This will help you lift the bars out of the pan after baking, making cutting easier.

To make the crust, place the pistachios, sweet rice flour, millet flour, tapioca flour, sugar and salt in the bowl of a food processor. Scatter the butter pieces over the top, sprinkle over the vanilla and pulse until the mixture begins to form large, coarse crumbs and holds together when squeezed, about 30 seconds. Dump the mixture into the lined pan, and use your hands to press it into an even layer. Bake the crust until golden and puffed, 25–35 minutes. Remove from the oven and gently press the hot crust down with the back of a spoon or the bottom of a flat measuring cup; this will help it hold together when sliced.

Decrease the oven temperature to 325ºF (165ºC).

To make the filling, wipe the food processor clean. Add the goat and cream cheeses, sugar, sweet rice flour, vanilla bean seeds, lemon zest and salt and blend just until smooth, 5–10 seconds. Add the eggs one at a time, processing until just smooth after each egg, and scraping down the sides and bottom of the bowl to prevent lumps. Add the cream and process briefly just until smooth. Scrape once more, and blend again if at all lumpy, taking care not to overprocess the mixture.

Scatter the berries evenly over the cooled crust, and pour the filling over, distributing it evenly. Bake the cheesecake until the edges are set and the center wobbles very slightly when you give the pan a gentle shake, 30–45 minutes. Remove to a cooling rack and let cool for 1 hour, then cover and chill for at least 3 hours or overnight, until firm and cold.

Gently loosen the sides of the cheesecake with a thin knife or offset spatula, and use the parchment paper handles to carefully lift the cheesecake out of the pan and onto a cutting board. Fill a pitcher with hot tap water and have some paper towels handy, or an old (but clean) dishtowel that you don't mind getting stained. With a large, sharp chef's knife dipped in the hot water and wiped completely dry between each cut, cut the cheesecake into bars.

Place each bar in a paper muffin liner if you like, arrange on a platter, and top with a pistachio, a halved raspberry and a blueberry. Cover and chill until needed. The bars are best within a day or two of baking when the crust is crisp, but extras store well, refrigerated airtight, for up to 4 days.

MEYER LEMON BARS WITH VANILLA-ALMOND CRUST

{ALMOND, SWEET RICE, MILLET}

Few baked goods get me grumpy like a bad lemon bar. At their worst, the crust is pale, bland and pasty. The topping is often a thin, gummy gel of overcooked curd. Since lemon curd needs sugar to help it set, the whole thing can be unbearably sweet to boot. These bars, on the other hand, boast a buttery-crisp crust laced with almond flour and vanilla, with a bit of added flavor from millet and vanilla bean seeds. A creamy, softly set topping bursts with the sunny flavor of Meyer lemons, a tangerine-lemon hybrid that grows abundantly throughout California. Meyers have a thinner, brighter skin that smells like flowers and sunshine, and their plentiful juice tastes sweeter than that of regular (Eureka) lemons. If you're Meyer-less, I've included a version of these bars made with regular lemon and orange juices below. And if you're lucky enough to possess a fresh bergamot, its zest and juice will make for the most fragrant lemon bars you've ever tasted.

Do note that the soft topping means that these bars need to be kept refrigerated, and be sure to allow a few hours for the initial chilling before cutting and serving the bars. You will need approximately 5 large Meyer lemons for this recipe.

MAKES 16 SMALL BUT RICH BARS

CRUST

½ cup (60 g) almond flour

¼ cup plus 2 tbsp (55 g) sweet white rice flour

¼ cup plus 2 tbsp (45 g) millet flour

Seeds from 1 vanilla bean (or 1 tsp vanilla extract)

¼ cup (50 g) organic granulated cane sugar

¼ tsp fine sea salt

5 tbsp (70 g) cold, unsalted butter, in ½-inch (1.3-cm) dice

LEMON CURD

8 tbsp (113 g) cool, unsalted butter, in ½-inch (1.3-cm) dice

2½ tsp (10 g) firmly packed finely grated Meyer lemon zest (from 2–3 large Meyer lemons)

1 cup plus 2 tbsp (225 g) organic granulated cane sugar

3 large eggs

2 large egg yolks

¾ cup plus 2 tbsp (205 ml) strained Meyer lemon juice (from 4–5 large Meyer lemons)

Powdered sugar, for dusting (optional)

To make the crust, position a rack in the center of the oven and preheat to 350°F (175°C). Line the bottom and sides of a 9-inch (23-cm) square baking pan with 2 crisscrossed pieces of parchment paper or aluminum foil, leaving an overhang on each side. This will help you lift the bars out of the pan after baking, making cutting easier.

In the bowl of a food processor, whizz together the almond, sweet rice and millet flours with the vanilla bean seeds, sugar, salt and cold butter until it begins to form large clumps, about 30 seconds. Dump the crumbs into the lined baking pan and pack it firmly and evenly with your hands or a flat-bottomed glass. Bake the crust until light golden all over and toasty smelling, 20–25 minutes. Use the back of a spoon to press the crust down firmly; this will help it hold together when the bars are cut.

Decrease the oven temperature to 325°F (165°C).

To make the curd, set a mesh strainer over a heatproof bowl or large measuring cup and set aside. Place the cool diced butter and lemon zest in a small bowl and set aside.

In a medium, heavy-bottomed saucepan, whisk together the sugar, eggs and egg yolks to combine. Whisk in the lemon juice. Place the pot over medium-low heat and cook, stirring constantly with a heatproof silicone spatula, until the mixture thickens slightly and reaches 160°F (71°C) on an instant-read thermometer, 5–10 minutes. As you stir, be sure to scrape the entire bottom and corners of the pan, so that the mixture heats as evenly as possible. It will start out thick and cloudy from the undissolved sugar, then will turn thin and translucent and finally begin to thicken and turn cloudy again as the eggs cook. If the mixture starts to curdle or bubble, immediately remove it from the heat and proceed to the next step.

Immediately pour the curd through the strainer and into the bowl to stop the cooking. Whisk in the butter pieces and zest until combined.

(continued)

MEYER LEMON BARS WITH
VANILLA-ALMOND CRUST (CONT.)

Pour the cooked curd over the warm, baked crust. Bake the bars until the sides are barely puffed and the center wobbles like firm Jell-O when you give it a gentle shake, 18–25 minutes. It should not be wet or watery looking (underbaked), nor should it be puffed in the center or cracking (overbaked). Remove the bars from the oven and let cool for about 30 minutes, then chill until firm, 2–3 hours.

Grasp the parchment and lift the bars from the pan and onto a cutting board; peel away the sides of the parchment. Trim away the outer edges of the bars, then use a large chef's knife to cut the bar into 16 squares, wiping the blade clean between cuts. Just before serving, dust the tops with a bit of powdered sugar.

The bars keep well, refrigerated, for up to 3 days, though the crust is the crispiest within the first 1–2 days.

VARIATIONS

BERGAMOT AND MEYER LEMON BARS

Fresh bergamots are becoming easier to find in specialty grocers when they come into season during the winter months, and their zest and juice make for a spectacularly unique lemon bar.

Use 1½ teaspoons (5 g) lemon zest and ½ teaspoon bergamot zest. Use ¾ cup (180 ml) Meyer lemon juice and 2 tablespoons (30 ml) bergamot juice. Make the recipe as instructed.

NO-MEYER LEMON BARS

A mix of orange juice and zest added to regular lemon juice and zest makes superb lemon bars, for those who don't have Meyers readily available. Do be sure to use freshly squeezed juice from regular (Eureka) lemons and a Valencia or navel orange.

Omit the Meyer lemon zest and juice, using instead 1 teaspoon each lemon and orange zests, ½ cup (120 ml) lemon juice, and ¼ cup plus 2 tablespoons (90 ml) orange juice.

SWEET POTATO BOURBON CHEESECAKE BITES WITH MESQUITE-PECAN CRUST

{SORGHUM, SWEET RICE, MESQUITE }

Mesquite's uniquely warm, earthy flavor pairs seamlessly with roasted sweet potatoes and freshly grated nutmeg, all rolled up in these dainty cheesecake bites. Keeping with the Southern theme, I add a splash of bourbon to the filling, and pecans and sorghum flour to the crust, which, when baked, reminds me of really amazing graham crackers. They make an ideal treat for holiday parties and potlucks. In fact, the nutmegy filling reminds me a little of eggnog crossed with pumpkin pie. These are deceptively simple to make, as the crust and filling can both be done in a food processor, with the sour cream whipped just before serving. Do be sure to allow a few hours for the bars to chill in the fridge to a sliceable consistency. They keep well for up to 3 days; in fact, they just seem to get better and better.

MAKES ONE 8-INCH (20-CM) SQUARE CHEESECAKE, 25 BITE-SIZED SERVINGS

CRUST
¼ cup plus 2 tbsp (50 g) sorghum flour

¼ cup plus 2 tbsp (50 g) sweet white rice flour

¼ cup plus 2 tbsp (35 g) mesquite flour

½ cup (55 g) pecan halves

6 tbsp (70 g) packed organic light brown sugar

¼ tsp fine sea salt

5 tbsp (70 g) cold, unsalted butter, in ½-inch (1.3-cm) dice

FILLING
1 cup (235 ml) packed roasted sweet potato flesh (see Notes)

8 oz (225 g) cream cheese, at room temperature

½ cup (100 g) packed organic light brown sugar

¼ tsp fine sea salt

½ tsp packed freshly grated nutmeg

2 large eggs

2 tbsp (30 ml) sour cream

1 tsp vanilla extract

2 tbsp (30 ml) bourbon or GF whiskey (such as Queen Jennie)

TOPPING
½ cup (120 ml) sour cream

½ cup (120 ml) heavy whipping cream

1 tbsp (12 g) organic granulated cane sugar

½ tsp vanilla extract

2 tsp (10 ml) bourbon or GF whiskey (such as Queen Jennie)

A handful toasted pecans, for garnish

Position a rack in the lower third of the oven and preheat to 350ºF (175ºC). Line the bottom and sides of an 8-inch (20-cm) square baking pan—or a 9-inch (23-cm) pan for slightly thinner bars—with a large piece of parchment paper or heavy-duty aluminum foil, leaving a 1-inch (2-cm) overhang on every side.

To make the crust, in the bowl of a food processor, whizz together the sorghum, sweet rice and mesquite flours with the pecans, brown sugar, salt and butter until it begins to clump together and looks like damp sand, about 30 seconds. Dump the crumbs into the lined baking pan and pack it firmly and evenly with your hands or a flat-bottomed glass. (No need to wash the food processor bowl—you'll use it again in the next step.) Bake the crust until golden and toasty smelling, 15–20 minutes.

Decrease the oven temperature to 325ºF (165ºC).

Meanwhile, to make the filling, in the bowl of the food processor, puree the sweet potato smooth, scraping down the sides of the bowl a few times. Add the cream cheese and puree smooth, then blend in the brown sugar, salt and nutmeg, pulsing until just smooth and combined, scraping down the sides of the bowl a few times. Add the eggs one at a time, pulsing until just combined after each addition. (Be careful not to overwork the cream cheese—doing so can break down the proteins and cause the mixture to become thin and watery.) Add the sour cream, vanilla and bourbon, pulsing to just combine. Remove the blade from the bowl, and give the mixture a final stir with a flexible spatula to make sure it's thoroughly combined.

Spread the cheesecake batter evenly over the hot crust and rap the pan on the counter a few times to pop any large air bubbles. Place the cheesecake in the oven on the lower rack. Bake for 25–35 minutes, until the sides are gently puffed and the cheesecake is set when you give it a shake. An instant-read thermometer inserted into the center should register 165ºF–170ºF (74ºC–76ºC). Let cool completely, then chill until firm, at least 3 hours and up to 1 day.

To cut the bars, grab the parchment paper handles and pull the whole thing out of the pan and onto a cutting board; it's okay if the crust cracks a little. Peel away the sides of the parchment. Use a large, sharp chef's knife, wiped clean after each cut, to trim away the edges, then cut the cheesecake into 25 squares. Cover and chill until ready to serve.

(continued)

SWEET POTATO BOURBON CHEESECAKE BITES
WITH MESQUITE-PECAN CRUST (CONT.)

To make the topping, in a large bowl with a balloon whisk (or with a handheld blender or stand mixer fitted with the whip attachment), whip together the sour cream, heavy cream and sugar until it holds soft peaks. Add the vanilla and bourbon, and whip until it holds soft peaks again.

Serve small squares of the cheesecake topped with dollops of the whipped cream and pecan pieces.

NOTES

- To roast the sweet potatoes, place 2 medium garnet or jewel sweet potatoes on a small, rimmed baking sheet, prick them a few times with the tines of a fork and bake them in a 375°F (190°C) oven until very soft when squeezed with a pair of tongs, about 45 minutes. Let cool completely, then scoop the flesh out of the skin and into a measuring cup. (Extra sweet potato is delicious warm with a dollop of sour cream—a little treat for the baker.)

- If you or your cheesecake biters are highly sensitive to trace amounts of gluten, be sure to source a GF whiskey (such as Queen Jennie). Otherwise, I like a tipple of Bulleit bourbon here. You can also leave off the booze altogether, or substitute GF brandy or dark or spiced rum.

BASICS AND ACCOMPANIMENTS

Sauces and toppings can take a dessert from good to amazing. Here are a few favorites that are a snap to make at home, as well as some DIY guidelines for turning out thick crème fraîche, potent vanilla extract and perfectly browned butter. Caramel is demystified with a few easy techniques that thwart crystallization. Making ice cream at home is as simple as churning a basic stirred custard in an ice cream maker; frozen yogurt is even simpler. And you'll never accidentally overwhip cream again with one simple trick. Read on!

HOW TO BROWN BUTTER

Brown butter, called *beurre noisette* in French for its hazelnut-like flavor, is simply butter that's been cooked until the milk solids caramelize. I like to add vanilla bean to the mix; as it cooks, it gives off the intoxicating aroma of baking cookies, and it adds incredible depth of flavor to anything you put it in. The first time I browned butter, I burned butter. So here's a bit of instruction to keep that from happening to you. Each recipe will have its own quantities, so none are given here.

Butter (see individual recipes)

Vanilla bean, split lengthwise and scraped (see individual recipes)

Place the butter and vanilla pod and scrapings in a medium, heavy-bottomed saucepan. Place the pan over medium-low heat and cook, swirling occasionally, to melt the butter. Continue cooking the butter. After 3–5 minutes, the butter will foam up, turn golden and smell nutty, with brown flecks mingling with black vanilla bean seeds on the bottom of the pan. It may be hard to see the color of the butter beneath the foam and in the pan, so if you're unsure, spoon a little of the butter into a white, heatproof bowl; it should be golden in color and the milk solids on the bottom of the pan should be chestnut brown from caramelization, with black specks from the vanilla bean. The butter should smell so delicious that you could eat your own arm from hunger. At this point, remove the pan from the heat and immediately pour the butter into a heatproof measuring cup to stop the cooking. When ready to use, remove the vanilla bean and discard. Brown butter can be cooled and refrigerated airtight for up to a week or two.

NOTE: If you don't have vanilla beans on hand, leave the vanilla out of the browning butter and add 1 teaspoon vanilla extract for every bean called for to the batter or dough with other liquid ingredients.

VANILLA EXTRACT

I pity the fool who utters the phrase "plain vanilla" in my presence. Vanilla is truly one of the more exotic flavorings that we have access to. It takes months to grow a single seedpod from the tropical vanilla orchid, and each pod must be harvested by hand and undergo a lengthy curing process. Vanilla beans are costly when purchased in single form at most grocers, but they can be ordered in bulk for a vastly lower price. (See Sources, page 260.) I save the pods to stick in a jar of alcohol (inexpensive brandy is my favorite) to make an ongoing batch of vanilla extract. I'm not very scientific about it, but I wanted to share my method here.

Inexpensive neutral-tasting alcohol (such as brandy, vodka or rum)

Vanilla beans

Put some booze in a bottle or canning jar; I usually use a 1-quart (1-L) jar as I go through a lot of beans, but you may wish to start smaller if you have only a few beans. Split a few vanilla beans lengthwise and add them to the jar to get this party started. When you end up with a stray vanilla pod, or one that you've steeped in a custard or brown butter, rinse it, let it dry and add it to the jar. Keep doing this, adding more booze to cover the beans if you need, and storing the jar in a dark place, such as a cupboard, for several months. Give it a shake occasionally when you think of it. When the liquid turns a dark brown after a few months, it's ready to use. Strain some of the liquid off and place it in a small bottle to use in your baking. Top off the jar with more booze. Continue this process indefinitely. After a few years, your beans will be spent of their flavor and you'll want to start the process over, decanting the extract and discarding the spent beans, to make room for fresh beans.

NOTE: If you have vanilla beans that have become dry and hard, here's a tip I learned recently: pour an inch (2.5 cm) of inexpensive alcohol into a jar tall enough to house the beans. Add the beans to the jar and seal. After several days, the beans will absorb the liquid and plump up again, and any alcohol left in the bottom can be used as vanilla extract.

CRÈME FRAÎCHE

Crème fraîche may sound fancy, but it's actually stupid-easy to make at home. This is technically mock crème fraîche, as real crème fraîche uses a more complicated culturing process, but this works just the same when baked into recipes, whipped with cream or spooned over warm biscuits or rustic fruit desserts.

MAKES A LITTLE OVER 1 CUP (245 ML)

1 cup (235 ml) heavy cream

1 tbsp (14 g) fresh buttermilk (or crème fraîche)

Stir together the cream and buttermilk in a jar to combine well, cover, and leave in a warm place (such as on top of the refrigerator) for 12–24 hours. The cultures in the buttermilk will go to work on the cream to thicken it. Give the mixture a shake or stir 2–3 times as it sits to discourage a hard layer of cream from forming on the top. After 12–24 hours the mixture should be slightly thicker and have a pleasant sour smell. Give it a final stir and chill until cold, 2 hours and up to 1 week. It will thicken further as it cools.

WHIPPED CREAM

Cream whipped with a splash of vanilla and a touch of sugar is traditionally called crème chantilly (pronounced shan-tee-yee) and its flavor is as smooth and classy as the name. When you're not eating it on spoons straight from the bowl, use whipped cream on any room temperature fruit dessert (pie, tart, cobbler, crisp, etc.) or fancy up breakfast by serving it alongside scones or peach oven pancake. I've included a couple of favorite variations, below. If you can find a locally produced, nonhomogenized cream, this will taste extra sweet and delicious. Make sure your cream contains 35–40 percent fat; any heavy cream, whipping cream or heavy whipping cream should do. See page 52 for a dairy-free version made with coconut cream.

Note: If you accidentally whip your cream too far and it begins to thicken and seize toward becoming butter, never fear—all is not lost. You can rescue it by gently folding in additional heavy cream until the mixture becomes smooth again. Start with 2 tablespoons (30 ml) and add more as needed.

MAKES ABOUT 2 CUPS (230 G)

1 cup (235 ml) cold heavy cream, whipping cream or heavy whipping cream (with a fat content of at least 35%)

2 tsp (10 g) organic granulated cane sugar, to taste

½ tsp vanilla extract (or seeds from ½ vanilla bean, added at the beginning)

Place the cream (and vanilla seeds, if using) in a large, chilled bowl or the bowl of a stand mixer fitted with the whip attachment. Whip on medium speed (with the stand mixer or with a balloon whisk, handheld blender or old-fashioned non-electric egg beater) until the cream mounds softly. Sprinkle in the sugar and vanilla extract (if using) and continue whipping until the cream holds soft peaks, meaning that when you lift the beater out of the cream and turn it upside down, the peak of cream will flop over. Keep the cream cold until using; it will separate as it sits and may need to be re-whipped if chilled for longer than an hour or two.

VARIATIONS

MAPLE BOURBON WHIPPED CREAM

The warm flavors of maple and whiskey make this well-suited to fall desserts such as pumpkin pie and pecan tart.

Omit the sugar, using 1 tablespoon (15 ml) maple syrup or maple sugar instead. Omit the vanilla and add 1–2 tablespoons (15–30 ml) bourbon or GF whiskey (such as Queen Jennie).

WHIPPED CRÈME FRAÎCHE (OR YOGURT OR SOUR CREAM)

This denser, tangier whipped cream makes a fabulous accompaniment to most any fruit dessert.

Use ½ cup (120 ml) Crème Fraîche (page 223) (or sour cream, or whole-milk Greek yogurt or skyr) in place of ½ cup (120 ml) of the cream and proceed with the recipe.

MASCARPONE WHIPPED CREAM

This thick whipped cream holds its shape well for up to several hours in the refrigerator and is a great do-ahead option. I especially like the vanilla bean seeds here.

Use ½ cup (120 ml) mascarpone in place of ½ cup (120 ml) of the cream and proceed with the recipe, using the vanilla seeds if you've got them and a tiny pinch of fine sea salt.

VANILLA BEAN ICE CREAM

Once you have an ice cream maker, ice cream is surprisingly easy to make. A few tools will help ensure a smooth custard: a heavy-bottomed saucepan will distribute the heat evenly as the custard cooks, a heatproof spatula will help you scrape the sides of the pot and an instant-read thermometer will ensure that the eggs reach a safe temperature. This ice cream pairs well with just about everything, from fruit pies to brownie sundaes. And don't miss the variations.

MAKES ABOUT 1 QUART (1 L)

1¼ cups (300 ml) whole milk

½ vanilla bean, split lengthwise and scraped

½ cup (100 g) organic granulated cane sugar

⅛ tsp fine sea salt

1¼ cups (300 ml) cold, heavy cream

4 large egg yolks

NOTES

- Save the egg whites for making Chestnut Plum Financiers (page 64) or Vanilla Chiffon Cake (page 49). They will keep, refrigerated airtight, for up to a week, or in the freezer for up to several months.

- For a richer ice cream, use 1 cup (235 ml) milk and 1½ cups (355 ml) heavy cream, or 1½ cups (355 ml) half-and-half and 1 cup (235 ml) heavy cream.

In a medium saucepan, heat the milk with the vanilla bean and scrapings, sugar and salt until steaming and small bubbles appear around the sides of the pan, stirring occasionally to dissolve the sugar and prevent the milk from scorching. Remove from the heat, cover and steep for 30–60 minutes to infuse with the vanilla.

Pour the heavy cream into a quart-sized (1 L) container, such as a mason jar, and set aside. If you have an instant-read thermometer, have it handy.

Place the egg yolks in a medium bowl set on a damp towel to stabilize it. Reheat the milk until hot and steamy. Whisking constantly with one hand, pour the hot dairy very slowly into the yolks. This is called tempering, and prevents the yolks from scrambling. Pour the mixture back into the pot and set the pot over low heat. Cook, stirring constantly with a heatproof silicone spatula, scraping the sides and bottom of the pot, until the custard just begins to "stick" (or form a thickened film) on the bottom of the pot (you may have to tilt the pan to see it), or registers 170ºF (76ºC) on an instant-read thermometer, 5–10 minutes.

Immediately pour the custard into the container of cold cream, stir to combine, and chill for at least 4 hours, or preferably overnight. For a quicker chill, pour the ice cream into a metal bowl and place over an ice water bath, stirring until the base is cold.

Place the ice cream base in the freezer for 30 minutes to get it really cold, stirring once or twice (this way the ice cream will take less time to churn, resulting in a denser, creamier ice cream). Strain the mixture through a fine mesh sieve, then pour into your ice cream maker and process as per the manufacturer's instructions. Mine takes about 20 minutes to churn.

When the ice cream is finished churning, scrape it into a container. Press a piece of parchment paper directly onto the surface (this will discourage crystals from forming), cover tightly and freeze until firm, at least 2 hours.

Homemade ice cream is best within the first week of being made, but will keep for a month or two in the freezer.

(continued)

VARIATIONS

FRESH GINGER ICE CREAM

Omit the vanilla bean and make the custard as directed, straining it directly into the cold heavy cream. Stir in 2 tablespoons (30 g) peeled, very finely grated fresh ginger (grated on a microplane grater or the smallest holes of a box grater to a fine pulp). Chill the ice cream base, don't re-strain and proceed with the recipe.

CARDAMOM ICE CREAM

Omit the vanilla bean, heating the milk, sugar and salt with 1 teaspoon ground cardamom. No need to steep the mixture. Proceed with the recipe.

CRÈME FRAÎCHE ICE CREAM

Omit the vanilla bean. Make the custard as directed and strain it into a heatproof bowl set over an ice water bath, stirring until cold. Omit the cream and stir 1¼ cups (300 ml) Crème Fraîche (page 223) into the cold ice cream. Chill until cold, then proceed with the recipe.

VANILLA BEAN FROZEN YOGURT

I grew up in the '80s, when frozen yogurt was touted as a healthier alternative to ice cream, and my family and I would frequent the many shops throughout L.A. for cups brimming with soft serve and all the toppings I could pile on. In reality, the frozen dessert in question was probably no healthier than real ice cream, and it was likely packed with sugar and preservatives, gums and stabilizers to keep it soft. This version, on the other hand, uses a combination of Greek yogurt and heavy cream to make it naturally rich and delicious. Just enough sugar balances the acidity in the tangy yogurt, and if you add a touch of alcohol, it gives the yogurt a slightly softer freeze. Enjoy this atop any warm fruit dessert or pie as a more refreshing and simpler alternative to ice cream. Or layer it with streusel and roasted berries for a thoroughly addictive dessert (page 175).

MAKES ABOUT 1 QUART (1 L)

1 cup (235 ml) heavy cream

½ vanilla bean, split lengthwise and scraped

½ cup (100 g) organic granulated cane sugar

Pinch of fine sea salt

2 cups (475 ml) plain, whole milk Greek yogurt (such as Straus Family Creamery)

2 tbsp (30 ml) GF whiskey or vodka (optional, for a softer freeze)

In a small saucepan over medium heat, combine the heavy cream, vanilla pod and scrapings, sugar and salt and heat until hot and steamy, stirring to dissolve the sugar. Cover and let steep for 20–60 minutes to infuse. Place the yogurt in a medium-sized bowl and whisk smooth.

Strain the cream into the yogurt, whisking to combine. Whisk in the whiskey. Chill until cold, 1 hour or up to 2 days. Churn the frozen yogurt according to the manufacturer's instructions, then scrape into a container, cover and chill until firm, at least 2 hours and up to several weeks.

SALTY VANILLA BEAN CARAMEL SAUCE

Organic granulated cane sugar, with its larger crystals, is more prone to crystallization than regular granulated sugar, thus a bit more care is needed to keep it liquid to make this silky smooth caramel sauce. Essentially, sugar crystals are prone to peer pressure, and the presence of just one sugar crystal can cause all the other dissolved sugar particles, necessary for making a liquid sauce, to snap into crystalline structure and turn your smooth caramel into a pot of sludge simply because all the cool crystals are doing it. So just say no to crystallization. Here are some tips I've picked up from various sources over the years, particularly *Cook's Illustrated*.

- Adding a bit of an invert sugar, such as corn syrup or honey, helps prevent crystallization.
- Placing water in the pan first, then adding the sugar to the center without letting any crystals get on the sides, helps moisten the sugar crystals and keep them from re-crystallizing.
- Leaving the lid on the pan for the first few minutes will wash away any wayward crystals.
- As always when making caramel, refrain from disturbing the pan too much during cooking, tilting it gently if it begins to caramelize unevenly.
- Worst case scenario, if your sauce does turn into a pot of sludge, you can sometimes dump a bunch of water in there and begin the dissolving process again; it will just take time for the water to cook off.

MAKES 1¼ CUPS (300 ML)

¾ cup (180 ml) heavy cream

1 vanilla bean, split lengthwise and scraped

¼ cup (60 ml) water

2 tbsp (30 ml) organic corn syrup (or honey)

1 cup (205 g) organic granulated cane sugar

2 tbsp (28 g) unsalted butter, in a few pieces

½ tsp flaky salt, such as Maldon, or more to taste

VARIATIONS

SALTY AND SMOKY CARAMEL SAUCE

Omit the vanilla bean and use black smoked salt in place of the Maldon salt, adding it to taste.

SALTY AND BOOZY CARAMEL SAUCE

Omit the vanilla bean. Add 2–4 tablespoons (30–60 ml), to taste, bourbon, scotch, brandy or dark rum to the sauce along with the flaky salt. (Make sure your spirits are GF if you or your caramel eaters are sensitive to trace amounts of gluten.)

Pour the cream into a small saucepan, add the vanilla pod and seeds, and heat over medium heat until hot and steamy, swirling the pan occasionally. Cover and let steep while you get on with the recipe.

Meanwhile, pour the water into a medium-sized, heavy-bottomed saucepan. Add the corn syrup, then carefully pour the sugar into the center of the pan. If any sugar crystals stick to the sides of the pan, brush them down into the water with moistened fingers. Cover the pot with a lid and, without disturbing the pan, cook over medium heat until the sugar is dissolved, about 3 minutes (the steam will wash down any wayward sugar crystals). Remove the lid and continue to boil, without stirring, until the mixture turns a deep amber, gently tilting the pan to encourage even caramelization and brushing down the sides of the pan with a damp pastry brush if you see any pesky sugar crystals forming on them. This will take only a few minutes; watch the pot carefully toward the end, and reduce the heat to low if you're nervous.

When the mixture turns a dark amber (if the mixture is bubbly, you may need to place a drop of caramel on a white, heatproof plate to check), immediately swirl in the butter, then gently and slowly whisk in the cream. Return the pot to low heat and whisk gently to dissolve any hardened caramel that may be hanging out on the bottom or corners of the pan. Strain the caramel into a heatproof bowl and let stand, stirring occasionally, until cooled and thickened slightly. (You can rinse and dry the vanilla bean and add it to Vanilla Extract, page 220.) Stir in the flaky salt, crushing any extra-large bits between your fingers and adding more if you feel the sauce needs it.

Store the caramel in an airtight jar. It will keep at room temperature for up to 1 day, or chilled for up to 1 month.

RHUBARB PRESERVES

This thick, jammy compote is made rosy from red rhubarb and deep burgundy blood orange juice. Garden-grown rhubarb isn't quite as rosy-hued as the forced stalks grown in hothouses that grace the pages of cookbooks and foodie magazines. It's hard to find the latter here in California, but I've learned a few tricks over the years to get a prettier puree from field-grown stalks. First, look for the reddest stalks you can find and use only the reddest parts of the stalk, closer to the root end. Second, don't peel the rhubarb, as some recipes instruct; it isn't necessary and only removes the pretty pigment we're after. Third, add something bright to the preserves. Blood orange juice is my favorite addition, as it doesn't change the texture or overpower the flavor of the rhubarb, but it does enhance its color. Blood oranges are waning just as rhubarb is beginning its season, but you can squirrel some away in the fridge and have this pretty preserve all through spring. Alternatively, use regular orange zest and juice in its place. You can leave it chunky or puree it smooth (see variation below). Either way, wrap these preserves up in Vanilla Chiffon Cake (page 49) and spread with Whipped Crème Fraîche (page 224) for a Rosy Rhubarb Roulade Cake (page 51), or enjoy it on toast, biscuits or yogurt.

MAKES ABOUT 2 CUPS (475 ML)

1 cup (205 g) organic granulated cane sugar

Finely grated zest from 1 medium-sized blood orange

Strained juice from 1 medium-sized blood orange (about 4 tbsp [60 ml])

½ vanilla bean, split lengthwise and scraped

2 lb (900 g) rhubarb, trimmed, sliced into ½-inch (1.3-cm) pieces (about 10 medium-sized stalks, 5 cups)

In a large saucepan over medium heat, combine the sugar, orange zest and juice, and vanilla pod and scrapings. Bring the mixture to a simmer, stirring occasionally to dissolve the sugar. Cook until thick and syrupy, 5 minutes, then dump in the rhubarb. Cook, stirring frequently with a long-handled spoon as the mixture will splutter, until the mixture has broken down into a thick, glossy jam that holds its shape, 15–20 minutes, lowering the heat as needed to maintain a rolling simmer. Remove from the heat and let cool, stirring occasionally. Transfer to a jar, cover and chill for up to 1 week. You can leave the vanilla pod in to continue flavoring the preserve, but remove it when you're ready to use.

VARIATION: RHUBARB PUREE

Remove the vanilla bean and puree the preserves in a food processor until silky smooth, scraping down the sides of the bowl as needed.

HONEY CANDIED KUMQUATS

It took me a while to warm to kumquats. I remember being handed one as a kid and told, "You can eat the whole thing, peel and all—they're sweet!" I then got a mouthful of heinously tart, bitter fruit, and I steered clear of the little buggers ever since. But my good friend Amelia is a kumquat fiend, and it was she who convinced me to give them another shot. Simmering the slices briefly in a syrup of sugar, water, honey and vanilla bean means that a bitter, tart mouthful is the last thing you'll get when you bite into one.

It takes a bit of effort to slice and seed the kumquats for this recipe, but doing so will preserve them for up to 2 months in the refrigerator. Use these to make dainty Fromage Blanc Tartlets with Honeyed Kumquats (page 135), chop them up into a cream cheese frosting to serve atop Vanilla Bean Cupcakes (page 83) or serve them over yogurt and sprinkled with granola for breakfast.

MAKES ABOUT 1½ CUPS (400 G)

8 oz (225 g) kumquats (2 cups)

½ cup (100 g) organic granulated cane sugar

½ cup (120 ml) water

¼ cup (60 ml) mild honey

½ vanilla bean, split lengthwise and scraped

Trim the ends off the kumquats and slice them ⅛-inch (3-mm) thick, removing the seeds as you go. In a medium saucepan, combine the sugar, water, honey and vanilla pod and scrapings. Bring to a boil over medium heat, swirling occasionally to dissolve the sugar. Add the sliced kumquats, and shuffle the pan to submerge them; there will barely be enough liquid to cover them at this point. Return the mixture to a simmer, simmer for 2 minutes, then turn off the heat, cover the pan and let the mixture steep for 15 minutes. Strain the kumquats, reserving their syrup, and place the fruit in a heatproof bowl or jar. Return the syrup to the pot and simmer over medium heat, swirling frequently, until it bubbles thickly and measures about ½ cup (120 ml), 10–15 minutes. Pour the syrup over the drained kumquats, and chill until cold. They will keep in the refrigerator for up to 1 month.

ALTERNATIVE GRAINS AND FLOURS

Alternative grains and flours have the ability to add not only structure but also a host of varying flavors and textures to baked goods. I've divided the flours used in this book into categories based on their common flavor profiles—neutral, earthy and grassy. Within those categories are unique flours with their own tastes and textures, histories and applications.

I've used Bob's Red Mill brand flours when possible for consistency, since different brands grind flours differently and this can have drastically different effects in baking. For the best results, I suggest sourcing the brands with which I've developed these recipes. Many can be found in your local health food store and all can be ordered online. And if you need to use a different brand, no worries—the results will still taste delicious even if the texture needs tweaking.

A NOTE ON SUBSTITUTING FLOURS

Alternative flours can vary hugely in weight, absorbency, starch, protein and fiber contents and thus can have dramatically different results in baking. For instance, 1 cup of oat flour weighs close to 100 grams, whereas the same amount of teff flour weighs 30 percent more, or 130 grams. For tried and tested results, make the recipes as written the first time around. If you need to substitute due to allergies, availability or personal preference, your best bet is to pick a flour with similar flavor characteristics and a similar weight per cup, and to substitute by weight rather than by volume. That said, I do hope you'll become comfortable enough with these recipes to experiment, and that you'll share your results and variations with me and my readers on AlternativeBaker.com and BojonGourmet.com.

NEUTRAL

These mild flours are easy to love and pair well with nearly everything; it's no wonder they're used frequently in alternative baking.

SWEET WHITE RICE FLOUR

AKA: Glutinous rice flour, sticky rice flour

Flavor profile: Sweet, bland, mild

Consistency: Soft, fine, starchy, sticky

Brand tested: Koda Farms' Blue Star Mochiko Sweet Rice Flour

Weight per cup: 5½ ounces (155 g)

Find it: In Asian markets and at health food stores with the other alternative flours or Asian foods

Store it: Airtight at room temperature in a cool, dry, dark place (such as a kitchen cupboard) for up to 1 year

Use it: In nearly anything; sweet rice has a neutral flavor that goes with everything. Don't use more than 50 percent sweet rice flour in any given recipe, or in recipes with a lot of moisture or acidity, which will often make for a gummy texture.

Health benefits: Sweet rice flour is mostly starch, with little nutritional value beyond ample carbohydrates and little fat.

Sweet white rice flour is my alternative baking secret weapon. Commonly used to make Japanese mochi and many other desserts throughout Asia, it is finely ground from a specific variety of rice referred to as sticky rice or glutinous rice (though it does not contain gluten). It helps hold baked goods together without the need to add many other starches or gums. Its sticky power is similar to gluten in that working or agitating the flour with liquid increases the stickiness. In contrast to gluten, acidity also seems to increase the stickiness, as I've found when I've added acidic ingredients (such as citrus juice, cocoa powder, rhubarb and cultured dairy) to recipes. For instance, biscuits made with buttermilk consistently baked up dense and gummy. But when I traded in regular milk, the texture improved dramatically. In other recipes, however, the extra stickiness is a boon. Either way, sweet rice flour makes possible many of the recipes in this book, such as fluffy biscuits and scones, flaky pie dough and pillowy cakes.

If you can't find sweet rice flour, you can order it online. In a pinch, try substituting a GF all-purpose, rice-based flour blend such as Bob's Red Mill 1:1 (in which sweet rice flour is the first ingredient) or King Arthur's GF Multi-Purpose Flour. Or substitute regular or superfine white rice flour by weight, though the texture will be much more brittle, especially in recipes that call for a lot of it. In this case, you might try adding in some tapioca flour or ground chia seed.

OATS AND OAT FLOUR

Flavor profile: Creamy, sweet, wheaty, nutty, a little earthy

Consistency: Soft, tender, starchy, delicate

Brand tested: Bob's Red Mill Gluten-Free Oat Flour and Old-Fashioned Rolled Oats

Weight per cup: Oat flour, 3½ ounces (100 g); old-fashioned rolled oats, 3¼ ounces (90 g)

Find it: With other alternative flours and/or in the bulk section at health food stores. Be sure to look for certified GF oats and oat flour, as they are traditionally grown and processed with wheat and can be contaminated with gluten. All oats used in this book are the old-fashioned rolled variety.

Store it: Airtight at room temperature in a cool, dry, dark place (such as a kitchen cupboard) for up to 3 months, or refrigerated airtight for up to 1 year

Use it: Anywhere you want a touch of whole-grain flavor and soft, delicate texture. Oat flour pairs well with comforting flavors such as apples, bananas, winter squash, spices, chocolate, caramel, brown sugar, honey, maple, nuts and dried fruits. When used in conjunction with sweet rice and millet flours, it makes an all-purpose-like flour with a fairly neutral taste and pillowy texture. Do note that some people with celiac disease or other severe gluten-intolerance also can't tolerate oats, even the certified GF variety.

Health benefits: Higher fat content than most cereal grains, high in fiber, only grain to contain globulin, a legume-like protein that can be a boon to vegetarians. These properties give oatmeal its "stick-to-your-ribs" reputation. Oats are also an excellent source of manganese, which helps build connective tissue in the body, regulate blood sugar and absorb calcium, and are a good source of other minerals.

It was a happy day when we all learned that oats are actually gluten-free. They were so commonly grown and processed with wheat, where they picked up fairly large amounts of gluten, that they were thought to inherently contain gluten. In fact, oats used to be considered weeds that grew among wheat and barley only to be uprooted and burned. They thrive in cool, wet climates such as northern Europe, Canada and

(continued)

NEUTRAL FLOURS FROM TOP: SWEET WHITE RICE, ALMOND, COCONUT, OAT

the northern United States. They are particularly loved in Scotland, where they feature in soups and stews, breakfast porridge, oatcakes and scones. We have Scottish settlers to thank for bringing oats to North America in the 1700s.

I now make frequent use of oat flour in alternative baking. It adds nutritional value and a bit of hearty depth to any and all baked goods. It absorbs moisture fairly well and bakes up soft and smooth, adding necessary starch to many GF baked goods and keeping them moist and tender due to its high fat content and stable protein. It makes pillowy biscuits and scones, springy cakes and hearty muffins. Old-fashioned rolled oats, which are made by steaming and rolling the grains flat, star in crisps, streusel, granola bars, oatmeal cookies and a pumpkin cranberry bread packed with seeds.

ALMOND FLOUR

Flavor profile: Mild, nutty, rich, buttery

Consistency: Slightly coarse and nubby, but soft and delicate, tends to clump

Brand tested: Bob's Red Mill Blanched Almond Flour/Meal

Weight per cup: 4¼ ounces (120 g)

Find it: With other alternative flours at health food stores

Store it: Refrigerated airtight for up to 6 months. Due to its volatile oils, almond flour can go rancid if left at room temperature.

Use it: In almost anything where you don't mind a slightly nutty flavor and a bit of nubby texture. Particularly tasty with stone fruit, berries, figs, apples, pears, citrus, chocolate, coffee, other nuts, honey, vanilla and spices. Do warn your dessert eaters of the presence of nut flour in baked goods in case of nut allergies. Don't use more than 50–75 percent almond flour in any given recipe lest you wind up with a dense, macaroon-like texture and assertive almond flavor (unless that's what you're going for).

Health benefits: High in protein, vitamins B and E, minerals, particularly calcium in levels nearly as high as in milk, fiber and good fats that purportedly lower cholesterol and blood pressure and decrease risk of blood clots.

The almond is not a true nut, but rather the seed of a fruit related to stone fruit (apricots, cherries and peaches) called a drupe. Almond trees are native to the Middle East and South Asia, and they have sustained Silk Route traders, Egyptian kings and biblical figures for millennia. King Tut was buried with almonds to munch during his journey to the afterlife. In Genesis, Jacob sends his sons to buy grain from the Egyptians, offering them almonds, among other gifts, in exchange. Almond-shaped halos surround saints in Renaissance paintings and frescos. Almonds played a part in nearly every ancient civilization and continue to be used in cuisines around the globe, particularly India, the Middle East and along the Mediterranean. They're pureed into a refreshing milk substitute, blended with sugar for marzipan and almond paste, ground into frangipane, made into macaroons and amaretti, candied, roasted and fried for snacks and coated in sugar and given at weddings to symbolize the sweetness of love coating the bitterness of life.

Today, almonds thrive in California's Mediterranean-like climate, where 80 percent of the world's almonds are produced. Recently, almond flour has become a popular ingredient in alternative baking and touted for its many health benefits. Blanched almond flour comes from almonds that have been slipped from their papery skins prior to grinding; it bakes up smooth, mild and light in color, and its high protein content handily replaces the missing proteins in gluten-free baking. Its high fat content produces tender, rich baked goods. Bob's Red Mill brand, used here, is advertised as finely ground, but it still has a bit of texture, which makes a pleasant addition to the tart crust and clafoutis in this book as well as many cakes such as financiers, buckle, olive oil cakes and madeleines.

HAZELNUT MEAL

Hazelnut meal has similar characteristics to almond flour. It is sold unblanched, thus has a higher fiber content, darker color and earthier flavor, but can often be used interchangeably where these characteristics are desired. I particularly like it with pears, buckwheat flour, chocolate and warming spices. The financier variation in this book was developed with Bob's Red Mill Finely Ground Hazelnut Flour/Meal.

COCONUT FLOUR

Flavor profile: Mild, sweet, slightly floral and tropical

Consistency: Powdery, fibrous, tends to clump

Brands tested: Let's Do Organic, Bob's Red Mill

Weight per cup: 4¼ ounces (120 g)

Find it: With other GF flours and/or the bulk section at health food stores

Store it: Airtight at room temperature in a cool, dry, dark place (such as a kitchen cupboard) for up to 1 year

Use it: In just about anything where you don't mind its distinctive taste and fibrous texture. Its light, floral flavor pairs especially well with other tropical, bright flavors, such as citrus, mango, berries, ginger, vanilla and chocolate. Don't use more than 30 percent coconut flour in a recipe or the results may be dry, crumbly and slightly gritty. Even with a small amount of coconut flour added, you will need to increase the moisture content in order to appease this thirsty flour.

Health benefits: Very high in fiber, nearly double the protein of wheat flour, high in healthy fats that are said to be antiviral and antimicrobial, rich in trace minerals

Like almonds, coconuts are not nuts at all, but the seed of a palm tree fruit, or a drupe. The name coconut comes from the Spanish word coco, meaning "skull," named for the three indentations in mature coconuts that resemble a face. Coconut palms thrive in hot, humid climates and are cultivated throughout tropical Asia, parts of India and Sri Lanka, the northern coast of Australia and in the United States (namely Florida and Hawaii). In Thailand and Malaysia, primates called pig-tailed macaques are trained to harvest coconuts. Culinarily, coconuts have many uses, including coconut oil and butter, shredded coconut, coconut milk and cream, coconut water and coconut flour.

Coconut flour is made from dried, unsweetened coconut that has had a large amount of its fat removed, making it very high in fiber. It ranges in color from stark white to beige. The texture of coconut flour from different brands varies wildly. All the recipes in this book were tested with Let's Do Organic, which is ground medium fine. Bob's Red Mill is ground more finely and will also work in these recipes.

Coconut flour is different to work with than other flours and takes some getting used to. The first cake that I tried, a chiffon recipe with some coconut flour traded in, went straight into the compost. The batter soaked up moisture like a parched sponge, but I soldiered ahead, folding the whipped egg whites into the cement-like batter and baking the cake. The abomination that I pulled from the oven was an inedible brick. The moral of this sad story is that coconut flour is thirsty, thirsty stuff that soaks up liquid like nobody's business. However, when tamed, it adds a delightfully hearty texture to baked goods and perfumes it with its delicate flavor. The blondies on page 206 have a pleasing chew that smacks of macaroons, and when baked into a (successful) chiffon cake and soaked with rum-kissed coconut milk, it makes a dreamily tender tres leches cake of sorts. And it makes a tender, shortbread-like crust for a coconut cream berry tart that also happens to be vegan.

EARTHY

I have a weakness for any and all earthy flavors: black tea, coffee, chocolate, caramel, mushrooms, smoke, molasses, you name it. The flours in this section are some of my very favorites. All boast rich, warm flavors, along with their nuanced textures and colors, and are particularly well suited to baking. Teff flour, with its malty milk chocolate notes, came as a particularly welcome surprise.

BUCKWHEAT FLOUR

Flavor profile: Deep, rich, warm, with notes of spice (cinnamon, allspice), coffee, chocolate, toasted hazelnuts

Consistency: Soft, starchy, delicate, cakey

Brand tested: Bob's Red Mill Buckwheat Flour (Note: Though buckwheat is inherently gluten-free, Bob's buckwheat flour is not processed in their dedicated GF facility. If you or your guests are highly sensitive, you'll want to go with a certified GF buckwheat flour, such as one from Arrowhead Mills.)

Weight per cup: 5 ounces (140 g)

Find it: With other alternative flours and/or the bulk section at health food stores

Store it: Airtight at room temperature in a cool, dry, dark place (such as a kitchen cupboard) for up to 3 months, or refrigerated airtight for up to 1 year

Use it: Where you want assertive flavor and a deep, charcoal hue. Buckwheat's robust flavor plays well with spices (especially cinnamon and cardamom), dark berries, fall fruits (such as figs, apples, pears and quinces), bananas, coffee, brown sugar, maple, winter squash and sweet potatoes, chocolate and nuts. It can also contrast nicely with lighter, brighter flavors such as rhubarb, red berries and stone fruit. Buckwheat flour can turn mushy if overmixed, so take care when working with it in recipes. With its strong flavor and delicate texture, I don't recommend using more than 30–50 percent buckwheat flour in most recipes.

Health benefits: High in protein, iron and other minerals, as well as the amino acid lysine, said to prevent canker sores. In traditional Chinese medicine, said to have warming properties and to aid digestion.

If I had to choose one alternative flour to use for the rest of my life, it would be buckwheat. My first experience with this grain occurred when I was about fifteen and went through a bread-baking phase wherein I went to town rummaging through my mom's flour cabinet and adding in all manner of things. Because of its confusing name, I assumed buckwheat was a variety of wheat, and it wasn't until many years later, when my interest in GF baking began, that I learned how wrong I was. I still remember that first rustic loaf baked with buckwheat and (thankfully) bread flours, which had a wildly earthy flavor unlike any I had ever experienced.

Buckwheat's pretty, pyramidal, greenish gray-brown grains are the seed of an herb plant related to rhubarb and sorrel that's native to northern Europe and Asia, where it has been used since the eighth millennium BCE; in fact, it isn't even a true grain. When toasted, it is referred to as kasha. Buckwheat flour is made from these toasted grains, thus the rich, roasty flavor and deep color flecked with charcoal-hued specks. Known as *blé noir* in French, meaning "black grain," it is commonly used to make savory crepes. In Japan it stars in soba noodles and buckwheat tea, and it's used widely in eastern Europe as both a flour and the cooked grain dish kasha.

Bob's Red Mill makes a finely ground buckwheat flour that doesn't clump and adds a soft, starchy texture to baked goods. In this book, it makes an intensely flavored and super flaky pie dough, adds tenderness to double chocolate cookies, and creates pliant crepes that are easy to wrap around sweetened cheese for blintzes.

TEFF FLOUR
AKA: Brown teff flour

Flavor profile: Warm, sweet, malty, milk chocolate, caramel, butterscotch

Consistency: Fairly soft and starchy with a bit of grainy texture

Brand tested: Bob's Red Mill (Note: This flour is not produced in a dedicated GF facility; if you or your guests are sensitive to trace amounts of gluten, you'll want to source a certified GF variety of teff flour.)

Weight per cup: 4½ ounces (130 g)

Find it: With other alternative flours and/or the bulk section at health food stores

Store it: Airtight at room temperature in a cool, dry, dark place (such as a kitchen cupboard) for up to 3 months, or refrigerated airtight for up to 1 year

Use it: Teff flour's warm, earthy flavor pairs well with chocolate, coffee, apples, pears, figs, spices (especially cinnamon and nutmeg), nuts, bananas, maple, caramel, brown sugar and spirits. Stone fruit such as peaches, plums and cherries contrast nicely with teff.

Health benefits: Very high in iron (nine times more than wheat) and calcium (five times more than other cereal grains), vitamin C (which is rare in grains) and protein (a 2-ounce [56-g] serving of teff has the same amount of protein as an extra-large egg).

The word teff means "lost" in Amharic, named for the tiny grains' ability to disappear when dropped. Teff was almost lost to the world for good when, in the 1970s, Ethiopia's socialist military government forced farmers to switch over to more profitable wheat production. As teff was grown in an isolated region of Ethiopia and hadn't yet made it to other parts of the world, teff might have disappeared forever if it hadn't been for an American aid worker who, having fallen in love with Ethiopian cuisine, brought the grain back to his home in Idaho, which boasted favorable growing conditions for this ancient grain. To the joy of many Ethiopian and Eritrean ex-pats, teff found a new home, and The Teff Company was born, spreading the deliciosity of teff throughout the United States.

(continued)

EARTHY FLOURS FROM TOP: BUCKWHEAT, CHESTNUT, TEFF, MESQUITE

With a rising interest in alternative grains, teff is gaining popularity, even being called The West's Latest Superfood Crush (Vice.com, 2014). The world's smallest grain boasts some of the biggest nutritional benefits, including high levels of protein, iron, calcium and vitamin C. Teff flour is ground from these tiny grains, each the size of a poppy seed and weighing in at 1 gram per 3,000 grains. It is most traditionally used to make injera, a fermented Ethiopian flatbread. Of the many varieties of teff, the two most common are brown and ivory, with brown being the most readily available in the United States. Bob's Red Mill teff flour is ground fairly fine, with a bit of texture still, and doesn't clump. The Teff Company, which I found in bulk at my co-op and can be ordered online, makes brown and ivory teff flours with a powder-fine consistency that bakes up super smooth. Since this brand is harder to find, however, recipes in this book have been formulated to work with Bob's coarser grind. The flour is a warm, medium brown hue and if you stick your nose in the bag and inhale, you'll be rewarded with the scents of malt, milk chocolate, baking bread and earth.

It took me years to give teff flour a try in sweets, linked as it was in my mind to super-savory Ethiopian curries. But once I did, I was hooked. With its warm notes of caramel and malted chocolate milk, teff flour was made for desserts. In this book, it gives oatmeal cookies an extra layer of earthy flavor, blends with roasted bananas and brown sugar in scones, forms craggy biscuits for peach cobbler, bakes into chocolate cherry pots and makes a flaky pie pastry base for hazelnut frangipane and plums.

CHESTNUT FLOUR

AKA: Chestnut flour powder, Italian chestnut flour, farina di castagne (not to be confused with water chestnut flour, which comes from a completely different plant and is not covered in this book)

Flavor profile: Sweet, nutty, sometimes slightly smoky with hints of bitterness

Consistency: Soft, starchy, cakey, tendency to clump

Weight per cup: 3¾ ounces (105 g)

Brands tested: Calleris and Ladd Hill

Find it: In Italian specialty shops or with other alternative flours in health food stores and upscale grocers. It tends to show up in the United States around the fall and winter holidays. If you can't find it locally, it can be ordered online (see Sources, page 260).

Store it: Refrigerated airtight for up to 1 year

Use it: Darker chestnut flour such as Calleris has an earthier flavor that pairs well with stone fruit, figs, apples, pears, other nuts, chocolate, coffee, rum and other brown spirits, brown butter, vanilla and caramel. Its flavor can be assertive on its own, so I recommend using only 50 percent chestnut flour in recipes that call for a high proportion of flour. Lighter flour, such as Ladd Hill, has a milder flavor that is closer to all-purpose flour; it pairs well with nearly any baking ingredients and fruits and can be used in baking up to 100 percent.

Health benefits: Low in fat and rich in vitamins (especially vitamin C, E and B-complex), minerals (iron, calcium, magnesium, manganese, phosphorus, zinc and potassium) and dietary fiber. Chestnut flour also contains high-quality protein with essential amino acids.

Chestnut flour is a rare find in the United States these days, but it was a staple food throughout both Europe and North America since ancient times, developing simultaneously on both continents. It featured in stews and preserves, and was often ground into a starchy flour and baked into bread. Chestnuts were particularly necessary in regions where other starchy foods (such as wheat and potatoes) wouldn't grow, such as in the mountainous regions of southern Europe. Chestnut flour fell out of favor due to a chestnut blight in the early 1900s in the United States, while Europeans grew to loathe it during wartimes, where it gained a reputation as peasant food. (This is all rather hilarious to any bakers who have shelled out for chestnut flour today; it's the most costly flour used in this book!)

Thankfully, modern cooks and bakers are rediscovering the positive qualities of chestnut flour, of which there are many. Chestnut flour is made by grinding either raw or roasted, dried chestnuts into a powder; most of the world's chestnut flour is produced in Italy (hence the high price tag and spotty availability in North America), but it's becoming more widely cultivated in the United States. The soft, starchy flour is low in fat, sweet in flavor and bakes up smooth and tender. With a similar starch content to wheat flour but without the gluten, it makes an excellent addition to all manner of baked goods. The Italian brand Calleris is the one I've found most commonly in Northern California at Italian markets as well as health food stores and specialty grocers, and I've used it in the recipes in this book. It has a deep, tan color and slightly smoky flavor that can be delicious in small quantities but overpowering if used too freely. Ladd Hill is a harder-to-find brand made in Oregon's Willamette Valley from organic, unroasted chestnuts. This bone-white flour has a sweet, mild flavor without a trace of smoke or bitterness and can be used mostly interchangeably with the roasted flour.

(continued)

Chestnut flour is fairly perishable, so do be sure to store it in the refrigerator. It tends to clump, so be sure to strain or sift when called for. It adds a warm, intriguing flavor and cakelike texture to baked goods, be it chocolate chip cookies laced with brown butter and milk chocolate, financiers topped with plums, apple tart covered in salty caramel or fig-stuffed scones.

MESQUITE FLOUR

AKA: Mesquite powder, raw mesquite powder

Flavor profile: Sweet, wild, warm, baked earth, cinnamon, vanilla, toasted nuts, graham crackers

Consistency: Powdery and fine, cakey, delicate, tends to clump

Weight per cup: 4¼ ounces (120 g)

Brand tested: Zócalo Gourmet Mesquite Algarroba Organic Flour

Find it: With other GF flours and/or the raw foods section at health food stores and upscale grocers

Store it: Airtight at room temperature in a cool, dry, dark place (such as a kitchen cupboard) for up to 3 months, or refrigerated airtight for up to 1 year

Use it: Pairs well with ginger, cinnamon, apples, bananas, sweet potato, winter squash, caramel, chocolate, nuts (especially walnuts and pecans), berries, stone fruit, maple, brown sugar. Because of its strong flavor, you won't want to use more than 50 percent mesquite flour in flour-heavy recipes. Mesquite can also be used more as a spice or sweetener in smaller quantities.

Health benefits: Despite its sweet flavor, mesquite flour has a low glycemic index and high protein (13 percent) and fiber content (25 percent). It contains only 3 percent fat. It is rich in calcium, magnesium and lysine, an amino acid said to prevent canker sores. It has proven effective in controlling diabetes as the soluble fiber from the seeds and pods forms a gel that slows nutrient absorption by three to four times after ingesting (4–6 hours rather than 1–2 hours). This slower digestion prevents the blood sugar spikes that result from eating other carbohydrates.

Mesquite flour always reminds me of Red Rock Canyon in Southern California in color and aroma: warm, baked earth with notes of cinnamon and a dusty reddish beige hue. I've heard it described as tasting like warm gingerbread or freshly baked bread.

Drought-tolerant mesquite trees are native to the southern United States and grow in arid regions such as Arizona and Mexico. The algarrobo variety grows in forests along the coast of northern Peru, where trees can reach upward of 100 feet tall. Mesquite's edible seedpods look a little like shelling beans. The tree's reddish brown wood was used to build Spanish ships; now, the trees are the most expensive to harvest in the United States and are used only in high-end furniture. The wood chips, which are mesquite's claim to fame, are sold for smoking and grilling foods, a practice used by Native Americans for ages, but only embraced by Western chefs since the 1980s. Native desert dwellers subsisted largely on mesquite flour, using stones to grind the seeds and pods by hand and often mixing this meal with corn. Today, the whole pods are dried and ground into mesquite flour, sometimes called raw mesquite powder. Despite its low glycemic index, this flour is naturally quite sweet and is sometimes used as a replacement for sugar. The pods can be boiled to make mesquite syrup, which can be ordered online.

Mesquite flour is embraced today for its beguiling flavor and health benefits, thanks in part to Heidi Swanson, who published a mesquite chocolate chip cookie recipe in her book *Super Natural Cooking* in 2007. This was my first experience with the flour, which I found at my co-op, and it baked up into the most flavorful chocolate chip cookies I'd ever tasted. Other common recipes include mesquite pancakes, quick breads, cornbread and even flan. Mesquite flour's warm flavor pairs especially well with earth and spice. It has a powder-fine texture that needs sifting to oust clumps, and it bakes up soft and smooth. Its high sugar content makes it prone to burning, so take care when baking with mesquite to not overcook. In this book, it complements little chocolate cakes topped with whipped crème fraîche and berries, forms a shortbread-like crust for banana cream tart and sweet potato cheesecake bites and adds oomph to gingersnaps and chewy ginger cookies.

GRASSY

These flours are characterized by a vegetal flavor, sometimes referred to as "green" or "grassy," which can range from freshly mowed lawn to straw or hay.

AMARANTH FLOUR

Flavor profile: Assertive, vegetal, earthy and slightly herbaceous

Consistency: Fairly fine and starchy with some sandy texture; similar to millet

Weight per cup: 4½ ounces (130 g)

Brand tested: Bob's Red Mill

Find it: With other alternative flours at health food stores and upscale grocers, or order online

Store it: Airtight at room temperature in a cool, dry, dark place (such as a kitchen cupboard) for up to 3 months, or refrigerated airtight for up to 1 year

Use it: I like blending amaranth with milder flours, such as sweet rice and oat, as well as other strong flavors and spices to temper its assertive taste and grainy texture. I don't recommend using more than 30 percent amaranth in a recipe because of its strong flavor and sandy texture. It pairs nicely with light, bright fruits and spices such as cinnamon, ginger, stone fruit, rhubarb, citrus and berries, as well as vegetables such as carrots, zucchini and winter squash.

Health benefits: Amaranth has 30 percent more protein than rice or sorghum; it is rich in calcium, iron and the amino acid lysine. Related to quinoa, amaranth is often hailed as a superfood.

Amaranth may be a nutritional powerhouse, but the flavor and texture can be an acquired taste. The tiny seeds can develop a viscous texture when steamed, making a better porridge than a substitute for fluffy rice or quinoa. Amaranth is a boutique ingredient today, but this was not the case for the ancient Aztecs, who derived 80 percent of their sustenance from the weedlike plant, even using the seeds bound with honey to build statues to their gods, which they used in religious rites (sometimes involving human sacrifice). Amaranth grows quickly and can bear seedpods weighing up to 2 pounds (900 g) and harboring half a million seeds. The pretty plants are often grown as ornamentals, and the burgundy leaves can be cooked like a heartier variety of spinach, to which it is related. Amaranth seed is used culinarily in South and Central America, where it is popped, mixed with honey and formed into cakes or added to a form of hot chocolate.

I'm still learning to love amaranth, whose flour has a fine texture but intense flavor. One tester described its taste as "musty," and another wrote that while she and her husband loved the flavor, her kids "noticed" the "earthy" taste of the amaranth. It is not a grain for the faint of heart. Rich dairy can help smooth amaranth's rough edges and bring out its buttery quality. When tamed by other bold ingredients, amaranth can add an intriguing depth of flavor to baked goods, offsetting sweetness with its bitter undertones. I like amaranth in moderation, baked into peachy scones kissed with cinnamon sugar and in gingered biscuits atop strawberry rhubarb cobbler. If you're amaranth-curious, try swapping it in for millet in any of the recipes in this book. Just don't try it with the ancient Aztec secret ingredient—trust me on this one.

CORN

AKA: Maize, polenta (yellow corn grits), cornmeal, corn flour

Flavor profile: Nutty, warm, vegetal, sunny, buttery, bitter undertones

Consistency: Polenta is the most coarsely ground of the corn products and needs a long cooking time to soften its hard grains. Cornmeal is medium ground and adds nubby texture to cornbread and the like. Corn flour is finely ground and tends to clump; it makes for delicate, tender baked goods that can be brittle if not combined with other stickier flours.

Weight per cup: Polenta, 5.65 ounces (160 g); cornmeal, 5.65 ounces (160 g); corn flour, 4¼ ounces (120 g)

Brands tested: Bob's Red Mill Corn Grits Polenta, Arrowhead Mills Organic Gluten-Free Cornmeal, Bob's Red Mill Organic Corn Flour

Find it: Cornmeal and corn flour can be found with other alternative flours at health food stores, and sometimes in bulk. Polenta or corn grits are sometimes sold with other hot cereals if not with GF flours.

Store it: Airtight at room temperature in a cool, dry, dark place (such as a kitchen cupboard) for up to 3 months, or refrigerated airtight for up to 1 year

Use it: With light, bright flavors: honey, rhubarb, berries, stone fruit, citrus, vanilla, dairy. Corn has a fairly brittle texture, so don't use more than 25 percent cornmeal or polenta, or 50 percent corn flour, in most baking recipes.

Health benefits: High in protein, fiber, iron and phosphorous

Edible corn comes in many forms, including coarse polenta or grits, cornmeal of various grinds and, the most finely ground, corn flour (not to be confused with cornstarch, which is referred to as corn flour in the UK and Australia). Corn or maize is thought to have been cultivated by the ancient Olmecs and Mayans, spreading to other parts of the Americas since 2500 BCE. European explorers brought it back home in the 1500s and 1600s, and it gained popularity around the globe for its ability to grow in diverse climates. Many varieties of corn are used today in myriad applications, edible and not, including starch, oil, animal feed, fuel and even compostable substitutes for plastic. In the kitchen, we pop the kernels into salty snacks, bake the meal into cornbread and use the syrup to sweeten baked goods. Latin cultures make masa harina by soaking the hominy variety of corn in limewater and grinding it into a fine meal for tamales and tortillas.

(continued)

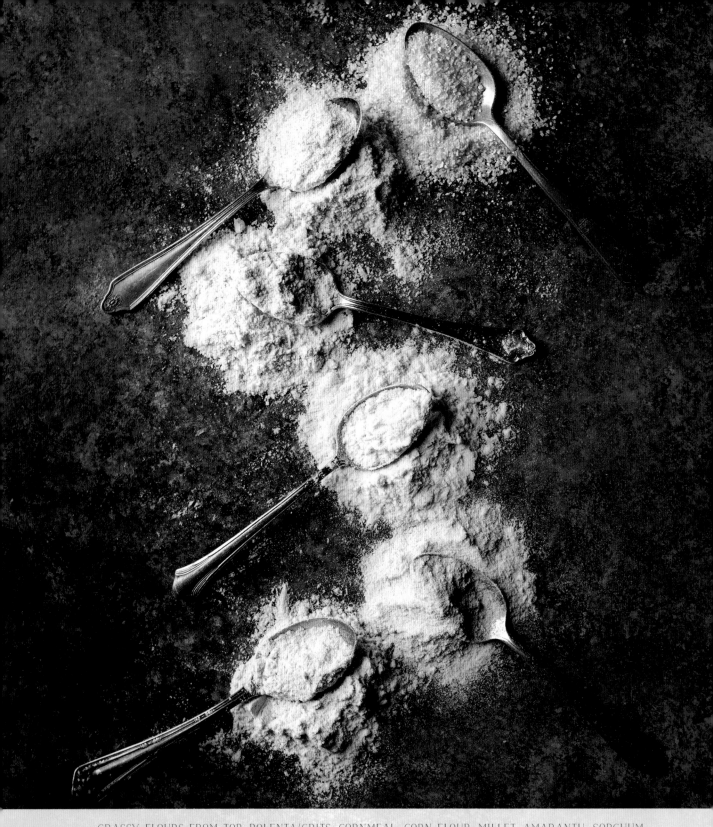

GRASSY FLOURS FROM TOP: POLENTA/GRITS, CORNMEAL, CORN FLOUR, MILLET, AMARANTH, SORGHUM

Polenta is a staple of northern Italy, where it gets a long, slow cook, becoming a savory porridge of sorts. And in the American South, hominy grits get a similar treatment. But corn isn't all sunshine and flours: many crops have been genetically modified and treated with pesticides, so do take care to buy corn products from small brands, organically grown if possible.

Corn is a sturdy grain that likes to soak up moisture, and its sunny taste is easy to love and complements a wide variety of foods and flavors. Polenta or corn grits, when baked long and slow with plenty of milk and honey, makes a sublime porridge to top with summer berries. Stone-ground cornmeal makes a nubby cake to sop up juices from blood oranges and a skillet cornbread studded with millet seed and cherries. Finely ground corn flour makes a fluffy topping for berry plum cobbler, and it bakes into pillowy muffins moistened by juicy blueberries.

MILLET FLOUR

Flavor profile: Warm, buttery, vegetal, nutty, some bitter notes

Consistency: Fairly fine and starchy with a bit of sandy texture, slightly clumpy

Brand tested: Bob's Red Mill GF Millet Flour

Weight per cup: 4½ ounces (130 g)

Find it: With other alternative flours and/or in the bulk section of health food stores and upscale grocers

Store it: Airtight at room temperature in a cool, dry, dark place (such as a kitchen cupboard) for up to 2 months, or refrigerated airtight for up to 1 year

Use it: Millet is one of my top three used flours for its mild flavor and starchy, finely milled texture. In conjunction with sweet rice and oat flour, it makes a neutral flour that mimics all-purpose but with more texture, flavor and nutritional value. Millet flour tastes a bit like cornmeal or corn flour and pairs well with similar flavors, such as honey, berries, stone fruit, citrus, vanilla and dairy. It can have some bitter undertones, however, which is why I recommend using no more than 30 percent in any given recipe.

Health benefits: High in protein, fiber and the minerals iron, phosphorous, manganese, magnesium and copper. Do beware of eating too much millet if you suffer from the condition hypothyroidism, which can be exacerbated by consuming large amounts of the grain.

Millet seed has been a food staple for humans for at least the last 10,000 years, particularly in India and parts of Africa, where it is thought to have evolved. Millet actually refers to several different varieties of a cereal grass, the most common in North America being the proso variety, while pearl millet is the most common variety cultivated worldwide. Primarily grown in the United States for use as animal feed or birdseed, millet has gained in popularity as an alternative grain in its own right. The seeds are butter yellow in color. They cook up light and fluffy, not unlike couscous, and make a good stand-in for steamed rice. The flour is well loved in gluten-free baking for its soft, starchy consistency, particularly in breads.

Millet flour does have notes of bitterness, however, which is why I recommend blending it with other, milder flours, particularly sweet rice and oat. Toasted millet seed takes center stage in Millet Skillet Cornbread with Cherries and Honey (page 29), and the flour features in countless recipes throughout this book, including buttery scones and biscuits, light cakes and flaky pie pastry.

SORGHUM FLOUR
AKA: Milo flour, sweet white sorghum flour

Flavor profile: Earthy, nutty, vegetal, mild, sweet

Consistency: Fairly fine with a bit of gritty/sandy texture

Weight per cup: 4¼ ounces (120 g)

Brand tested: Bob's Red Mill Sweet White Sorghum Flour

Find it: With other alternative flours and/or in the bulk section of health food stores and upscale grocers

Store it: Airtight at room temperature in a cool, dry, dark place (such as a kitchen cupboard) for up to 3 months, or refrigerated airtight for up to 1 year

Use it: Where you don't mind a bit of texture and whole-grain flavor in conjunction with softer, milder flours such as sweet rice and oat; don't use more than 30–50 percent in most recipes. Pairs well with stone fruit, berries, apples, pears, chocolate, spices (especially cinnamon), honey, dairy and nuts

Health benefits: High in antioxidants (more per serving than blueberries and pomegranate) as well as fiber, protein, unsaturated fat and the minerals phosphorus, calcium, potassium and iron

(continued)

Sorghum is an ancient, drought-resistant grain that hails from southern Egypt and remains a staple throughout Africa. It clocks in as the fifth most important grain worldwide. Though the United States is the biggest producer, many Americans are not familiar with this small, gluten-free grain. Sorghum can be found in many gluten-free flour blends. It reminds me very much of brown rice flour: nutty, grassy, with some bitter whole-grain notes and a slightly coarse texture. It is naturally sweet and was often boiled into a syrup popular in the southern United States before the rise of corn syrup.

Bob's Red Mill makes sorghum flour that is ground fairly fine with a bit of sandy texture. I find it slightly troublesome to work with; it doesn't absorb moisture well and it has a distinct flavor that isn't always welcome. I tested it in several cake and biscuit recipes that baked up brittle and with a cornbread-like texture that staled quickly, before returning to softer millet and oat flours. Azure Farm, which I found in bulk at my co-op, makes a powder-fine sorghum flour that, when combined 50:50 with sweet rice, makes an all-purpose-like blend. Since this brand is less widely available, all recipes in this book have been formulated to work with Bob's coarser grind. It does add a warm, cornlike flavor and custardy texture to oven pancakes, and its grassy flavor blends beautifully with Chocolate Zucchini Cake and Matcha Cream Cheese Frosting (page 60).

STARCHES

Starches can be a necessary addition to whole-grain baking to absorb moisture, create structure and add stickiness to baked goods. These are the two I keep in my pantry.

TAPIOCA FLOUR/STARCH

Powdered tapioca is sometimes labeled flour or starch, but it is all the same. Made from the root of the cassava plant, tapioca is a powerful binder and thickener and can add much-needed chew and stickiness to alternative baking. It's traditionally used to make the Brazilian cheese bread pao de queijo or rolled into balls for Japanese boba tea and tapioca pudding. It does have an assertive flavor in large quantities, which is why I prefer the softer flavor of cornstarch for thickening fruit. However, tapioca adds essential chewiness in chestnut chocolate chip cookies, helps crisp topping clump together and makes pie dough extensible and stretchy, easier to roll out and handle.

CORNSTARCH (CALLED CORN FLOUR IN THE UK AND AUSTRALIA)

Just to confuse things, the starchy powder known as cornstarch in the United States and Canada is called corn flour in the UK and several other countries, while corn flour in this book refers to finely ground cornmeal, which is yellow in color and contains the whole grain. Cornstarch is made solely from the endosperm or starchy component of the corn kernel through a process called wet milling, which removes the outer parts of the kernel. The resulting slurry is washed of protein, then dried in centrifuges to remove moisture before being ground and packaged. The starch has no nutritional value, but small amounts can add big improvements to alternative baking. Cornstarch promotes browning and crisping, and can help absorb excess moisture. In my pie dough, it promotes flaking and helps the dough stand up to moisture. I use it to thicken fruit in pies and rustic fruit desserts, where it softens into a silky texture and leaves behind a more neutral flavor than tapioca. Do be sure to source organic cornstarch, which is GMO free.

FLOURS NOT COVERED IN THIS BOOK

These ingredients commonly used in alternative baking just don't float my boat. Here's why.

REGULAR WHITE AND BROWN RICE FLOURS

These two are the most widely used flours in GF baking. I've found that using sweet white rice flour rather than regular rice flour gives baked goods better texture, and allows me to use less of it, and fewer other starches or gums, than regular white rice flour. Brown rice flour tends to keep a gritty texture in baked goods that I dislike. There is superfine brown rice flour available, but I have yet to see it carried at any of my local grocers. Furthermore, rice has been found to contain arsenic and should not be consumed in large quantities (brown rice flour has higher levels of arsenic, as the arsenic likes to hang out on the outside of the whole grain, which is buffed away to make white rice, removing much of the arsenic). These findings are part of what led me to explore other alternative grains; I feared we were getting into the same situation with rice flour as we did with wheat flour, relying on it too much and edging closer to a mono diet. For all of these reasons, I prefer to use a small amount of sweet rice in conjunction with millet and oat as my neutral flours.

QUINOA FLOUR

Quinoa has a strong, fairly bitter flavor thanks to saponins that coat and protect the grain. I often rinse and cook the grain whole for savory sides and salads, but I haven't found the flour to work well in sweets, preferring milder millet or complex-tasting amaranth. That said, quinoa flour's texture is similar to both, so feel free to trade it in for either if you're quinoa-curious.

BEAN AND LEGUME FLOURS (SUCH AS CHICKPEA)

Chickpea flour works beautifully in savory baked goods due to its soft texture and high protein content, but its assertive bean flavor tends to take over when used in sweets. Chickpea flour is classically used in socca, a delicious flatbread from the south of France.

POTATO FLOUR AND STARCH

These two can add softness and moisture to baked goods. However, I've found that they both cause baked goods to go stale more quickly due to being hygroscopic, meaning that they grab water molecules from out of the air and hold on. You'll find them both in many GF flour blends and products, but I prefer to do without them in my own kitchen.

GUAR AND XANTHAN GUMS

These gums are often used to replace the gluten in gluten-free baked goods. However, some people can't tolerate these, they can be hard to source and I've found that they are usually not necessary anyway. When some extra sticky power is needed in a recipe beyond what sweet rice, tapioca, almond flour or egg can offer, I use ground chia seed, which has a similar effect as these gums but also adds a pleasant nutty flavor and is full of good-for-you fiber and nutrients to boot.

OTHERS

There are new-to-me alternative flours popping up every day that I have not yet experimented with, including wild rice flour, kaniwa, benne seed, purple corn, tiger nut, plantain, banana, coffee, water chestnut and sweet potato, among others.

OTHER
INGREDIENTS

I generally try to use organic, seasonal and locally grown ingredients whenever possible—they taste better, are healthier for our bodies and benefit our communities and the planet as a whole. Besides, if you're going to go to the trouble of shopping for groceries, making a recipe and cleaning up, you might as well stack the deck in your favor and start with the most flavorful ingredients possible. And, to quote an old hair commercial: You're worth it. Here's a little bit about the ingredients that went into developing these recipes; starting with similar products when possible will help you achieve the best results.

SEASONAL FRUITS AND VEGETABLES

Produce tastes best when it's grown close by, picked when ripe and eaten soon thereafter. Farmers' markets, CSAs, co-ops and health food stores tend to provide the best produce. When picking out fruit for recipes, use your nose as well as your eyes; you can often tell a ripe pear or tasty peach by its scent, even when the fruit feels hard when you give it a gentle squeeze. Ask for samples and recommendations when you can. As a bonus, fruit at the peak of its season usually costs less than flavorless, out-of-season fruit grown halfway across the world.

Fruits and vegetables can vary in size a lot, so I recommend using the weight or volume measurements that I've included whenever possible for the best results in recipes. If you don't have a scale at home, you can weigh produce when you shop and then you won't have to guess.

What's in season when will vary regionally as well as year to year depending on weather patterns. Here are some general guidelines for when the produce used in this book are in season in California and similar regions.

SPRING

Rhubarb, strawberries, cherries, apricots, early peaches, blueberries

SUMMER

Peaches, nectarines, plums, raspberries, blackberries (and berry hybrids such as tayberries and loganberries), marionberries, olallieberries, corn, zucchini, first crop of figs

FALL

Figs, huckleberries, pears, apples, quinces, cranberries, pomegranates, persimmons, winter squash, sweet potatoes

WINTER

Lemons, oranges, tangerines, grapefruit, blood oranges, kumquats, foods that keep such as nuts, dried fruit

DAIRY

Nasty stuff like pesticides tend to gather in the fat portion of dairy, which is why I feel that it's particularly important to use organic dairy. Also, I like cows, and I prefer to use dairy made from mama cows who are treated kindly, which is more likely to occur in smaller dairies. Additionally, dairy from cows that have grazed on grass tends to be more flavorful and higher in nutrients, and dairy that is fresh and hasn't been ultra-pasteurized tastes sweeter and cleaner.

I don't have much experience with dairy substitutes, but much information can be found online if you need to make trades in these recipes. Look for ingredients that have similar consistencies and fat and water contents for the best results. For example, coconut oil contains nearly 100 percent fat to butter's 80 to 85 percent and will usually not make a good 1:1 substitute. To develop a coconut oil–based tart crust (page 119), I had to add water and tweak the other ingredients to make it work. I hope you'll feel free to play around based on your own dietary needs and preferences (and share your results with me at BojonGourmet.com and AlternativeBaker.com!). Don't be discouraged if it takes a few tries to get it right.

CHEESES

Whole-milk ricotta cheese tastes like heaven, and is nothing like cheap, part-skim supermarket ricotta. Spring for the good stuff for these recipes. I use Bellwether Farm's basket-dipped ricotta when I make the ricotta biscuits and shortcakes in this book (and much of it also goes directly into my mouth).

The farmer cheese used in blintzes should have the texture of a firm ricotta with more bite and is sometimes labeled fromage blanc (which is used in the Fromage Blanc Tartlets with Honeyed Kumquats, page 135)—the two are interchangeable.

I'm a fan of artisan, **crumbly cream cheese** for eating, which is free from gums and stabilizers and has a goat cheese–like texture. But when it comes to cheesecakes and cream cheese frostings, the silky-smooth foil-wrapped sort is your best bet. I don't recommend using whipped cream cheese, as it may give you different results.

Goat cheese in this book is usually the fresh, crumbly variety, sometimes called chèvre. It makes tasty cheesecake bites studded with berries. This will work in the fig bites (page 104) as well, but a funky, aged goat cheese will taste extra complex and delicious there.

Mascarpone is a creamy Italian cheese sold in tubs, with a consistency similar to sour cream but with a sweet flavor. I have yet to find an adequate substitute for this delicious stuff that's classically used in tiramisù and features in this book whipped with cream and spread into a couple of cakes.

I use two kinds of **yogurt** in baking: plain whole-milk yogurt and plain, whole-milk Greek yogurt, which is strained of some liquid and has a thicker texture and higher fat content. Both make delicious accompaniments to crisps, cobblers and breakfast treats when you want something creamy but less sweet.

(continued)

Different types of **cream** contain different levels of fat; all recipes in this book were tested with organic heavy whipping cream (also called heavy cream) with a fat content of about 40 percent, but regular whipping cream, with a fat content of about 35 percent, will work, too. Just don't go for something labeled simply "cream," which could have a fat content as low as 18 percent and could give different results in recipes, particularly whipped cream and ice cream. For the record, "double cream" in the UK has an even higher fat content of 48 percent.

Butter in this book is always European-style unsalted butter, which contains 85 percent butterfat. Regular butters in the United States have a fat content closer to 80 percent, with a higher water content. Pie and tart doughs, scones, biscuits, butter-based cakes and cookies will all taste richer and more flavorful when made with excellent butter: their textures tend to be more tender and flaky and they won't burn as easily. I've found European-style butter to be superior particularly when browning butter. All recipes in this book were developed with Straus brand butter; other brands with a similar fat content are Plugrá, Kerrygold and Organic Valley European-Style Butter. That said, most of these recipes should work fine with regular butter in a pinch. Ghee is butter that has been clarified and cooked until it takes on a warm, toasty flavor. With a high smoke point, it's your friend for frying blintzes (page 34).

Crème fraîche and sour cream are usually interchangeable in recipes. Crème fraîche has a milder flavor and softer texture, and is easy to make at home with just cream and buttermilk (or a spoonful of Crème Fraîche, see page 223).

Buttermilk as we know it today is different from old-school buttermilk, which was literally the liquid left over after churning butter. Buttermilk in Northern California is all low-fat, cultured and fairly thick in texture, like watered-down yogurt. When measuring buttermilk, it's important to give it a good shake first, as the solids tend to settle to the bottom of the container. Shaking the buttermilk also aerates it a bit. If you don't have access to buttermilk, plain, unsweetened kefir, which is a sort of liquid, yogurtlike substance, usually makes a good substitute. You can also water down plain, whole-milk yogurt. Another common buttermilk substitution is to mix a tablespoon (15 ml) of lemon juice into a scant cup (230 ml) of milk, stir and let sit until thickened, 5 minutes. Do note that the watered-down yogurt and thickened milk won't be aerated the way shaken buttermilk or kefir are, so you'll want to use a little less than is called for.

Eggs in my recipes are always "large" (2 ounces [57 g] by weight in the shell). "Pastured" eggs are currently the gold standard of eggs (second only to eggs from your or a neighbor's own chickens). These chickens are allowed to run around outside, beaks intact, pecking at bugs and eating lots of yummy things. These eggs have firm whites and bright orange yolks, and vastly more nutrients than conventional eggs (two to three times more vitamin A, two times more omega-3 fatty acids, three times

more vitamin E, four to six times as much vitamin D and seven times more beta-carotene). They even have less cholesterol (by one-third) and saturated fat (by one-fourth) than conventional eggs. Organic, free-range eggs are the next grade down. These chickens are allowed some access to the outdoors and their feed is free of pesticides. All recipes in this book were tested with either pastured or organic eggs. Egg whites from both types will whip up better for use in chiffon cakes, and the yolks will add more color and flavor to custards and ice creams. I tend to stay away from commercial eggs because the way the chickens are treated makes me sad, as do their pale yolks and watery whites.

SWEETENERS

Sweeteners are part of the panoply of flavors we bakers get to play with. At home and on my blog I revel in all of them: unrefined muscovado sugar, buckwheat honey, coconut nectar, bourbon smoked sugar … To make the recipes in this book more accessible, I stuck with only a handful of easier-to-find sweeteners.

Organic granulated cane sugar is my go-to sweetener. Wholesome Sweeteners and Florida Crystals are two commonly found brands. This sugar has crystals that are slightly larger and more irregular than conventional granulated sugar and an off-white color with a hint of caramel flavor and tiny amounts of trace minerals. (This sugar is also vegan, whereas conventional granulated cane sugar gets a final whitening process involving animal bones—creepy.) Its mild flavor allows other ingredients to star, and its delicate texture melts into baked goods. If you substitute regular granulated sugar, be sure to substitute by weight or take down the sugar by 1 tablespoon for every ½ cup called for; a cup of organic granulated cane sugar weighs 7 ounces (200 g) whereas the same amount of regular granulated sugar weighs 8 ounces (225 g).

Organic light and dark brown sugars are also slightly different from their conventional counterparts. All kinds of brown sugars have been refined to the point of being granulated, then mixed with varying amounts of molasses to add back its rich, earthy taste and some trace minerals. If you compare organic and conventional brown sugars side by side, you'll see that the organic sugar (even light brown) is many shades darker than even conventional dark brown sugar. The sugar crystals are coarser, and the sugar is moister. For this reason, I specify organic in recipes. Substituting conventional brown sugar will result in slightly sweeter, drier baked goods with less depth of flavor. If that's all you've got, your best bet is to substitute by weight, or reduce the brown sugar by 1 tablespoon for every ½ cup called for. That said, organic light and dark brown sugars can be used interchangeably; I've specified where I have a flavor preference, though. Whatever you use, be sure to pack the sugar into the cup for the correct measure; when you turn the packed cup out into the mixing bowl, it should crack apart just a bit, signifying a properly packed cup.

If you want even more oomph in your sugar, trade out the brown sugars in any recipe for light or dark muscovado sugar (sometimes marketed as natural dark brown molasses sugar, Barbados sugar or unrefined cane sugar). Unlike brown sugar, these sugars haven't had the molasses removed in the first place, and they have a richer flavor and are usually less refined (though there is no standard process for making muscovado sugar). Dark muscovado is a deep, chocolate brown in color and has the highest molasses content of the brown sugars. Light muscovado is closer in color to light brown sugar and can stand in for it in any recipe. India Tree and Billingtons are two commonly available brands

Powdered sugar (AKA confectioners' sugar, or in the UK, icing sugar) is a combination of pulverized granulated sugar mixed with cornstarch to prevent clumping. Recipes in this book were tested using organic powdered sugar from Wholesome Sweeteners, which comes from the slightly less refined organic granulated cane sugar (above) and has an off-white hue when moistened. It's an essential ingredient in frostings and glazes, where it dissolves easily and adds starch at the same time. Sifting powdered sugar over a cake or pastry can give it a pretty, sweet finish.

For finishing baked goods, I often add a sprinkle of **coarse sugar** (either demerara or turbinado, AKA Sugar in the Raw). These sugars have large, crunchy crystals that are semi-refined and retain a bit of caramel flavor. They make scones and muffin tops look pretty. But if you don't have any on hand, organic granulated cane sugar works just fine.

Maple is perhaps my favorite sweetener. A nutritionist friend considers it the healthiest of the lot, insisting that it thwarts blood-sugar spikes and contains healthy trace minerals. I like its rich flavor (particularly in grade B syrup, which is darker and extra-delicious) that pairs well with other warm flavors, particularly summer and fall fruits, earthy grains and flours, chocolate, nuts and spirits. Maple syrup is about as sweet as sugar by volume, but it contains much more liquid. For this reason, substituting maple syrup for sugar in recipes is not advised without some research, trial and error. If you want to trade sugar out for maple in a recipe, maple sugar is a better bet. It isn't cheap, but it has had the liquid removed and will give much better results, so think of the extra cost as money saved on potentially failed recipe tests. Maple sugar has a condensed maple flavor and if it weren't so darn expensive, I'd use it instead of organic granulated cane sugar in many recipes. It can sometimes be substituted 1:1 by volume in recipes, though some experimentation will still be required.

Honey, the sticky, golden nectar produced by bees, is about 33 percent sweeter than sugar by volume. It has intoxicating floral notes reminiscent of ripe apricots and citrus and, depending on what sort of flowers the bees have access to, can contain flavors ranging from buckwheat to orange blossom to lavender. Honey's complexity makes it excellent for finishing sweet dishes, the way freshly ground pepper lends flavor to a savory dish, and it adds a beautiful gloss and sheen to tarts, trifles and cakes. Its wild flavors are best preserved in raw

honey added as a finish, but I occasionally bake it into cornbread or upside-down cakes, or stir it into candied kumquats, to give them a little more oomph and natural sweetness. Buying honey in bulk from your local co-op can be the least expensive option, and eating very local honey is said to help prevent seasonal allergies.

I use **corn syrup** (an organic variety from Wholesome Sweeteners) in only one application, and that is when making caramel. This invert sugar helps prevent the crystallization that can especially plague caramel made from coarser organic granulated cane sugar. Honey has a similar effect and can be used interchangeably there.

SALT, SPICE AND ALL THINGS NICE

Salt may be the smallest volumetric ingredient used in any given recipe, but it has a big effect on the outcome. Most sweets made without salt taste flat, regardless of other flavors. Fine sea salt is my salt of choice for baking; it is pure white with crystals similar in size to organic granulated cane sugar, and I get it in bulk at my co-op. Kosher salt has larger, less regular crystals; if you substitute this, you'll want to add a little extra than is called for. Conversely, table salt has finer crystals, and you'll want to use a little less of this. I don't recommend using iodized table salt, as it can have a harsh flavor. Unrefined salts such as pink salt can have intense oceanic flavor and I also don't recommend them for baking.

For finishing both sweet and savory dishes, I love **Maldon salt** for its crunchy, pyramidal crystals and clean flavor. A sprinkle is the perfect addition to salty caramel or to chocolate cookies. Maldon is made in Essex, England, but Jacobsen Salt Co., in Portland, Oregon, makes a similarly shaped flake salt.

Cinnamon comes in several different varieties. Ceylon (*Cinnamomum verum*) is considered "true" cinnamon and has a subtler, floral flavor. I usually prefer using regular "cassia" cinnamon (*Cinnamomum burmannii*), the type most widely sold in the United States, in baking, however, as it has that classic cinnamon flavor that carries through better in baked goods such as apple pie and cinnamon swirl biscuits.

I use several different forms of **ginger** in this book: fresh ginger root, ground/powdered ginger and candied or crystallized ginger, which are chunks of ginger that have been blanched and preserved in sugar.

If you've ever tried freshly grated **nutmeg,** you'll know how different it tastes from the pre-ground stuff. Fresh nutmeg has a peppery, floral, spicy flavor; these nuances get lost in pre-ground nutmeg. So buy whole nutmegs and grate them with a microplane-type grater for best results. To measure, grate it onto a small piece of paper, then use the paper to slide the nutmeg into a measuring spoon and pack lightly.

(continued)

Other spices gracing these pages are **cardamom, cloves and allspice.** When stored airtight in (preferably) glass jars, these hold their flavors well pre-ground; just make sure they're no older than 6 months.

Vanilla beans make appearances in many of my recipes. Don't buy the über-pricey beans in the supermarket; order them in bulk online (see Sources, page 260). I rinse and dry used beans and stick them in a mason jar covered with alcohol to make my own vanilla extract and get the most bang for my buck. Vanilla extract can be substituted at about 1 teaspoon per vanilla bean. And it goes without saying, but only use real vanilla extract, not the fake stuff. I haven't worked with vanilla paste or ground vanilla yet, but they are other options for getting your vanilla on in recipes.

LEAVENERS

Baking soda (called bicarbonate of soda in the UK) and **baking powder** (currently marketed as double-acting) are the two leavening agents used throughout this book. My teacher in pastry school explained that soda promotes spreading (such as in drop cookies) while powder provides lift (in things like scones and biscuits). Baking soda reacts with acidic ingredients (such as cultured dairy, citrus and even sugar) to produce carbon dioxide, which aerates batters and doughs. It is used in smaller quantities than baking powder and can leave an aftertaste if not properly neutralized by acidity in recipes. It also increases browning in cakes and muffins. In gluten-free baking, I've found that baking soda can improve the texture in cakes due, I think, to changing the pH. In short, don't leave out the soda when it's called for, as even a small amount can have a big effect on baked goods. Baking powder is a mixture of baking soda, cream of tartar and sometimes cornstarch, and it reacts not only with acidity but also with heat to create lift (hence the "double-acting" bit). Some recipes call for one or the other, while others need both, so take care to use the right leavening for the job. Do be sure to source gluten-free, aluminum-free baking powder, and see that your leaveners are not more than 3 months old; their lifting powers could be compromised and result in dense, gummy baked goods.

Cream of tartar is another, lesser-used leavener. In this book, it is used as an acid in the whipped egg whites for chiffon cake, which helps create a stable mixture that makes the cake light and pillowy.

CHOCOLATE

Chocolate comes from the fruit of the theobroma cacao tree (*theobroma* meaning "food of the gods"). The seeds undergo a lengthy process to become what we know as chocolate, as well as cocoa powder and cacao nibs, all used extensively in this book. Here's how to tell them apart.

Cacao nibs are the least processed form of chocolate: the cacao bean is simply roasted, slipped from its husk and broken into small pieces. They taste a little like coffee beans, earthy and bitter (except more chocolaty, of course). They work beautifully wherever you want a little crunch, such as the no-bake oat bars (page 41) or atop little chocolate cakes dolloped with berries and crème fraîche (page 56).

Cocoa powder comes in two forms: natural and Dutch-processed. The latter has been processed with an alkalizing ingredient to neutralize the natural acidity of the cocoa. I prefer the flavor of the Dutch variety, which has a darker color and mellower flavor (think Oreos). Regular and Dutch cocoa powders react differently to leavening in recipes; sometimes they are interchangeable, but other times not. So to be safe, go for Dutch-processed in these recipes. Most European brands are processed with alkali. If you're not sure, look for alkali in the ingredients list. Valrhona, Guittard, Frontier and Equal Exchange are four readily available brands in the United States.

When using chocolate, I always go for bars (or baking drops) over chips. Chips have higher amounts of lecithin that keep them from melting in cookies, but I don't even like these in cookies! Chopping up a bar leaves you with irregular pieces and some chocolate dust that disperses better throughout the cookie. Plus, bar chocolate is generally higher quality than chips. Percentage matters when chocolate is melted into a batter, such as in brownies or double chocolate cookies, so take care to use the right chocolate for the job, detailed below. But when chopped and stirred in, such as in blondies or chocolate chip cookies, use any percentage you like.

Dark milk chocolate with around 40 percent cacao mass tastes nothing like the cheap candy bars we all ate as kids. Milk can smooth rough edges and bring out the fruity notes in the chocolate. I love Recchiuti and Scharffen Berger, and more and more artisanal brands are coming out with dark milk chocolates, too. Try this in the chestnut chocolate chip cookies on page 193.

Semisweet chocolate usually has a lower cacao mass than bittersweet, (roughly 35 to 60 percent), though there are no real standards. I usually skip this in favor of bittersweet.

Bittersweet chocolate is the darkest of the chocolates, with a cacao mass usually between 60 and 75 percent. (There are higher percentage chocolates out there, too, but those usually make better eating than they do baking.) Recipes in this book that call for bittersweet chocolate were tested with either Tcho's 66 percent or Guittard's 72 percent bittersweet chocolate. Other excellent brands for baking are Scharffen Berger, Alter Eco, Valrhona and Callebaut, among countless others.

White chocolate has a bad rap due to the cheap stuff being made without any cacao butter at all. But there are some delicious white chocolates out there, my favorite being Green & Black's Organic. It isn't toothachingly sweet and is studded with specks of vanilla seeds for big flavor. When baked into blondies, it enhances their butterscotch flavor.

NUTS, DRUPES AND SEEDS

These tend to be highly perishable and their oils can go rancid at room temperature. Buy them from stores with high turnover (such as the bulk bins at well-attended co-ops and grocers) and keep as many as you can fit in the refrigerator, particularly pistachios, cashews, pecans, walnuts, hazelnuts, hemp seeds and chia seeds, which are the most volatile. Toasting nuts can go from raw to burnt quickly, so keep an eye on them and set a timer if you're forgetful (like me!). Sunflower, flax and pumpkin seeds make up the pumpkin cranberry loaf on page 38 and are also delicious toasted and sprinkled over salads or yogurt.

Almonds are used here not only as a flour (discussed more in "Alternative Grains and Flours"), but in other forms, too. Unblanched sliced almonds add texture and a pretty topping to oat bars and buckles, and sweet almond paste (marzipan's less-sweet cousin) makes a wildly flavorful crisp topping.

Chia seeds are no longer just for chia pets. They are related to flaxseeds and have similar properties with a milder flavor. Black and white chia seeds both work well in recipes and are interchangeable; I tend to buy the white seeds because they make a lighter-colored pie pastry. They're featured in the pumpkin loaf (page 38), helping to bind the ingredients together, and when ground they take the place of xanthan gum in flaky pie dough (page 87) while adding their own nutty flavor. If you have extra seeds lying around that you don't know how to use, try throwing a tablespoon (10 g) of them into your smoothie or stirring them into oatmeal.

NOTE: To grind chia seeds, place about ¼ cup (40 g) of seeds in a clean spice grinder or coffee grinder. Grind the seeds until they're the consistency of a fine meal, being careful not to take them so far that they become pasty. Dump the seeds into a jar and store, refrigerated airtight, for up to 1–2 months.

Coconut is used here not only as a flour (as discussed in the "Alternative Grains and Flours" section) but also as an oil and a milk. Coconut oil is solid at cool room temperature, but if it's too hot in your kitchen, store it in the refrigerator to keep it firm. Always buy raw, extra-virgin coconut oil. I always use canned, full-fat coconut milk unless otherwise specified. This can be chilled, the cream scraped from the top and whipped into a dairy-free whipped cream (page 52) to top any dessert or fill roulade cakes.

OILS

Sunflower oil and **olive oil** can make fabulously moist and flavorful cakes. Sunflower has a neutral flavor, while olive oil will add a complex edge. Always use extra-virgin olive oil. Store both at room temperature in a cool, dark place.

SPIRITS

Wine and spirits make frequent appearances in my recipes, which, in addition to giving the chef a little treat while she bakes, can build layers of flavor into baked goods. There is some confusion as to which spirits are GF because even distilled spirits made from rye or barley should have the gluten removed during the distillation process, which takes out all the solids. Sometimes this process gets botched, however, or caramel color is added, which can contain trace amounts of gluten. This is only an issue if you or your guests have celiac or an extreme sensitivity to gluten, however. (For instance, my sister, who gets hives from gluten, can—and does—drink all the whiskey she wants.) I've noted which spirits you should source GF versions of and made note of brands that are certified GF, such as St-Germain elderflower liqueur, The Kraken black rum and Queen Jennie Whiskey, which is made entirely from sorghum. Lillet Blanc and white wine, also used in recipes here, are GF as well.

GEAR

I try to minimize the amount of equipment I cram into our tiny kitchen, but here are some tools and equipment that I don't like to be without. Having them on hand will make baking exponentially more fun and functional.

STAND MIXER

These big mixers usually come with three different attachments: paddle, for beating buttery batters; whip, for fluffing up egg whites and whipping cream; and hook, for kneading bread (not used in this book). I bought my KitchenAid mixer used from a friend who was upgrading hers, and I use it often when I want to get a batter started and keep my hands free, whip up cream without breaking a sweat or churn ice cream in the ice cream making attachment. I've given alternate instructions for recipes that can be made in different ways.

RIMMED BAKING SHEETS AND RIMLESS COOKIE SHEETS

At the very least, have in your kitchen two rimmed baking sheets. Called "half-sheet pans" in commercial kitchens, these measure 12 by 17 inches (30 by 43 cm) and are the ones I reach for most often. Having a pan half that size (called a quarter-sheet pan) often comes in handy for toasting smaller amounts of nuts and the like. And if you have a couple of rimless cookie sheets, these are handy for (obviously) baking cookies because, if you line your pans with parchment, you can grab the whole thing and slide it onto a cooling rack to quickly stop the cookies from overbaking. Do stay away from dark pans in favor of good ol' stainless steel; dark pans can promote excessive browning and result in burnt cookie bottoms.

WHISKS

I have a few different whisks that come in handy for different things, but one will do in a pinch.

A small, skinny whisk is great for getting into the corners of pots when making curds or grits. A medium whisk works well for stirring batters. And a larger balloon whisk is a good thing to have if you like to whip cream or egg whites by hand.

OVEN THERMOMETER AND INSTANT-READ THERMOMETER

Since my oven is nearly as ancient as some of the grains in this book, I never bake without an oven thermometer (or two) firmly in place. These can be inaccurate, but they're better than nothing. Replace every six months for the most accuracy. An instant-read thermometer is nice to have for checking that custards and curds have reached the proper temperature to kill any nasty germs.

MEASURING CUPS AND SPOONS

There are two types of measuring cups: wet (glass or plastic pitchers for measuring liquids) and dry (metal or plastic cups in ¼-cup [60-ml] increments for measuring flours, sugars and other dry ingredients). (See more on measuring on page 13.) Measuring spoons are for smaller measurements such as baking powder and salt. Not all measuring cups are created equal! Check your measures against each other (or better yet, against a kitchen scale) to see that everything matches up.

ELECTRIC KITCHEN SCALE

This can be a lifesaver for weighing things like fruit that are hard to get an accurate volumetric measure on. Baking by weight saves time and dishes because you can simply spoon all the ingredients right into the bowls rather than having to dirty a variety of measuring cups and spoons. Plus, baking by weight tends to yield more consistent results.

SPATULAS

My number one favorite kitchen tool is my small, offset spatula. It has a skinny, metal spatula bit that sits lower than its handle, and it's the perfect tool for just about everything—lifting bars out of pans, flipping crepes, spreading icing. A regular, thin metal spatula is another essential tool for cooking things in skillets, lifting oven pancakes out of pans and transferring cookies from baking sheets. A few flexible, silicone spatulas are essential for folding batters, scraping doughs out of bowls, and stirring stove-top custards. I have a couple of standard-sized ones, plus a smaller one for coaxing honey out of jars and that sort of thing.

PIE PAN

Look for a standard 9-inch (23-cm) pie pan with a flat lip around the edge; this will give your crust something to rest on and hold it up as it bakes. All pies in this book were tested with glass pie pans; if you have a metal pan, that's fine, just decrease the baking time, as metal conducts heat differently than glass does.

TART PANS

The two I use most often are a 9-inch (23-cm) pan with a removable bottom and a 10-inch (25-cm) ceramic pan that is perfect for baking clafoutis and cobblers. Smaller 4-inch (10-cm) pans with removable bottoms are nice for individual tarts, too.

CAKE PANS

Look for cake pans with 2-inch (5-cm) high sides made from sturdy metal and with straight sides. I prefer to stay away from nonstick coating when possible. Having the following will give you the most versatility:

- one 6-inch (15-cm) round pan (for making small cakes)
- two 8-inch (20-cm) round pans (for making the layer cakes in this book)
- one 9-inch (23-cm) round pan
- one 9-inch (23-cm) round springform pan (which has a bottom that detaches from the sides)
- one 8-inch (20-cm) square pan
- one 9-inch (20-cm) square pan

And a couple of specialty pans:

- one 8 by 4–inch (20 by 10–cm) loaf pan
- one 10-cup (2.4-L) Bundt pan

CANNING JARS AND/OR RAMEKINS

These are the perfect vessels for baking individual puddings, cheesecakes and crisps. Ball mason jars are quite affordable and can be found at hardware stores. Weck makes an assortment of cute canning jars, too. And ramekins can be found at kitchen supply stores.

CAST-IRON SKILLETS

Aside from having a sort of old-timey charm, these skillets conduct heat brilliantly and are just the thing for baking cornbread, oven pancakes and tarte tatins. The sizes I use most often are 8 and 10 inches (20 and 25 cm). To season a skillet, rub the inside with a teaspoon of oil (I use sunflower) and place the pan over medium heat until it's very hot. Let cool. Acidic ingredients, soap and abrasive sponges can all strip away the seasoning, so take care to keep those things far away from your cast iron.

FOOD PROCESSOR

This is your friend for grinding nuts and making frangipane. I tend to use my stand mixer more often (and call for it in recipes), but a food processor can also help pulse cold butter into biscuit and scone doughs.

MICROPLANE GRATER

Ever grate citrus zest on a block grater and spend hours trying to scrape it out of those obnoxious little holes? Well now you'll never have to again. Microplanes are ideal for zesting citrus and grating fresh ginger and nutmeg.

SPRING-LOADED ICE CREAM SCOOPS

These come in a variety of sizes and make quick work of portioning out cookies, muffins and cupcakes.

PASTRY BLENDER

I use my pastry blender, which has a handle attached to four curved metal blades, for working butter into pie, scone and biscuit doughs. It's the perfect tool for the job, as it gives you more control over the final product without the heat from your fingertips, which causes the butter to soften prematurely. Stay away from the flimsy, wire types, which don't work as well.

BENCH SCRAPERS

These may seem like a luxury, but for certain tasks, like working with GF pie dough, they're essential. These come in both plastic and metal, and I recommend having one of each. The plastic ones have a bit of flex and are great when working with stiff doughs, like scones and biscuits. A metal scraper is your friend for scraping fraisaged pie dough off the counter, folding the dough and cleaning off a floury countertop in one fell swoop.

PARCHMENT PAPER

I have a slight addiction to parchment paper that comes from having worked in bakeries and restaurants most of my life. It makes life so much easier: fewer dishes to do, fewer pastries sticking to pans. Additionally, layering baked goods with parchment for storage helps keep them fresh, as the parchment absorbs excess moisture that leads to stale sweets. And it makes measuring things like freshly grated nutmeg or citrus zest a breeze because you can grate it onto a small piece of parchment, then use the parchment to slide the zest or spice into a measuring spoon. Look for natural, precut sheets of parchment paper. To line a pan with parchment, you can either do it the neat way (cutting the parchment to fit precisely) or the messy way (shoving the parchment in the pan, creasing the corners and trimming excess overhang). I've given the neat way as the instruction in most recipes, but if you can't be bothered to measure and trim, most of the time it's fine not to. To line a round pan with parchment, place the pan on a sheet of parchment, use a pencil to trace a circle around the pan, cut out with scissors and voilà.

ROLLING PIN

This comes in handy for rolling out pie dough and biscuit dough for swirl biscuits. I prefer the tapered pin with no handles, but anything will do. (I even used a wine bottle once in a pinch!)

KITCHEN SHEARS

These are great for cutting parchment paper, trimming pie dough and opening up bags of flour so you don't ruin your knives!

KNIVES

It definitely pays to splurge on a few good knives. I recommend:

- A large, sharp chef's knife, for general chopping and cutting
- A large serrated knife, for sawing away at things like roulade cakes
- A small, sharp paring knife for cutting the hulls from strawberries or cutting into oven pancakes
- A small serrated knife for cutting delicate fruits

T-SHAPED VEGETABLE PEELER

This is the perfect tool for peeling apples and pears or making chocolate shavings.

STRAINERS

A medium-mesh strainer is the thing to use for sifting clumpy flours, rinsing berries and straining batters—more useful and user-friendly than a traditional sifter. A fine-mesh strainer works well for straining custards, such as ice cream bases.

COOLING RACKS

These allow baked goods to cool, letting air circulate beneath them. I like to have at least one round rack and one large rectangular rack on hand.

BISCUIT CUTTERS

A set of fluted biscuit cutters is just the thing for cutting out rounds of dough for fig bites, cutout pie lids and pandowdies. (But a small glass works in a pinch, too.)

PASTRY BRUSH

You'll be glad to have a small pastry brush on hand; nothing else quite does the trick for brushing the tops of scones or pastries or sweeping away excess flour when rolling out pie dough.

MADELEINE PAN

This specialty pan makes the pretty little cookies on page 202. If you don't have one, however, you can bake the batter as little cakes in a muffin pan instead.

MUFFIN AND CUPCAKE PAPER LINERS

These are you friends for making muffins, cupcakes and financiers. Small paper liners can also hold cheesecake bites or other bar cookies for serving.

KITCHEN TORCH

This not only makes you look like a badass in the kitchen, but it also caramelizes figs for the tartlets on page 124.

BAKING STONE

Never have a soggy-bottomed pie again with one of these. It'll give your pie bottom some extra oomph, keeping it nice and crisp. (Plus, you can use it to make the alternative flour pizza recipe on my blog.)

PASTRY BAG AND TIPS

If you want to look fancy, pipe frosting for cakes or cupcakes from a bag fitted with a plain or star tip. If you don't have one of these, a plastic baggie with the top cut off will work in a pinch.

SOURCES

The best place to shop for the ingredients and materials in this book is your local co-op, farmers' market, health food store, upscale grocer and kitchen supply store. When all else fails, here are some good online resources.

ARROWHEAD MILLS
Alternative flours, many organic and GF
www.arrowheadmills.com

BOB'S RED MILL
Alternative flours, grains and starches
www.bobsredmill.com

CHEF SHOP
Calleris Chestnut Flour
www.chefshop.com

CRATE & BARREL
Kitchen supplies, bakeware and cookware
www.crateandbarrel.com

FRONTIER CO-OP
Whole and ground spices
www.frontiercoop.com

INDIA TREE
Light and dark muscovado sugars
www.indiatree.com

KEREKES BAKEDECO.COM
Hard-to-find tartlet pans with loose bottoms in all sizes
www.bakedeco.com/a/gobel-round-fluted-t-258.htm

K+L WINE MERCHANTS
Specialty spirits such as St-Germain and nocino
www.KLWines.com

KODA FARMS
Blue Star Mochiko Sweet Rice Flour
www.kodafarms.com

LADD HILL ORCHARDS
Delicious, organic chestnut flour that isn't smoky
www.laddhillchestnuts.com

OLD SUGAR DISTILLERY
Queen Jennie Gluten-Free Whiskey, made from sorghum
www.oldsugardistillery.com

SINGING DOG VANILLA
Organic vanilla beans, vanilla extract and even some yummy vanilla-infused teas
www.singingdogvanilla.com

SUR LA TABLE
Kitchen supplies, bakeware and cookware
www.surlatable.com

THE TEFF COMPANY
Teff grains and flour
www.teffco.com

WHOLESOME!
Organic granulated, brown and powdered sugars, molasses and corn syrup
www.wholesomesweet.com

WILLIAMS-SONOMA
Kitchen supplies, bakeware and cookware
www.williams-sonoma.com

ZÓCALO GOURMET
Algarrobo mesquite flour
www.zocalogourmet.com

ACKNOWLEDGMENTS

It truly takes a village to raise a book baby! This book couldn't have happened without:

My editor Marissa's kindness, patience and encouragement;

Danielle Svetcov's killer title and subtitle, advice and calm demeanor;

My dad's teaching me to love both food and health;

My mom's endless support, research and proofreading assistance;

Cierra's personal assistance and cheerleading;

My yoga and dance teachers keeping me (semi-) fit and (mostly) sane, and eating the desserts I bring them;

Sarah M's friendship, advice, recipe guidance, help with process photos and perfecting the cover design;

Adam Salomone's endless generosity of time, support and guidance to a complete stranger;

Stephen, Shelley, Craig and Pete's photography schooling;

Claire making me embrace chiffon cake and teaching me how to master pie pastry;

My amazing community of readers and fellow bloggers' encouragement and support over the years;

Amelia's unwavering friendship, support and recipe testing skillz;

My army of kind and generous recipe testers who made these recipes rock solid: Kelly O, Ann L, Malavika, Jemma, Lea, Celia, Deanne, Tara, Ana, Emma, Stacy, Lukas, Zané, Kelly H, Joelle, Max, Tori, Christine, Emily, Daria, Morgan, Sienna, Sharon, Karen, Vanessa, William E, Maria, Suzuki, Tracy, Todd, Jen M, Cassy, Emilie, Ellen, Nicole, Jessica, Ashley and Tara;

With special thanks to Caterina, Michelle R, Janet, Erika, Lawre, Maureen, Shanna, Rebecca G, Kathy, Michelle D, Alanna L and Jaime for testing loads of recipes and even helping develop, brainstorm and problem solve;

And especially Jay's willingness to "taste" insane amounts of sweets without complaining (much), washing approximately a million dishes, supporting me through many years of Bojon and encouraging me to pursue my passion.

ABOUT THE AUTHOR

Photo credit: Shelley Eades

Alanna Taylor-Tobin is a food stylist, photographer and trained pastry chef. In 2009, she founded the popular recipe blog The Bojon Gourmet (bojon = no job, backwards), where she plays with uncommon ingredients and alternative grains and flours in her spare time. Her recipes, food styling and photography have been featured in countless web and print publications, including the *New York Times*, *Food and Wine*, Food52, The Huffington Post, *GFF: Gluten-Free Forever Magazine* and Williams-Sonoma. She lives and works in San Francisco with her other half, Jay, and a sassy feline named Catamus. Find her at BojonGourmet.com or follow along on Instagram (@the_bojon_gourmet).

FLOUR INDEX

INDEX